SOVIET
LITERATURE
TO-DAY

SOVIET

LITERATURE

TO-DAY

BY

GEORGE REAVEY

GREENWOOD PRESS, PUBLISHERS
NEW YORK

THE CALVIN CHAPIN MEMORIAL PUBLICATION FUND

The present volume is the tenth work published by the Yale University Press on the Calvin Chapin Memorial Publication Fund. This Foundation was established November 17, 1916, by a gift to Yale University from Arthur R. Kimball, of the Class of 1877, Yale College, in memory of his great grandfather, Calvin Chapin, of the Class of 1788, Yale College, who died March 16, 1851. He was born on July 22, 1763, and at the age of fifteen served for six months as fifer of a militia company in the Revolution. His preparation for College was delayed by the war but was finally completed, and after entering Yale he became one of the best scholars in his Class. Following his graduation he spent two years as a successful teacher in Hartford, Connecticut, and then began the study of theology, though meantime continuing to teach. From 1791 to 1794 he served as a tutor in Yale College, and then accepted a call to Stepnay Parish in Wethersfield, now the town of Rocky Hill, Connecticut. From 1805 to 1831 he served as a Trustee of the Missionary Society of Connecticut; took a prominent part in the formation of the Connecticut Bible Society in 1809; and was one of the five organizers of the American Board of Commissioners for Foreign Missions in 1810, holding the office of Recording Secretary of the Board for thirty-two years. In September, 1820, he was elected a member of the Yale Corporation, serving thereon until his resignation in October, 1846.

CONTENTS

548436

Contents—*continued*

CHAPTER VII
THE WRITER AND THE CRITIC.

CHAPTER VIII
WAR, POETRY AND OPTIMISM.

CHAPTER IX
THE LITERATURE OF THE NATIONALITIES

CHAPTER X
THE NEW DEMIURGE AND THE WINDOW OF EUROPE.

PREFACE

I FIRST became interested in Soviet literature when at Cambridge in the late twenties, though I did not read Russian at the University. I had, however, a smattering of the language, acquired as a result of a sojourn of some years (1912-18) in Russia as a child, and I proceeded to revive my knowledge of it, rusty and half-forgotten as it was, at first through the medium of the poets I then discovered. The world of Blok, Khlebnikov, Mayakovsky, Pasternak* and Essenin, which was then revealed to me, proved an exciting adventure, and both coincided with and complemented that of the modern French poets and, of course, that of our poets of the era, Hopkins, Yeats, Eliot, Joyce and Lawrence. There was much in common in that early phase (1912-27) between Russia and European poets in their general æsthetic trend and both schools shared a common background of Symbolism, Imagism and Futurism. It was also true that traditionally the function of Russian literature was to deal more directly with the problems of life in their social setting and the peculiar nature of the immense Russian revolutionary experiment was to stress still further social factors and a belief in the possibility of "transforming the world" in practical ways at the expense of a more purely æsthetic attitude towards life. The poets I had discovered really belonged to an earlier phase of the Revolution which was dominated by a battle of ideas : the break between this world and that other one to come of a more stabilized and organized revolutionary society was already on the eve of occurring and was soon apparent in the mobilization of writers to record the achievements of the First Five Year Plan (1929). In an Anthology, which I edited and which was published in 1933,† this transition was already clearly indicated. By that time, the modernist movement was on the wane in Europe generally or was assuming new forms, but in the Soviet Union it was brought to a formal and more drastic end by an official and exclusive acceptance of the canons of Socialist Realism from 1932 onwards.

---

*First Essay Towards Pasternak, published in Experiment, No. 6, Cambridge, 1930.
†Soviet Literature (ed. Reavey and Slonim): Wishart, London ; Covici Friede, N.Y. ; N.R.F., Paris ; Mondadori, Milan.

I confess that for a time I lost some of my interest in Soviet literature and was more attracted by the French scene.* This was doubtlessly due to the fact that, since the death of Mayakovsky and apart from the continued but to me familiar mode of Pasternak, who also published very rarely at this time, there appeared no new poetic genius to excite me sufficiently, with the exception, perhaps, in a minor key, of Bagritzky and the momentary but lively fancy of Zabolotsky (1933), a poet who has since mysteriously vanished from the scene of Soviet letters. Gone were the fire and the drama associated with the names of Blok, Essenin and Mayakovsky, and the whole of the debate of their time. Instead, Soviet literature was in the throes of internal reforms which, essential or useful as they have been in the light of the fundamental, industrial and national developments of the period, had far less colour and literary genius to symbolize them. New foundations were being laid and the great achievements lay rather in the sphere of industry, agriculture and social reorganization, rather than in that of literary talent or brilliance : the country was being radically transformed from a backward and primitive agricultural land to one of great potential industrial power. And, as a corollary, the links with the past, with literary and political traditions that had at first been ruthlessly severed, were now being reforged again in a careful and deliberate manner.

But, in 1941, I again turned to the land where by then terrific battles were raging against the invading German armies, and I wrote several feature programmes broadcast by the B.B.C. and somewhat optimistic in tone considering the situation at the time. By April, 1942, on board an Arctic convoy bound for Murmansk on the way to join the British Embassy in Kuibyshev on the Volga in an official capacity, I felt more like an ancient traveller into the unknown than a potential Embassy Secretary. Having reached my destination, though not without adventure, I remained in the Soviet Union for over three years, until the summer of 1945, and had some share in starting and directing that novel venture, the *Britansky Soyuznik* or *British Ally*, the first British and foreign paper to be published in the U.S.S.R.

To have spent the war years in the Soviet Union and to have observed the Russian people in their distress and resolution is an unforgettable experience as is, indeed, the discovery that in their homes and behind the barrier of dogma and officialdom they are still a most human people, hospitable and full of kindness when their peculiar shyness of the foreigner is in abeyance. Their society, too, is far more fluid than one would suppose from the outside staring at a façade of rigid pronouncements and acts. But the importance of

*Thorns of Thunder. Selected Poems of Paul Eluard (ed. George Reavey): Europa Press, London, 1936.

these latter must not be underestimated either, for they set the tone and underline the purpose of the whole experiment.

Russia has always been a land notoriously difficult for a foreigner to assess, and since the Revolution the Soviet Union has been constantly the subject of controversial debate and partisan passion. Three years is a none too long period for a first hand acquaintance—one just begins to arrive at scratching the surface by that time. On the other hand, a longer stay without re-emerging into the outer world would also be fraught with peril—that of losing one's sense of proportion. This peculiar world has a pressure all its own and life in it may be compared to that of a deep sea fish that is in danger of bursting when it emerges to the surface. I almost felt like that myself when I was whisked off in an aeroplane and landed back in a strange enough post-war Western world of another density. After a few months of readjustment, I decided to write this book analysing the trend of Soviet literature over the past decade and in its post-war mood, and also in so far as it reflects the march of Soviet life. In stressing the background of the literary scene, in contrasting the goal with the achievement, in elaborating on the relation between writer and critic, and in touching upon the Soviet dialectical attitude to the West, I have tried to make the book a little more than a narrow "literary history." If it also helps to throw some light on the processes at work, their direction, and the general movement of Soviet Society—that "unprecedented and unbelievable State, rushing headlong into the ages," as Pasternak called it in his *Safe Conduct* (1931)—then my purpose will be doubly served. And I have done my best to give a balanced account based on my observations and on the reading of Russian texts which, on the whole, are not enough known or studied abroad with the result that critical comment is often ten or fifteen years out of date. If, here and there, a note of friction has to be recorded instead of one of co-operation after the war, that is a situation that has to be squarely faced. It is no use shirking differences when they are emphasized just as it is foolish to magnify them when they are not. The problem of the present and the future is how to resolve these differences in a reasonable and human way.

My thanks are due to Mr. Michael Apletin, Vice-President of the Foreign Commission of the Union of Soviet Writers in Moscow, for answering a number of queries and supplying me with some books which it would have been impossible otherwise to get, to Madame Alexei Tolstoy, Madame Afinogenova, and those Soviet writers whose hospitality I enjoyed; and to the Librarian of the School of Slavonic Studies at the University of London for the use of the Library.

GEORGE REAVEY.

1st July, 1946.

A*

CHAPTER I

THE TRADITIONS, HISTORY AND CHARACTER
OF SOVIET LITERATURE OF TO-DAY

I

Traditions in the Making

THE background, achievements, and aspirations of Soviet literature are not easy to assess for a number of reasons. In no literature are theory and practice more closely related or at least nowhere is there such insistence on their identity. This both simplifies and complicates the task : while there may be a certain number of constants to guide one, there is also a perpetual interplay of theory and reality on an evolving foundation and every now and. again a slight or more emphatic modulation of line. In approaching this literature, two ways are open to the critic. One is to consider only those Soviet works that have been translated into English and to pronounce critical judgment upon them; and here no doubt the standard of comparison would be our knowledge of the Russian classics. Another would be to study Soviet literature in its native environment and in the process of development—in the background of a whole complex of factors making up the society of which that literature is the product and reflection. Here we shall attempt the latter approach and we shall try to situate the literature of the war period and the first year of peace in their appropriate background. It is to be hoped that as a result a clearer picture will emerge of the problems and tasks, the directives and trends, of this literature, and of the life and work of the writers who compose it.

An added reason for insisting so much on the background is that the eclectic method has not yet done full justice to the Russian literature of the 19th century. While writers like Gogol and Turgeniev, Dostoievsky and Tolstoy, have been given all the limelight, other writers of quality and importance like Lieskov and Saltykov-Schedrin, for example, have long been ignored. Writing in 1914, Maurice Baring said : " There is no translation of Saltykov-Schedrin, the greatest of Russian satirists; there is no complete translation of

Lieskov, one of her greatest novelists. . . ." Thirty years later, we find these writers still comparatively unknown. The same is true of the critic-philosophers, Herzen and Bielinsky, Chernyshevsky and Dobroliubov, who are now regarded as the founders and precursors of the realist attitudes of to-day.

We must warn the reader in advance that this will not be a book about great literary geniuses. The Soviet literature of to-day reveals no such outstanding figures as had graced Russian literature in the past. But we do not wish to imply that this literature is without its talent, variety and interest, or that it may not have its geniuses in the offing. The period we are dealing with was a particularly difficult one and had very special problems of its own; but whatever might be said about its total contribution, it was full of developments and trends that are significant for the future. In any case, the lack of great literary geniuses at present does not appear to be an exclusively Soviet phenomenon if we are to judge by the rest of the world in the past ten years. There may be good social reasons for this universal state of affairs, but it is outside our province to embark upon a discussion of them here. The dearth of great literary genius is as apparent in the Soviet Union as it is elsewhere. Another reason we have for insisting on background and atmosphere is that Soviet literature in its development has exhibited certain organizational and other characteristics which distinguish it sharply from other literatures; and it would be difficult or impossible otherwise to understand it as a whole or the relative importance attached to some of its works.

It might be argued that a great deal of Russian 19th century literature was concerned with a potential or imminent Revolution; a great deal of it was certainly critical of society or the Tsarist government in one form or another. But its impact on the rest of the world through fiction mainly was due to the boldly drawn and essentially human characters it portrayed, and the spiritual issues it raised. By way of contrast, the Russian literature of to-day finds itself in a state of society where the Revolution is a premise of life. The initial revolutionary act did not just involve a change of system, it also stimulated all sorts of social processes; and moreover, it has as its basis a dynamic theory in the principles of " dialectic and historical materialism." And these principles are instrumental in their turn in stimulating further changes. Anyhow, their relation to literature and their influence on its development cannot be ignored.

There has been another and no less important change since the Revolution of 1917, and that is the industrial and agricultural revolution of 1929-32. If, by the theory of historical materialism, the prevailing system of means of production in any given social order is the key to social forms, it is then clear that this industrial and agricultural revolution of the 1930's had an enormous determining effect on the social life of the Soviet Union from then onward, and in fact it has transformed this society and is still transforming it in a degree no less than that in which it was altered in 1917-21. We shall not dwell on the details of this transformation except in so far as they affect literature, and that will emerge in due course. If we generalize, we might say that the trend has been from an "experimental" society to a more settled social order, which is working out its own traditions and social forms based on a blend of old and new.

The question of traditions looms very large in Russian life to-day and is by no means confined to literature or the arts; it is closely bound up with the re-discovery of history as a source of experience and example and the rich store of "national heritage." This trend became marked in the middle 1930's but during the war it was even more strongly in evidence; and it no doubt reflected the need felt, in the light of present success, for more solid national foundations. Thus, the note of to-day is "the moral greatness of the Soviet people and its uninterrupted ties with the glorious past, the heroic present and the great future." To the Soviet citizen are now attributed all the finest traditional qualities of the Russian character and the "moral superiority" and positive outlook that are claimed to be the products of the new Socialist order. Significantly, too, "spiritual values" are now often quoted as the essential part of both the revived human personality and of artistic works; and the personality of the artist is assuming a new validity in relation to the work of art, whereas some twenty years ago the work of art was regarded as a purely "social phenomenon" and the rôle of the artist's personality was denied.

The last decade has been spent largely in building up national traditions in the army and in statecraft as well as in the arts. The army and navy now have their Suvorov-Kutuzov and Ushakov-Nahimov ancestry; and the problem of the "traditions of the Soviet officer" is a typical one. The ballet has gone back to a solid classical repertoire, and the outstanding new productions of recent years, such as *The Fountain of Bakshisaray, Romeo and Juliet, Crimson Sails,* and *Cinderella,* are all interpretations of literary legends or fairy tales. Similarly, historical subjects in drama and fiction are being treated more and more; there is a tendency to emphasize historical detail and make it ceremonious at every opportunity whether in classical Opera or in period plays; and court scenes are especially popular.

At the same time, national differences in style and traditions are being given added emphasis. By this we mean the distinction, which was smothered in the early days of the Revolution, between the Great Russian and the other Soviet nationalities. In architecture, for example, it was recently decided not to apply a universal style in rebuilding all over the Union but to take into account national and local traditions of style and material. This coincides with the granting of a greater measure of formal autonomy to the Republics such as their diplomatic services and national armies (1944). These processes are only in their initial stages; but it is as well to remember that there are now sixteen constituent Republics and over a hundred other smaller nationalities within the orbit of the U.S.S.R. This already has some effect, and no doubt will have even greater influence, on the development of Soviet literature as a whole; these national literatures are being encouraged and a complicated network of inter-translation has been set up. The level of development among them is naturally most varied, but about forty of these literatures are considered to be "established" and they are in the process of rapid development. Each one of them, too, on the principle of the central Russian literature, is sifting its past and building up a tradition of its own. In this connection, it is interesting to note V. Shklovsky's statement made in his book *Meetings,* that "Khlebnikov (the poet) in 1912 wrote that Russian literature must make a further advance after having learnt anew the old Slavonic and the Eastern literatures. . . . Khlebnikov said that it was now necessary to study the songs of the Adriatic Slavs and the Mongolian epics." These possibilities open up new and strange vistas for the future. In the meantime, as we shall see in a later chapter, a lot of spadework is already being done.

But to return to Great Russian traditions which are our leading theme. We last mentioned the ballet and the insistence on historical detail. But history does not stop there; it is beginning to excavate deeper into the past, and the Slavonic origins are much to the fore as well as earlier Slav connections with the outside world, the Balkans and Byzantium. The traces of Greek colonization and civilization on the shores of the Black Sea and elsewhere are receiving renewed attention. During the war something was made of the Slav origins in anti-German pamphlets, and the Slav theme has gained added importance as a result of the new connections established with other Slav nations. In literature, this theme has been barely touched but it is bound to be given more prominence.

In music it is Chaikovsky who holds the place of honour as the most national of composers; there may be some debate about his priority among intellectuals but there can be no doubt as to his general popularity. His *Swan Lake* is the most attended of ballets and his *Eugene Onyegin,* the most popular of operas. The image of Tatyana both in Pushkin's poem and in this opera is the ideal of the younger generation of Soviet women, who are sentimental and unsophisticated, and believe in romantic love rather than in any notion of sexual freedom. It is not surprising then that the love theme has made its reappearance in Soviet poetry, in that of Simonov, who, as Shklovsky said, was the first "to open the secret of his heart." The same young Russians, when you ask them who is their favourite author, will almost invariably reply Pushkin or it may be Tolstoy or Dostoievsky. In their affections, contemporary authors, with a few exceptions such as Essenin, Mayakovsky, and Ostrovsky, do not rank very high; and the reasons are not very far to seek, for in them the simpler emotional world is refracted in the stormy mirror of day to day events, and the wholeness of an image is lost.

In architecture, that fundamental index of social trends and achievements, two periods now lie behind. They are the modern Le Corbusier style of the 1920's and the pseudo-classical, rather nondescript style of the middle 1930's in which Gorky street was rebuilt. From all that one can see of the projects for rebuilding the war-damaged cities and from all that one can read of statements made by architects to-day, there is a marked return to the classical 18th century and the Empire style of the early 19th century with a dash of English 18th century Bath thrown in. In the words of a Soviet architect, A. Burov, which we quote from his article, *War and Architecture,* published in Znamya No. 9, 1945, there is an argument between those who hold that " Constructivism is bad and ugly. By Constructivism I mean the new architecture. . . . Therefore let us return to the beautiful and tried old styles," and those who wish to create a new style befitting the age.

In architecture the plans are more concrete and visible. But is there a plan for post-war literature? There would appear to be one in the broadest of outlines, and it would seem to consist in suggesting the possibility of " classical revival " or a new literary age, and in preparing the ground for it by the actual and intensive revival of the classics as models and by encouraging all sorts of new or neglected *genres.* The general feeling often expressed by the critics and summed up by V. Shklovsky is that " After the war literature will change and it is already changing. The whole of the great Russian 19th century was determined by the storm of 1812." This is the commonly drawn parallel : the Napoleonic war had been followed by the Alexandrine Age of Pushkin and later by the birth of the Russian novel. The impact of Napoleon was still felt by Dostoievsky and Leo Tolstoy. The whole of Russian thought was stimulated by this experience. In the same way, it is now felt that the war will have exercised the same stirring effect and will produce somewhat parallel results in a post-war flowering of all the arts. Thus, every sort of stimulation is being offered, and the critics and writers are being told, and are telling one another, to bestir themselves. But the genius of the future is still unknown—" he who will write the new Iliad " or produce a new prose epic. But the critics are calling for him. This is at least a sign of great optimism : and that indeed is one of the fundamental features of Soviet literature which distinguish it from the more sceptically and pessimistically minded literatures of the West. This optimism may be explained in various ways and it may be attributed to pioneering success, but its note may be detected in most Soviet writing and particularly in the poetry.

2

A Brief Outline of the Evolution of Soviet Literature until 1941

WHEN surveying Soviet literature of the past six years, many subtle differences and contrasts will elude us unless we can fix in our mind a clear picture of its previous evolution. For the sake of brevity at this stage, we shall have to generalize; but this generalization will appear less forced when it is realized how closely Soviet literature has followed political and social trends and how faithfully it has recorded some of the leading problems of the time. In this section, we shall outline the structure of a sometimes abrupt but nevertheless organic plot, the later acts of which are now being played. If after June, 1941, Soviet literature assumes certain new features as a result of the war, and thus enters a new phase, then prior to 1941 it can be divided into *four* no less distinctive creative periods, each of which is distinctive in its themes and problems, its criticism and style.

The *first* was the period of the *Great Divide* or *Militant Communism* (1918-22). This phase, which was also that of the Civil War and the war with Poland, was a seething cauldron of ideas and conflicting theories. In it we have the reactions of many of the older writers, who had not yet emigrated; the Symbolism of Blok and the Imaginism of Essenin; the rise of the proletcult and of proletarian writers; the Darwinian theory of the survival of the fittest as expressed in Pilnyak's kaleidoscopic novel, *The Naked Year,* and the revolutionary romanticism of an Artiom Vesioly and an Andrei Malyshkin; the lyrical portrayal of mass effects as in Serafimovich's *The Iron Torrent* and the esoteric word-symphonies of Andrei Biely; the carefully constructed stories of Evgenyi Zamyatin and the dynamic Left Futurism of Mayakovsky. The tone of all these writers was exalted, lyrical, or militant, whatever their political persuasion, and the notion of the destiny of Russia, as then seen in the light of Revolution, was much debated; at the same time, the prose of this phase on the whole reflected the last stages of the disintegration of the classical narrative style, the dissolution of symbolism, as well as new experimental trends.

The *second* period was that of the Reconstruction or N.E.P. (1922-28). At this stage stock began to be taken after the wear and tear of a stirring beginning; and the experience was being digested. Now, under the auspices of Gorky, the foundations were laid of a new and young (in the literal sense, for by now many of the older writers and intellectuals had migrated and inexperienced novices had emerged out of the upheaval) literature. This was a time of groups and literary apprentices centred round some master or theory : there were the *Serapion Brothers,* with their charter of artistic liberties, the *Left,* the *Constructivists,* the *Formalists,* the communist *On Guard,* and the *Proletarian* associations. It was a time of literary and political debate, and the various groups were trying to impress their own panaceas on the public and on each other. The non-communist but sympathetic writers (and they were the majority) became known as Fellow Travellers; but the communist and proletarian writers, though less important from a literary point of view, were making various and repeated attempts to assert themselves. Their moment finally came in 1929. But before leaving this period, we must note that it saw the re-birth of the novel and the real beginnings of Soviet fiction. These early novels were either satirical and humorous as in Katayev and Ilf and Petrov, Zoshchenko and Romanov; or psychological and romantic as in Leonov and Fedin, Olesha and Kaverin; or crudely naturalistic as in Lydia Seifullina; but by 1926-28, in the first works of Fadeyev and Sholokhov, we observe a revival of Tolstoyan realism and the epic-narrative form which was ultimately to prove the steady ideal and backbone of the prose of the years to come. Thematically, most of these writers were preoccupied either with some aspect of the Civil War or of reconstruction as Gladkov was in his *Cement,* 1926, or with the intellectual's dilemma in face of a changing world as were Essenin and Olesha, or again in poetry with the affirmation of a new political and social consciousness as was Mayakovsky.

The *third* or the *Five Year Plan Period* (1929-32), made a sharp break with the comparatively free and easy Nep period. The Russian Association of Proletarian Writers (R.A.P.P.) now succeeded in establishing themselves as dictators in the literary field and insisted that it was the immediate duty of writers, whether Fellow Travellers or others, to " report " on the achievements of the Plan. In addition to Fellow Travellers and proletarian writers, shock brigades of workers were also mobilized as writers for the purpose; but these latter produced little or nothing of value. The best works of the period turned out to be those of writers already known such as Katayev with his *Speed Up, Time,* Gladkov with his *Power,* Leonov with *Sotj* and *Skutarevsky,* Panferov with *Brusski,* and Sholokhov with his collectivization novel, *Virgin Soil Upturned.* Some of these works had quality, but generally speaking the experiment of shock brigades and rapid tempos failed, and by 1932 it was admitted that there had been a decline in the general standard of performance and that the R.A.P.P.

dictatorship had proved unnecessarily irksome. But it had a permanent effect: it dispersed and broke up the groups. And when, on April 23rd, 1932, by a Resolution of the Central Committee, R.A.P.P. and other proletarian groups were themselves dissolved for fear that "these organizations might be turned from a means of intensive mobilization of writers and artists around the problems of Socialist construction into a means of cultivating hermetic grouping and of alienating considerable groups of writers and artists. . . .," Soviet literature (and the arts, too) were given a new organization. Its base was broadened and made more uniform. A single "Union of Soviet Writers of the U.S.S.R." was now established; but it took a year or two to work out the details of this new system. They were finally approved at the first general Congress of Writers in 1934, and Gorky became the first President of the Union, while Scherbakov was made the first Secretary—a political and administrative post. Henceforth and until our day, this basis of organization has persisted, with, of course, occasional modifications in matters of detail. The base had been broadened: the labels and distinctions between writers were removed; there were now no "proletarians" and "Fellow Travellers," but only "Soviet writers." The Union, however, like all similar organizations of the post-1932 period, had its simple and effective controls subtly interwoven into the fabric of the whole as part of the administrative machinery.

A new and fourth period, that of *Socialist Realism*, was inaugurated as a result of these reforms. As in the early 1920's, Gorky, who had by 1932 finally returned from Sorrento, played an active and directing part in these reforms which were to remove some of the elements of theoretical conflict between writers. But it is also true that Gorky was acting in close consultation with Stalin himself, and that these reforms were but part of a much wider reorganization of national life that had started partly as a result of the initial successes of the plans to industrialize and to collectivize the countryside, and by 1934, in literature and the arts, a new common theoretical principle and slogan had been propounded, that of Socialist Realism. We shall examine the implications of this theory more closely in the following section, but it may be said here that its three tenets were: *Socialist content, national form,* and *realistic representation*; thereby a clear and definite stand was made against any expressions or survivals of "leftist," "formalistic," or wilfully "experimental" trends; and this, by way of contrast, opened the door for the revival of the national classics.

These are the four periods, each distinctive enough, which succeeded each other between 1918 and 1941. To them we must add a *fifth,* that of the "*Great Patriotic War*" (1941-45); and the beginnings of a *sixth*—that of the post-war period, the character of which is being gradually defined and which points to a fuller national and revolutionary synthesis, and a revived ideological militancy. It is with the fifth period and the later transition stage that this book mainly deals. Whatever one's ultimate judgment may be of the works actually produced in this period, it is undoubtedly one of great formative significance, emphasizing as it does more roundly and more vitally the reformist trends of the past decade, its patriotic and moral motifs, and at the same time reopening more traditional windows and encouraging an increased dialectical awareness of the historical implication of events. Socialist Realism remains the guiding principle, but its range of interpretation and definition has widened. There is a new stress on Soviet Humanism as the fundamental philosophy. The war also helped to unify Soviet literature still further; it is now clear that it can be brought to bear on a given theme, in this case the "patriotic war," without that obvious compulsion which had manifested itself during the period of the R.A.P.P. dictatorship. This sense of national awareness, and the new consciousness of the power and function of the State, as well as the sudden realization of new horizons now opening out before the astonished gaze, all made themselves felt in different ways during this period. In the transition year following the war, stock was being taken of the achievement and discoveries; new literary *genres* were being tried out; and a new critical attitude was being worked out dialectically in relation to the outside world.

The balance between nationalism and the revolutionary dialectic was also being redressed. If, during the war, the feeling of "patriotism" was given full rein, from 1944 onwards there was increasing tendency to remind the public of the fundamental dialectical principles. This did not, as some foreign observers assumed, imply that the national past was being jettisoned; it was a reminder that the past must not be accepted uncritically and must be interpreted in the light of the pressing post-war problems, of which the new Five Year Plan is one.

3

The Principle of Socialist Realism

AS we have seen, the Resolution of April 23rd, 1932, had marked a new stage in the organization of Soviet writers and in the development of the arts as a whole as well as Soviet literature in particular. From now on this evolution was determined by the adoption of the general principle of Socialist Realism as the guiding theory of artistic expression. In the statutes of the Union of Soviet Writers, we find a Ruling to the effect that: "Socialist Realism, being the fundamental method of Soviet artistic literature and literary criticism, it demands of the artists a truthful, historico-concrete portrayal of *reality in its revolutionary development*. In this connection, the truthfulness and the historical concreteness of the artistic portrayal must take into account the problem of *ideological transformation* and *the education* of the workers in the spirit of Socialism."

This Realism is qualified : it is a particular type of " Realism "; it is " Socialist," and this implies that it should concern itself with the aims, qualities and manifestations of Socialist society as it exists and as it is in the making. Further, this " Realism " implies a faithful reflection of those human situations, facts and processes which are manifest in this Socialist complex, the foundation of which is the life and striving of the Soviet people. The terms " historical and concrete " are also used, and they must be taken to mean that the events and characters described should bear a close relation to this " Socialist complex " and that they should not be abstract, or just æsthetic, or unconnected with the problems of to-day. The use of the term " historical " further emphasizes the view that life is an historical process, that the present must be conceived as part of this process, and that the writer must therefore be conscious of *whither* this present is moving and *whence* it has originated, in other words, the writer must have an historical perspective that is neither a personal one nor one based on an " objective " approach to history, which has been so popular in the West and among British historians in particular, but having its root in a dialectical interpretation of reality and its criterion in the needs and aims of an evolving Socialist society. That this society is not conceived in static terms, but is on the contrary regarded as a dynamic complex of men and events, is further brought out by the reference in the Ruling to " the problem of ideological *transformation* and *education* of workers in the spirit of Socialism." In this context, the term Socialism itself is not a narrow concept or formula but is capable of wide interpretation in the light of historical development; and lastly, society and reality are seen in their *revolutionary development,* that is, in the light of a conscious aim—and this is the pivot of the whole dialectical system.

Socialist Realism is therefore a complex rather than a simple theory from the point of view of interpretation, and it implies above all development, analysis and the re-interpretation of " reality " from time to time. Thus, among Soviet critics and writers, we may find different and sometimes divergent interpretations of reality and realism; and there has been constant debate and definition on this subject. One aspect of broadly interpreted reality has been to re-incorporate more and more of the past under the sign of present-day approval. Thus, about 1936, the term *narodny* or national came increasingly into vogue when applied to writers of the past who were now re-admitted into the literary tradition; this term was a broader substitute for the class distinctions that had marked the criticism of the 1920's.

Similarly, in 1944, a new interpretation of Realism was given during a discussion on the theatre by Iury Golovashenko in his article on *The Diversity of Realism*. His interpretation, which was in turn criticized and dubbed "panrealism," was of the widest and attempted to prove that all art was essentially realistic and of present-day validity. He also complained of "the monotony of the devices of our stage." Golovashenko was, of course, criticized for his "dispassionate approach," "liberal toleration of everything," and "super-objectivity." This criticism was natural enough in the circumstances, for although Socialist Realism rested on expanding foundations, it could not give up its criteria or build up its specific traditions without exercising a selective principle where past or present works were concerned. But this discussion demonstrated once again that the principle was subject to debate and re-interpretation.

Many instances of such debate are available and reflect the evolution of critical thought that is going on. But, of course, when we examine the term "Realism" and the present attempt to make of it a canon and a tradition, we have to admit that there already was a very strong tradition of realism both in Russian art and criticism in the 19th century. In painting this was especially evident in the work of Repin and Surikov, and they have now become the "great masters" and tradition of Soviet painting. In speaking of contemporary art in his *Notes of an Artist*,* B. Ioganson says : "Realistic art exists when an artist in definite and clear form communicates his thought to the beholder in a form so high that the latter does not at first notice it but only hears the beating of his excited heart. The artist, overcoming form, rejoicing in his victory over nature, communicates his thought and feeling to the beholder. Here, then, comes the moment when it is necessary to consider what is realistic form, what is authentic innovation, what is pointedness of form. If in their time, Renoir or Dégas portrayed the woman of Paris, then for the expression of the essence of our Soviet woman, another form is essential corresponding to our contemporary state. This form we must seek. Has any one of us found it yet—that is still a question. On one point we shall all agree, that the high form of realistic art implies the blending of musical and plastic principles together with a profound psychological content. Moreover, the psychological content cannot be expressed without making use of these musical and plastic principles of painting. . . ."

Further Ioganson discusses a number of topical problems. He thinks *genre* is the Achilles heel of Soviet painting and he gives his reasons for its "impoverishment" after the Impressionists : "But soon

---

Soviet Art, of 16th November, 1945.

painters . . . laid a bridge towards monumental form, but instead of turning to the great traditions of the old masters (as Manet did when he opened the eyes of the world to Velazquez), they suddenly followed the path of formalism and went as far as Picasso in the West and Malevich's *Black Square* with us. There was nowhere left to go . . . . And we finally ask ourselves when the picture will appear, or more exactly pictures, in which artists of different formations—tragedians, lyrics, romantics, each according to his gifts, and on the basis of all the conquests of painting in the past and in late years, will say their word about our reality, but such a word as will reflect living man with all his passions and the subtle movements of his soul. . . ." Discussing genius and the innovations implicit in it, Ioganson says : " One need not fear that the people will not understand something. The people will not understand what it does not need, and what is incomprehensible to and remote from it will never be a work of genius, a classic. But it is possible that the people will not accept many artists—individualists, who have nevertheless exercised a great influence on painting. Should it wholly repudiate these innovators or be grateful to them? If many do not understand or value such an artist, then the artists themselves cannot, of course, agree with that. There are artists for artists. They exist lawfully as the seekers of new ways, as experimentalists revealing new possibilities."

Here on the whole, we have a generous interpretation of the problem of realism. The only touchstone is that the work should be *comprehensible to the people* and that it should reflect its best aspirations. Otherwise, it allows room for a variety of moods and stylistic approaches, realistic and romantic, as long as the form is fused with the content, and not paraded for its own sake or for the purpose of *formal* research only. The subject of painting and indeed of literature according to this theory should be man first and foremost, *the human passions set in their social background.* The human passions are, of course, the subject of all great art and the distinction here lies in the emphasis on the social background, that is, again, on the Socialist complex; or rather on the notion that you cannot separate man from his environment and that there is the closest of ties between his spiritual qualities and the order of society which has shaped him. This notion also finds its expression in another term, used often and concurrently with that of Socialist Realism—that is, Humanism. It is obvious that this term refers precisely to this emphasis on the qualities and spiritual values of " the new man in the new social order." But, like Socialist Realism itself, this very stress on the *moral, spiritual,* and *historic* character of man is a phenomenon of the past decade, and it gained increased currency during the war. Soviet art and literature then in *intention* at least, for Soviet critics admit dissatisfaction with the *performance,* appears to aim at something like a contemporary " Renaissance," one of the aspects of which is the liberation of art from the thrall of " formalism " just as the Italian Renaissance gradually freed painting from its Byzantine restrictions.

By " formalism " in this context Soviet critics now mean any art that is abstract, mechanical or experimental for its own sake, and which does not throw into prominence the human passions and the social background. Meierhold's " constructivist " theatre and Shostakovich's *Lady Macbeth* are typical examples of such " formalism " to be condemned. The Soviet ballet, too, was reconstituted on purely classical lines. Much of modern Western art, therefore, strikes the contemporary Russian as " formalism " and is consequently " unacceptable." If Soviet art cannot rise above a merely academic approach, of which we had so many examples in the 19th century, we shall not be very impressed. If, on the other hand, it can produce works offering a modern parallel to those of the Renaissance, they will not fail to have wide repercussions. In literature, Soviet writers are still overshadowed by giants such as Tolstoy and Dostoievsky, and if they get anywhere near to them we shall not fail to be stirred.

It is evident from the foregoing that the principle of Socialist Realism is not a simple formula but rather a succession of problems. When it is interpreted too literally it degenerates into what critics have called " naïve realism," which makes of " the hero " an easy victor and of the plot a mechanical achievement of success without any real problems or psychological difficulties to overcome. Examples of this easy method abound in literature and drama, but they do not correspond to the present demands for " greater psychological depth and more profound treatment " of difficulties and problems arising out of life. If, as it is claimed, " Literature lays down the laws of the future, the image of future man," then the obvious corollary is a " clear understanding of the meaning and dynamic of to-day's struggle." And art becomes " operative when an artist clearly sees the historical perspective and has the ability, when speaking of the present and past, to see the future." Great writers and artists in the past have often had some inkling of the future. Soviet writers claim to have a dialectical method by which this can be achieved; but the fact that many of them are criticized for not seeing far enough is perhaps another indication that the method is not a simple one and requires some genius in interpretation. It is easier to define than to interpret or create.

Another definition, that of A. Gurstein in his *Problems of Socialist Realism,* reads : " The fundamental features of Socialist Realism as an artistic method are Realism in the authentic meaning of the word, in the sense of the deepest expression and understanding of the processes of reality in its revolutionary development, the basis of the people freed from the distortions of capitalist society and the socialist content of art. Socialist Realism justifies the prognosis of Engels, who said that in the future in art will be achieved ' a complete fusion of ideological depth, of perceived historical meaning . . . with a Shakespearean liveliness and effectiveness (from Engels' letter to Lassalle of 18th May, 1859).' "

The mention of Shakespeare is significant as is his present popularity in the U.S.S.R. He is no longer interpreted from the point of view of class analysis as in the early days of the Revolution, but is regarded rather an example and model of what an artist can do for his age and how fully he can express it.* Balzac is another example often quoted of the artist's ability to sum up his age, and one is left with the impression that Shakespeare and Balzac, Pushkin and Leo Tolstoy, are the chief though not the only models which are being held up before contemporaries in an attempt to stimulate a bolder and more varied interpretation of the age. Or, as one of the critics says : " Advanced Soviet art should make an organic synthesis of all that is best. . . ."

So far, with a few exceptions, when translated and divested of their home environment, most Soviet works have failed to stir the imagination greatly or to reverberate round the world. This may be due to the absence as yet of a full-voiced body of work where the " historical perspectives " have been entirely assimilated and only human characters are left to speak. This problem is now realized by many of the critics. On the other hand, there remains the question of the writer's relation to reality on the principle of Socialist Realism, and this can only be solved satisfactorily by a very great writer who has passed out of a state of tutelage and has not got to readjust his perspective too often. As a minor example of what we mean, we may mention Prishvin, a miniaturist of nature, who is working in a limited field, but who through undeviating concentration has achieved greater depth of reality than most of his contemporaries.

4

Soviet Literature and the Problem of Education

THE integration of Soviet life and the orientation of its literature towards contemporary problems make of this literature an educative force not only in itself but in the rôle it is expected to play. Whereas any literature is part of a man's education in both the

---

*In *Transformation*, No. 4, Prof. Remenyi shows that he is fifteen or more years out of date when he says that Shakespeare is staged with " Marxist commentaries," by which he presumably means the " class analysis " common in the 1920's.

narrower school sense and the broader humanistic one, the Soviet writer and his critic are more immediately conscious of this aspect of their work. The reasons are not far to seek and they are to be found in the historic conditions of Russia and her evolution.

In the first place, as the result of the abolition of serfdom in 1861, and especially of the Revolution of 1917, we have the emergence into a gradual state of political consciousness of many millions of people, the majority of whom had previously been denied any possibility of even being able to read; and this emergent mass is the source of the new intellectual and technical cadres, since the old foundations had been mostly swept away. In addition, as a result of the Five Year Plans, Russia became for the first time an industrialized country, so that by 1940 a new type of Soviet citizen was already in existence; and his requirements would be different and increasingly more varied than those of his predecessors. For obvious reasons, this mass of people has been more backward technically and intellectually than its contemporaries in the advanced Western countries, which had experienced their industrial revolutions in the 19th century and which are now, on the contrary, suffering from industrial crises of the established system, on the one hand, and are alarmed rather than enthusiastic about the further developments of the new atomic revolution on the other. The fundamental problem of this new age of Russia was, therefore, "to catch up and then surpass" the rest of the world in technique, efficiency, and culture. And these problems are inevitably reflected in literature.

In the second place, the Revolution and its social developments, while they were based on and had the support of the masses or, in later terminology, "the people," have been and are still directed by a close-knit body of men, the leaders and other members of the omnipotent Party. This latter has its ideology, which has also evolved and broadened on the basis of dialectical materialism, but which still remains the measure of all things. This obviously affects the structure and nature of the educational system in its broad outlines and to some extent in its particular application. But it would be a mistake to assume that there is in practice a universal, very rigid and up-to-date interpretation of this ideology throughout the educational system as we find in 1946. On the contrary, the now national basis of education is so broad and the dialectical implications are so often ignored or misinterpreted, that we find a recurrent party criticism that the ideological education of various social groups or workers is being neglected and that something must be done about it. The Soviet idea of education spreads far beyond the school age and in its further stages is concerned mainly with the inculcation of a sense of awareness of "topical problems" seen in the right dialectical perspective. The Party is, therefore, still in the position of educator in chief when confronted with the mass of the people or its representatives in all spheres of society; for the Party is still about 3% of the total population. The awareness and perspective of history which the Party is striving to inculcate are also reflected in Soviet literature, though here, as in other spheres, we often come across the complaint that writers are not fully aware of or they have not fully grasped the import of the age they are living in.

The educative importance attached to the arts is illustrated by the following statement from a leader of the *Literary Gazette* of March 10th, 1945 : " Among all the means at the disposal of the Soviet State in the matter of national education, the upbringing of youth, and the re-education of the masses, *literature, the theatre,* and *the cinema, are the most powerful in their emotional impact.* Within their possibilities they must all be called upon to propagate the knowledge of natural sciences. . . ." Here literature is called upon to popularize the natural sciences, which are much publicized as an educative element and which have also now become the main weapon against " superstition." Another quotation from a leader of June, 1944, entitled *The Ideological and Political Education of the Artistic Intelligentsia,* reveals dissatisfaction with the present state of affairs : " The development of literature and art during the epoch of the Patriotic War is the first and principal evidence of the maturity of the political consciousness of the artistic intelligentsia. Art resolved and assimilated the problems posed by the times : the theme of our country, the idea of patriotism, was given a new and deeper exposition; the moving feeling of the national pride of the Soviet peoples was expressed with new force and their unbreakable friendship, as the source of the might of the Soviet State, was confirmed; the intelligentsia has also worked fruitfully to depict the hero of our time—the Soviet man, whose virility, moral beauty and integrity, are the basis of the eternal glory of our country. . . . But it would be naïve to think that experience alone is a source of the political maturity of the intelligentsia. Without serious work of the consciousness, without a deep study of the theory of Marx, Lenin, and Stalin, without the clarification of the essence of the contemporary process of struggle, the artist cannot fulfil his high mission, that of being ' the engineer of human souls,' *of being the educator and teacher of the people.* The fact cannot be ignored that the Patriotic War is accompanied by an enormous raising of the political activity and consciousness of the broad national masses. The intelligentsia can only satisfy the questions asked by the politically matured national masses if it itself ceaselessly works to raise the level of its own theoretical background. The neglect of theory, any arrest in ideological development, has in it the danger that the intelligentsia will get out of step with the people and will lose *its significance as the educator of the soul of the people* and this will lead to ideological as well as artistic breaks."

The passage we have quoted epitomizes the Soviet conception of the writer as a teacher, which is so different from our own. It is, however, a conception which is not only Soviet but traditionally Russian, with this difference that the writer has now become much more closely integrated with the people and the State, whereas in the 19th century he stood between them. A 19th century critic, N. Chernyshevsky, when writing of the difference between Russian and other literatures, produced the following significant analysis having direct bearing on the above : " In countries where intellectual and social life has reached a high development, *there exists a division of labour* between various branches of intellectual activity, *but of these we only know one—literature.* Therefore, however we may discuss our literature in comparison with others, nevertheless in our mind it plays a more important rôle than either French, German or English literatures play in that of their peoples; *and upon it are placed more responsibilities than on any other literature.* Up to now our literature concentrates in itself the whole of the intellectual life of the people, and for that reason *it has the duty to pre-occupy itself with such questions as in other countries have already been transferred to special spheres* concerned with other intellectual activities."

Chernyshevsky's analysis explains a great deal in the situation and psychology of Russian literature as we find it to-day, and in the *privileged but duty-bound* position of the Soviet writer, upon whom so many social demands are made. The passage on education previously quoted also reveals that, while the " teacher " is expected to be ideologically aware, the basis of reality is steadily changing through the appearance of new factors, and that the secret of dialectical interpretation lies in being able to give a just estimate of the historical perspective in its latest phase of development; otherwise the " teacher " would get out of touch with reality.

The main task now is the education and formation of the post-war generation of Russians. The basis of a broader national education had been laid down in the 1930's following the liquidation of the various experiments in this line in the 1920's. The war only strengthened the national position, and emphasized both the need for and the value of the classics. The young Russian of to-day will be largely brought up on these, with the salt and pepper of " dialectical and historical marxism " thrown in to sharpen his taste. The classics will be mainly but not exclusively Russian, since the theory is that all the masterpieces of the world should be absorbed. Lozinsky's outstanding translation of the *Divina Commedia* is proof of this. The popularity of Shakespeare—there were four or five of his plays running simultaneously in Moscow during the war—not only in the capital but also in the provinces and the Republics is another; Sheridan and Goldsmith were also staged during the war. Recently a new trend, the revival of Latin classics, has made itself apparent : Horace, Propertius and others have been translated. And there are, as we shall see, frequent references to Homer's *Iliad* not only as a " classic," but as a work the parallel of which Soviet literature should strive to create. There is no doubt that other Greeks besides Homer will not fail to re-appear; and so the horizon of vision and of example will be considerably extended. We cannot here go into all the details of this, but what is undoubtedly happening is the sowing time of a " renaissance " of its kind. The " re-discoveries " of old worlds and new worlds as well as the emphasis on the fundamentals of a Russian tradition are all signs of a feverish activity tending that way. How varied or rich the results will be is for the future to assess.

But let us return to education and the Russian tradition. These are again stressed in an article, *The Mighty Educative Force,* of August 25, 1945, which says : " The works of our biggest writers were always a mighty educative force. They taught the reader to love his country, to fight for high social ideals, and they brought out in him the best traits of man and citizen. *These fine traditions* have been continued and developed by Soviet literature, filling them with a new content dictated by Socialist reality. All these characteristics of our literature determine its enormous rôle in the formation of Soviet man. At school already the future citizens of our country become familiar with the lofty thoughts and feelings incarnated in the great works of the classics of Russian literature and in the writings of the best con- temporary writers. Historical songs and traditions, the images of the *bogatyry* (or champions of the *bylinyi* or heroic legends), the inspired lines of *The Raid of Prince Igor,* the genius-reflecting pages of Pushkin's *Poltava* and of Gogol's *Taras Bulba,* the immortal epics of Leo Tolstoy, resurrect before us the pictures of the heroic past of the Russian land, teach us to love our native history, its glorious actors and national heroes. . . . In the war years as never before, we felt how close to us was the work of the best writers of the past, how deeply are revealed in their work the best traits of the national character of the people, how stable are those traditions binding our classical litera- ture with the contemporary one. . . . We must never forget what a mighty influence the artistic word has on the human soul and especially on the youthful soul. And on this depends the further growth of our literature, the further heightening of *its rôle in the formation of the moral outlook* of the man of the Stalin age. . . ."

This passage speaks for itself and is a good indication of the temper and atmosphere prevailing in those circles which guide the evolution of Soviet literature. The insistence on tradition, patriotism, and morality, are almost Victorian in tone; but instead of a vague and optimistic notion of social and mechanical progress, the historically conscious Russian is aware that dialectically a next stage must not only be reached but that he must help the historical process to that end. In this setting the writer is and remains in a special position : he is the *teacher*, but he has teachers above him who remind him that he too must learn and refresh his knowledge at the dialectical source.

CHAPTER II

THE LIFE AND ORGANIZATION OF SOVIET WRITERS

I

The Writer at Home and Abroad

THERE 'has been comparatively little contact between Soviet writers as human beings and other writers or individuals outside Soviet Russia. When Soviet writers go abroad it has usually been as members of a delegation to an anti-Fascist Congress or a conference of some kind; and the duties of representation have appeared to weigh on them too much to make them more accessible to normal intercourse. There have been exceptions of course : Gorky lived for a long time in Sorrento for health reasons, Mayakovsky did his grand tour of Europe and the Americas in his own inimitable style, Essenin did some travelling with Isadora Duncan and created consternation by his unconventional behaviour, Evgenyi Petrov made his journey of " One-Storied America," and Afinogenov did a bicycle tour of Europe. A writer like Alexei Tolstoy was not only a war correspondent in Europe during the last war but also spent some years in emigration in the early days of the Revolution, and has since also visited Czechoslovakia, France and England. Lidin and Fedin, too, have been abroad and have written books on European themes. But it may be said in general that until the end of the war Soviet writers have been very little out of their country, and, if they have travelled, they have done so rather in the vast interior of their country which offers quite interesting contrasts in the North, in Asia and in the Caucasus. Since the war there has been more travelling in Europe but this has so far been confined to the zone of the Soviet armies or to visits with delegations.* It is interesting that a number of these

---

*Since the war a number of writers like Bajan, Perventzev and Kuleshov, have been to London but they came as members either of UNO or youth delegations. In each case parties to meet them were arranged only on the eve of their departure.

writers hold responsible government posts or may be members of the government like the Ukrainian poet Bajan, who is vice-chairman of the Supreme Soviet.

There has therefore been little opportunity for contact between these two worlds, and little or no idea of how Soviet writers live at home or earn their living. In considering the life and work of these writers, we must take into account three aspects : their everyday life, their membership or non-membership of the Party, and their obligations as members of the Writers' Union and other organizations. As far as their everyday life is concerned, it is just Russian and human : there are all the features of normal family life, including in some cases the presence in the family circle of the traditional Russian *nyanya* or children's nurse, servants or chauffeurs. A writer may have a flat in Moscow or Leningrad and a *dacha* or cottage in the country; the only peculiarity in this respect is that since they have to get their accommodation through the Writers' Union and since this latter has to bargain for space with the Town Soviet or the " County Council," it usually happens that a block or several blocks of flats are allotted to the Union with the result that a group of writers find themselves inhabiting the same block. And similarly in the country a particular spot or village may have been chosen for the erection of the writers' cottages as was the case near Moscow where many of the writers, though not all, find themselves living in the summer in the " writers' village " of Peredelkino. Besides the cottages this contains a so-called House of Rest to which writers may retire and isolate themselves either for work or when recovering from illness. There is a children's centre here too. The *dachas* are all of wood as are most Russian houses of this kind, and they are intended for the summer mainly although they can also be lived in in the winter. Peredelkino, though quite a countrified place, is only half-an-hour's drive by car from the centre of Moscow. During the war most writers, except a few like Alexei Tolstoy, had to do without cars, but normally many writers have them. The *dachas* are not all of the same size or character, and may be rented or bought; or a writer may have a house constructed for himself and instal open fires if he likes them. Alexei Tolstoy did not share communal blocks of flats, he had his *dacha* in another spot, and he did like open fires, which are not common in Russia.

There is an organizational tendency, however, to group intellectual workers in available accommodation under their professions, and this applies not only to writers but also to architects, actors and painters. Thus, seeing a large modern block of flats in Moscow, one may be told, " That belongs to the Bolshoy Theatre or the Arts Theatre, or that's where the architects live." In some of these cases the block has been specially built for a particular organization. This does not mean that all the workers of such an organization live in a particular block; some may have their own flats or rooms elsewhere; and also certain distinctions of status are observed. The more " deserving " one is the more chance one has of better accommodation. This arises mainly because accommodation is very short. The same was true of rationing during the war and even writers were split up into categories. A writer of A. Tolstoy's standing would get more than a young poet or novelist, or a " literary worker " like a translator. But then in wartime this was a general feature of the Soviet rationing system, so that, for example, a " Hero of Soviet Labour " might be able to buy a thousand roubles' worth of extra food at fixed prices over and above his normal monthly ration, which would already be above that of, say, the clerical worker, who, with the " dependant " or non-working person, got least of all. A lot more might be said about the intricacies and distinctions of this system but this is not the place, and it was also a wartime measure which will presumably gradually give way to the pre-war system where anybody could buy anything in shops which were not limited to various categories of individuals.

During the war the writer's life was far from normal : many writers were at the front; others were evacuated to places like Kazan, Kuibyshev, Alm Ata and Tashkent. But by the middle of 1943 there was a general return to Moscow, and an increasing sense of normality. It may be asked how does the Soviet writer make his living? Here we must take into account the enormous expansion since the Revolution in the ranks of the readers. Literally millions of people, who before the Revolution could neither read nor write, are now enthusiastically interested in literature. In fact, the publishing houses cannot keep up with the demand and this was, of course, especially true of the war years when shortage of paper severely limited the size of the editions and the variety of published material. The vast reading public is also a factor to be considered in the matter of literary taste and that of education which the State has always in view. An edition of ten thousand copies is just a drop in the ocean here. An edition of 100,000 to 500,000 is more like the norm for more popular books. And this leaves out all the other possibilities such as the translations into the forty odd literary languages of the U.S.S.R. Thus a writer can do very well. But some, of course, will do better than others. If he does not publish much or is not much published, or if he is a beginner or a young poet, the writer may have to struggle and will find it difficult to buy enough wood for heating at the exorbitant open market war-time prices; and he may have to try his hand at translation or some of the other literary jobs. The established writer can, on the other hand, be very well off, or if he is hard up he can get an advance from his publishers. The writer gets royalties and the poet is paid eight to twelve roubles a line; but the price of the book is very often low, so that he earns mainly on the large size of the editions and the frequency of them. A poet, for example, will not wait until he has accumulated a large and impressive work, but will publish as often as he can in small, cheap editions, and then follow up as quickly as he can with selected and collected editions of them; and these will be bought up over-night. It is also customary for the main literary periodicals to print leading novels serially and, in some cases, even simultaneously with the published edition. This is a steady extra source of income. And the public is so large and clamourous that this does not affect the sales of the book. There are also the *Stalin Prizes* awarded annually for the "best works," and they have a sum of a 100,000 or 50,000 roubles attached to them.

But the theatre is one of the best sources of income. Here the author receives seven and a half per cent. royalty for each act of his play when it is performed. Of the war-time successes, we learn that Simonov's *Russian Folk* was staged by one hundred and thirty theatres while Leonov's *Invasion* was put on by ninety-six (this was between 1942 and 1945). In these particular cases the authors are a poet and a novelist respectively, and not professional dramatists. It is nothing uncommon for several Moscow theatres to stage one and the same play simultaneously, since there is an equally great run on the theatres and they are all repertories performing at least three or four different plays a week. The total figures of productions given for three of the war years are five hundred plays produced in the theatres of the R.S.F.S.R., of which three hundred were by Soviet playwrights. The rest were presumably made up by Shakespeare and the other classics.

Membership of the Party carries with it certain duties : one of them is no doubt to interpret correctly the " line " at any given moment; a second is to be dialectically aware of what is happening; a third is to be active socially; and a fourth is to play the part of educator to less conscious elements. Now just as all members of the Privy Council are not cabinet ministers, while all cabinet ministers are *de facto* members of the Privy Council, so not all or even the majority of Soviet writers are Party members; but the Writers' Union has its Party nucleus with a secretary. Since 1932 there have been no separate groupings such as " proletarian writers " or " communist writers " or " Fellow Travellers "; instead there has been general grouping of " Soviet Writers " on an equal basis but with the administrative leadership usually going to the Party men as the most active and authoritative. Many of the writers, however, are not Party members either because they do not feel the vocation or for other reasons. Every now and again a writer may decide that he has the vocation or has done something which will qualify him, and he may apply for membership. An instance of this is Vera Inber's application for membership while she, a poetess, was writing and making herself socially active in besieged Leningrad. She describes the occasion in her *Leningrad Diary*, one of the interesting documents of this period.

Let us see then how a Soviet writer may become a Party member, though in Vera Inber's case it was under exceptional circumstances. Here is a quotation from the Diary : " The bureau of the Regional Commission was in session round an oval table in a large and beautiful room : the floor was laid with carpets, and the table was covered with green material. Questions were put to me and I replied standing.

Question : Why did you not apply to the Party organization of the Writers' Union?

Answer : The Leningrad section of the Writers' Union has not got at present its own Party organization. The front-line writers are attached to military Party organizations. The rest to those of the factories in which they are working.

Question : What social work have you been doing lately?

Answer : I have been lecturing in factories, clubs, military units, in hospitals and schools.

Question : How do you imagine to yourself your future Party work?

Answer : As before I shall continue to write and lecture. But I shall try and do this much better from the point of view of a writer's craft. Besides, I shall do everything that the Party may require of me.

Question : Are you not frightened of the strict Party discipline?

Answer : No, that does not frighten me. I am an organized sort of person by nature.

On the way home from the Regional Committee I asked myself : how did the year of stage as candidate (i.e., there is a year of pre-liminary candidature when the applicant's conduct is checked) really pass? What changes occurred in me in that time?

I lectured in factories, works and in military units. I wrote. That is all true. But I did all that before. Where is the difference?

It is not easy to formulate, but there *is* a difference. Formerly it was like this : I would write, let us say, a successful thing, and I was glad. Failure was bitter. But it was my personal sorrow and joy only. But now I think : *in what measure is that which I write useful for Soviet literature,* which in its turn, appears only as a part of the great thing—the flourishing of my country, the first Socialist country in the world? *Each literary work, if logically continued, must be transformed into action.* Or at least, it can be. I tried to develop this thought and guess what happens beyond that chasm at the end of a page where life begins. What effect have my verses now? How did my pen, my weapon, work in besieged Leningrad? Had I managed to be in any way useful to it? I answer for it. This work was entrusted to me by the Party, it is my Party work."

This passage should throw some light on the psychology of a Party member, and on the relations of Party writers and non-Party writers. It is an important element in the background of Soviet literature as a whole. Vera Inber's case, that of a person who joined the Party as a result of war experience, was common enough at this time when soldiers often did the same before going into desperate action at the front; and the result of it has been that the Party more than doubled its membership during the war, and now numbers well over five million. This contrasts with the figure of six hundred and forty three thousand in December of 1925.

While we are on this subject, it will also be illuminating to quote an ideal portrait of a Soviet writer as it appears in A. Kron's belated obituary* of Iury Krymov, author of *Tanker Derbent*, who was killed in action in 1941 : " Iury Krymov," says Kron, " was in the highest degree an integrated nature; he was guided by the same laws in personal life, in his social relationships and in his creative work. With him there was no division between his literary credo and his personal life. Those citizen's ideals and ethical principles which he affirmed in his work were at the same time the organic attributes of his nature. . . . Probably this quality must be inherent in any writer, whose life and creative work are indissolubly bound with the construction of a new Socialist society. If this thought is true, then we can say for certain that we find vividly expressed in Iury Krymov the features of the new man. . . . The highest happiness is the exploit for the good of mankind in the name of its advanced ideas. For this exploit it is necessary to prepare during the whole of one's life and to seek it, for in it lies the highest value and sense of human existence. Life without struggle or the pathos of creativeness, a consumer's life wingless and moved only by egotistical impulses, degrades man, impoverishes his spiritual world and can afford no real happiness, which is only known to those *men who move history forward*."

Some of the elements of this characterization, and especially the concluding passage, are, as the reader will discover, the *leit motif* of both Soviet literature and its criticism to-day. It represents, of course, the militant outlook of the Party which is the pivot of the whole structure. The non-Party writers, however, remain the majority, and they are varied enough both in their work and attitudes, and range from the writer who is about to realize his vocation to the one who is not given much space in periodicals or who may be ostracized.

Literature and Art, of 16th September, 1944.

2

Anniversaries, Deaths and Funerals

THE scale of the Pushkin centenary celebrations in 1936-37 was a sign of a new orientation not only in Soviet literature but also in Soviet life as a whole. From now on the national heritage, when it was acceptable, was to be made full use of and emphasized. The achievements of the past were to be held up as an example, morals were to be drawn from them, and the foundations of a Russian tradition, of which contemporary Soviet contributions had proved the continuation, were to be consolidated. The war years only confirmed and strengthened this tendency. Russian traditions were sought out and given a new authority in all spheres, scientific and artistic, military and political. In painting, the biographies and the realistic traditions of Repin and Surikov were given a new halo of fame, and these painters were mentioned by Stalin himself in one of his speeches. In the art of war, Suvorov and Kutuzov were claimed as the great ancestors. In the domain of statesmanship, the figure of Ivan the Terrible assumed a new dignity and validity. In science, the discoveries of obscure and neglected Russians were now brought to light : Popov was claimed to have discovered wireless, and Polzunov the steam engine. A new field was now opened to the biographer and the popularizer of past achievements. The process is still going on, and it has a great and immediate educative significance, while at the same time affirming the " originality and independence of Russian thought "—a claim now systematically made.

An example of this trend in the sphere of science is afforded by a statement made by A. Komarov, President of the Academy of Sciences, following an interview he had with Stalin in February, 1945. Here it is : " In view of Stalin's wishes, it is now necessary to broaden the basis of scientific propaganda and to organize a cycle of lectures on the history of Russian science, and about the great Russian scholars, Lomonosov, Mendeleyev, Lobachevsky, Timiryaziev, Pavlov, Michurin and others. In these lectures particular stress must be laid on the greatness and progressive character of Russian science and culture, its indivisible ties with materialistic philosophy, and the struggle of the Russian people against foreign invaders and the reactionary forces of the Tsarist régime."

This is an *ex cathedra* statement, but similar pronouncements can be multiplied to infinity. In the background of these newly formed traditions the celebration of anniversaries plays a prominent part. In literature it affords an opportunity for the frequent re-assessment or emphasis on the qualities and achievements which appear most significant to the contemporary. Forgotten figures also emerge into the limelight. The Gogols, Turgenievs, Tolstoys and Chekhovs, stand on solid pedestals; but new emphasis is given to writers like Griboyedov and Saltykov-Schedrin, who are less well known outside Russia too. Poets of more recent vintage, like Bryusov and Essenin, are also being rescued from neglect. But the tradition that is being built up is not a " house for all," and the selection of ancestors is not an indiscriminate one; it stresses the outlook and qualities that can serve as a model for the present. And when an anniversary such as Griboyedov's is celebrated (January, 1945), it is done with all pomp and ceremony at a special session of the intelligentsia assembled in the Bolshoy Theatre for the purpose; and speeches like Leonov's on the occasion have a solemn " destiny of Russia " note about them faintly reminiscent of Dostoievsky's famous oration on Pushkin in 1880.

These anniversaries remind us of things achieved; but they are also the bell of tolling time. And the ground is being prepared for new anniversaries of contemporaries who were with us but yesterday. The war claimed victims among writers : Krymov, Stavsky, Evgenyi Petrov, Joseph Utkin, and others. A. Novikov-Priboy died in 1944. And there was an extraordinary number of deaths among writers in the few months preceding and following the end of the war with Germany. In a short space of time the deaths were announced of Alexei Tolstoy, V. Shishkov, K. Treniev, Demyan Biedny, V. Veresayev, and Djambul, the Kazakh bard. These months were a succession of funerals and, since Soviet writers are buried with ceremony, it may be of interest to see what happens on these sad occasions.

Let us take Alexei Tolstoy's death as an example. The ceremony in his case falls into three parts : the lying in state, the cremation, and the funeral proper, when the urn with the ashes is deposited at the Novyi Dievychy cemetery, where most prominent Soviet personalities are buried. The lying in state was thus described in the Soviet Press : " At twelve noon, on February 25th, the small hall of the Trades Union House was opened to the public. Thousands of Muscovites came to pay their last respects to their favourite writer. The guard of honour consisted of the members of the government committee for the organization of the funeral, Popov, Gorkin, Tikhonov and Leonov, the Academicians Meschaninov and Obnorsky, the writers Ehrenburg and Ivanov, and the People's artist of the U.S.S.R. Moskvin and many others. At six o'clock the doors were closed to the public and the body was removed for cremation. . . . On February 26th the urn containing the ashes will be placed in the Trades Union Hall, which will be open to the public from 11 a.m. to 2 p.m."

This is what happened on February 26th : " At 11 a.m. the doors were opened to the public. Leading art workers, who came to pay their last respects to the great writer, rendered Tolstoy's favourite pieces of music : the Honoured artists of the R.S.F.S.R. Maksakova sang Chopin's *Sorrow*, People's artist of the U.S.S.R. Kozlovsky sang Beethoven's *Death* and the State Symphony Orchestra of the U.S.S.R. played the finale from Chaikovsky's *Pathetic Symphony*. At 2.15 p.m. members of the funeral committee as well as Shvernik, Vyshinsky and Meschaninov, carried the urn from the Hall and outside a military escort formed up. At the Novyi Dievychy cemetery, the ceremony was opened by comrade Popov (chairman of the Moscow Soviets), who was followed by Shvernik, speaking in the name of the Council of People's Commissars of the U.S.S.R. and the Central Committee. Shvernik referred to the great social work carried on by Tolstoy as a member of the Academy and of the Praesidium of the Union of Soviet Writers, as a deputy of the Supreme Soviet and as a member of the Praesidium of the All-Slav Committee and the Extraordinary State Commission for Investigating German Atrocities. He also spoke of the importance of the articles written by Tolstoy during the war, the most outstanding of which were *My Country, The Blood of the People, Russian Warriors* and *The Brown Drug*. Speeches were also delivered by N. Tikhonov, President of the Writers' Union, the writer and Academician M. Sholokhov, and the People's artist of the R.S.F.S.R., K. Zubov."

Tolstoy's funeral was of course that of the leading Soviet writer. Not all writers' funerals are so impressive, or attended by such a galaxy of personalities, but the ritual is similar in other cases, and the lying in state takes place in the Conference Hall of the Writers' Union. Shvernik's enumeration of Tolstoy's " social " activities is interesting and illustrates once again the attention paid to this aspect of a writer's life. In such cases, a state pension is often granted the widow of the deceased and the nearest relatives.

The following government decree, that of the Council of People's Commissars, on the *Perpetuation of the Memory of A. N. Tolstoy,* was also published on February 28th, and its provisions were : " 1. To erect a monument to A. N. Tolstoy in Moscow; 2. To place a memorial tablet on house No. 2 in Spiridoneyevskaya street where A. N. Tolstoy lived; 3. To rename Spiridoneyevskaya street Alexei Tolstoy street; 4. To charge the State Publishing House of the R.S.F.S.R. (O.G.I.Z.) with the publication of Tolstoy's complete works in 1945-46; 5. To establish the following scholarships in his honour, (a) At the Moscow State University two stipends of 400 roubles each for students of the philological faculty. (b) At the Literary Institue of the Writers' Union two stipends of 400 roubles each."

It is hoped that these details will throw some additional light on the general position of Soviet writers and the atmosphere in which they live. From the Decree we also glean that the Writers' Union has a Literary Institute attached to it which trains budding critics and *literati*; and here students undergo a five-year course.

3

The Structure and Organization of the Writers' Union

THE Union of Soviet Writers of the U.S.S.R. came into being as a result of a Resolution of the Central Committee of the Party published on 23rd April, 1932. It has been in existence therefore for fourteen years and has a look of permanency about it. By the Resolution the various proletarian organizations which were dictating to writers during the years of the first Five Year Plan were abolished and in their place it was decided " To unite all writers upholding the platform of Soviet power and striving to participate in Socialist construction into a single Union of Soviet Writers with a communist fraction within it." This was one of the fundamental literary reforms of the 1930's and created a basis of unity among writers, which had not previously existed when it was a question of proletarian writers versus the rest or of other conflicting movements. By the new measure equal status was granted to all and by 1934, when the first All-Union Congress was held, attended by the representatives of 52 Soviet nationalities, and when reports on 23 national literatures were read, a common platform was worked out on the principle of Socialist Realism. Maxim Gorky had a lot to do with the laying of these new foundations, and it was therefore natural that he should have been elected as the first President.

How then is this Union organized and how does it function? Let us first of all examine the administrative organs. It has a President, who is a noted writer and usually a Party member. It also has a secretary : the first was Scherbakov, who was later to rise very high in the Party hierarchy; during the war he was in charge of the Political Directorate of the Red Army and Head of the Soviet Information Bureau, and by the time of his death in 1945 he also held the rank of " Lieutenant General " in the army. These key posts also appear to be the link in matters of higher policy between the Union and the Department of Propaganda and Agitation of the Central Committee, which is the body that exercises ultimate powers of initiation and control of policy in the world of art as a whole. Its present head, G. F. Alexandrov, does not normally write about literature or criticize it in print,—his range is political, doctrinal and dialectical, and he interprets higher policies and points the direction; but when necessary he puts in an appearance at a Writer's Plenum. Behind Alexandrov and his department there are the Central Committee and Generalissimo

Stalin himself, of whom it has been said, in *A Short Biography*, published in Moscow in 1943, that "The questions which engage his attention range from complex problems of Marxist-Leninist theory to school text-books; from problems of Soviet foreign policy to the municipal affairs of Moscow; from the development of the Great Northern Sea Route to the reclamation of the Colchian marshes; *from the development of Soviet literature and art* to the editing of rules for collective farms." Thus a link is forged between this world of higher policies, which may require at intervals a new modulation or emphasis on a theme, and the world of writers.

We have considered the President and the Secretary, and their authoritative background. Next comes the Praesidium, to which are elected a given number of both Party and non-Party members; and this, with the President and Secretary, constitutes the cabinet of the Union. Let us see what sort of affairs the Praesidium deals with. "The Praesidium discussed the provisional plan of the work of the Writers' Union for the next few months. This plan includes discussions on contemporary literature, on the plans of publishing houses and periodicals for the year 1945, the review of the work of the Bashkir, Lithuanian and Estonian Unions of Writers. The plan has arranged for a number of 'creative evenings' devoted to the best works published in the preceding year, for a conference of the Regional writers of the R.S.F.S.R., for a conference on the question of translations, etc."* The Praesidium also institutes new Commissions and Sections, which are another feature of this Union; and it studies and discusses their reports.

The Commissions have increased in number of late and among them are the Foreign Commission, the Regional, the Nationalities, the Pushkin, the Military, and that of Children's Literature. The Foreign Commission acts as a clearing house for information about "trends" in foreign literatures and it also publishes *International Literature* in several languages. The Regional Commission, which is one of the busiest, links the Praesidium with the provinces. Until 1944 there were several Commissions, each dealing with a particular region, but in that year these were re-organized into one larger Commission covering all the regions of the R.S.F.S.R. and all regional writers, whether in Irkutsk, Novosibirsk, Ivanov, Gorky or Kamchatka. The regional writers are of course distinct from those of the various national Republics, such as Georgia, the Ukraine and Turkmenistan, and of which there are now sixteen including the Baltic Republics and Moldavia; to maintain contact with them there is the distinct Nationalities Commission. The Military Commission was set up to study the literary manifestations of the Red Army and various military problems as they affected literature.

*Literary Gazette of 24th December, 1944.

The Sections are multiplying and reflect a desire to initiate and foster literary *genres*. Thus to the original drama section have been added that of historical fiction, detective fiction, scientific fantasy, and poetry. The sections are a form of specialization and their members meet to discuss newly-written or already-published works, or for auditions of them. Specialists from outside may be called for discussions, and historians may be invited to give their view of a particular historical novel.

It is evident that the life of a Soviet writer is a busy one, for quite a portion of his time is or can be spent in criticism and committee discussions at the Writers' Union, as well as in public lectures and all sorts of commemoration ceremonies and anniversary celebrations. On the other hand he cannot complain of isolation, for once he is established his views are sought for on the most varied topics. However, he can always partially retire when the creative urge is uppermost; and some writers live in greater seclusion; Sholokhov, for example, is rarely seen in Moscow or in the vortex of the Union, for he prefers to live and write in his native Cossack country.

The organization we have described is the headquarters of the Union of Writers of the whole of the U.S.S.R. But we must now imagine it branching out in two directions: the Regions of the R.S.F.S.R. and the Republics. In the former, we find branch Unions in all the leading towns which may have their local writers, such as Leningrad, Smolensk, Gorky, Kuibyshev; in the latter, there are national Unions centred in Kiev, Tashkent, Tiflis, and Alma Ata, which have their own regional ramifications. The connection with the Moscow Headquarters is achieved through the Regional and the Nationalities Commissions. The number of these Unions has increased since new territories have been brought within the orbit. Thus from Kiev we have extensions into the Carpathians, into what was Ruthenia. Similiarly Writers' Unions on the Soviet model have sprung up in Poland, Yugoslavia, Bulgaria and Iran.

In describing the Writers' Union we have omitted to say that the Praesidium is situated in what was formerly the town house of one of the families which figure in Tolstoy's *War and Peace,* and that next door to it is the Writers' Club where the Sections meet and where public lectures or literary evenings are also regularly held.

At regular intervals, too, usually every year, the Praesidium holds a Plenum of the "administration of the Union of Soviet Writers of the U.S.S.R." This is attended by the leading administrative officers of the Republican and Regional Unions, and for several days problems are thrashed out, policies laid down and administrative changes approved. Thus a Plenum was held in Moscow on 16th April, 1945, and prior to that on 5th February, 1944. The latter, which was also the ninth Plenum, was important for certain administrative changes which were introduced. Here it should be noted that since Maxim Gorky's death in 1936, the practice of having a President *and* a Secretary was for the time being dispensed with, and that up to the time of the 1944 Plenum, A. Fedeyev, the novelist, fulfilled the functions of both. But now, to quote part of the proceedings, " In order *to improve* the work of our Writers' organization, the Praesidium has decided to revive the Gorky traditions, those of the First Congress of Writers, when at the head of the Union we had a President and a responsible Secretary. . . ."

L. Sobolev proposed Nicolai Tikhonov as President and the latter was unanimously elected. Tikhonov in his turn then proposed the election of D. Polykarpov as Secretary, who was likewise unanimously elected. Polykarpov was until then Chairman of the All-Union Radio Committee or the Soviet B.B.C. In our terms this appointment would be equivalent to that of, say, Lord Reith or a similar figure as the secretary of a Union of British Writers. It is clear that great importance is attached to this position and, as we have already seen in the case of Scherbakov, this post may become a stepping stone to even higher functions in the Party hierarchy. In themselves these changes obviously made for a stronger administration and increased awareness of current problems; and, as we hear, the work of the Union apparently needed " improvement." Since then various measures such as an increase in the number of sections and commissions, the encouragement of neglected *genres* and of more critical discussions have made themselves apparent. In this connection, we may note that there were many references at the Plenum to the " weak work of literary critics," and Nicolai Tikhonov stressed this in his *Report on Soviet Literature in Wartime*. G. F. Alexandrov also made a speech on the last day of the session; but it was not published in the press.

4

Publishing Houses and Literary Periodicals

A FEW words must be said about the Publishing Houses. In this domain we seem to encounter both centralization and autonomy. There are the associated Publishing Houses of the R.S.F.S.R. (OGIZ). And there is also the main publisher, The State Literary Publishing House (GOSLITIZDAT), with wide ramifications. But we also find that the Union of Soviet Writers has its own publisher, The Soviet Writer; and in the same way, the Academy of Architecture, the Army, and other organizations, are to be found publishing under their own imprint. " The Soviet Writer " has now become the chief publisher for contemporary literature.

Similarly, there are regional Publishing Houses in the main provincial and Republican centres, though Goslitizdat has its branches in all the capitals. From the newly-elected editorial board of Goslitizdat for 1945, we see that it is composed of a mixture of publisher-officials and writers. Of noted writers, we observe that Leonov was elected Vice-Chairman of the Board, while among the members we find Gladkov, Surkov, Sobolev, Tikhonov, Fadeyev, Fedin and Shaginyan. Polykarpov is also a member; and the chairman is one, Golovenchenko. It is evident from this that the writer figures prominently in an advisory capacity to the Publisher, or, in other words, that the Union of Soviet Writers has a large say in the matter. The impression one gets is that while there is a diversity of committees of all sorts covering the network of literary life, it is usually the same small and efficient nucleus of writers and administrators who reappear in all of them as the leaders and they are thus able to ensure a continuity of policy in all spheres.

Turning to the literary periodicals, we find first of all the weekly, *The Literary Gazette (Literaturnaya Gazeta)*. Owing to the shortage of paper during the war, this was merged with another weekly, *Soviet Art,* and the combined weekly appeared as *Literature and Art* (Literatura i Isskustvo). Towards the end of 1944 *The Literary Gazette* resumed independent publication. It is officially described as " the organ of the administration of the Union of Soviet Writers of the U.S.S.R.", and its editors now are B. Gorbatov, E. Kovalchik, V. Kozhevnikov, S. Marshak, D. Polykarpov, L. Sobolev, and A. Surkov, the editor-in-chief. It covers new publications and the activities of writers in the Republics, in Moscow and in the provinces.

The chief monthly periodicals are three in number, for the Leningrad *Zvezda* has been most irregular while *Krasnaya Nov* ceased publication : *Znamya (Banner)*, *Oktyabr (October)*, *and Novyi Mir (New World)*. They are described as "monthly literary-artistic and social-political journals" and they are all "organs of the Union of Soviet Writers of the U.S.S.R." They are edited by different sets of writers and critics, but there is no obvious difference of trend between them though there may be a difference of taste. The editorial board of *Znamya,* for example, is composed of Vs. Vishnevsky, editor-in-chief, K. Simonov, A. Tarasenkov, L. Timofeyev, N. Tikhov and M. Tolchenov, while that of *October* is made up of V. Ilyenkov, P. Pavlenko, F. Panferov, I. Shamorikov, S. Schipachev and M. Iunovich. All these periodicals are more bulky than the average British periodical of the type, and run to some 150 to 200 pages. They are usually divided into a current poetry and fiction section, and into a critical and bibliographical one. Many of the leading novels are first printed in their pages prior to book production. The periodicals are published in editions of twenty-five to fifty thousand; but during the war they tended to appear with delays and frequently two issues were merged into one.

These are the main literary periodicals, but after the war there are signs that a greater variety of publications will become available; and there are interesting developments in the provinces and the Republics. Thus a Tuvinian and a Buriat Mongol review have made their appearance, and there will be many óther such essays. An important step, in June, 1946, was the publication of a new periodical *Cultura i Zhizn* (Culture and Life), edited by the Department of Propaganda and Agitation of the Central Committee. Its aim was to " assist the Press, propaganda and culture, in their activity to further the Communistic education of the workers." But we are left with the impression that, apart from the development among the nationalities and in the regions, the literary life of the capital and centre is a very centralized and concentrated one.

CHAPTER III

THE RE-DISCOVERY OF HISTORY AND THE HISTORICAL NOVEL

I

The Background of the Historical Novel

THE historical novel, the historical biography, and, indeed, the notion of history itself, as a necessary background to present-day events, were all a striking feature of the war years in the Soviet Union, but they require some explanation because of their comparatively recent origin. The interest in historical subjects taken from the national past was already becoming marked especially in the latter 1930's; and it is in the fundamental reforms of that period that we must seek the clue; for in the early years of the Revolution the tendency was to be anti-traditional and to evoke only such figures of the past as were rebels or revolutionaries. In the war years the historical theme really comes into its own, and assumes a position of great importance not only as a literary *genre,* but also as a means of general and political education expressed through the various media of textbook, lecture, films and plays. To Russians, Stalingrad was not merely a turning point in the Russian-German war, it was also a turning point in world history. A new awareness had been born, and then consciously stimulated, of the greatness of Russia not only as the Soviet Union of to-day but also as the past source and "mother" of the many national virtues. During the war the question was asked : what and whence are these virtues that have made the common Russian superior to the German, who used to be regarded as the advanced type of Westerner, both technically and artistically? When he turns to the national past, a Soviet writer now performs an act of national self-awareness, and he seeks to extract from the past both example and inspiration which may illumine the present.

This is a new and important trend; it must be remembered that until about 1932, as will be shown more fully later, quite a different conception of history predominated. This latter also called itself marxist and was based on the theory of economic materialism; Pokrovsky was its chief protagonist; and in his works history was shorn of most of its natural attributes such as the rôle of the personality, the play of human values and loyalties, statesmanship, chronology, and the subtle complex of social, political, economic and religious considerations. Instead, all was economic determinism and class warfare on dogmatic lines irrespective of the period or the age.

The reforms of the 1930's, of which a revised conception of history was one, laid the foundation for the re-birth of the historical novel as a more than accidental manifestation of the aspirations of the new Russia that was emerging in these years. In the beginning, writers were slow and not too sure of themselves. They no doubt remembered that they were liable to make mistakes and might involuntarily "misrepresent" history, and so unleash the fury of official critics. The first Soviet historical novel, Olga Forsh's *Clad in Stone,* depicting some of the 19th century revolutionaries, had been literary in its approach. So were the historical novels, *Khukhlya* about the Decembrists, and *The Death of Vazir Mukhtar* about Griboyedov, of Tinyanov, talented writer, critic and once a member of the Formalist group. Historical themes, when they did appear in the 1920's, were usually associated with early revolutionaries or rebels such as Stenka Razin; and it was the dualism of oppression and revolt that was stressed rather than the significance of the age in relation to national history as in the later works.

The pioneer of the new trend of the historical novel was, of course, Alexei Tolstoy, with his *Peter the Great,* Volume I (1930) and Volume II (1934), and his play on the same subject. It is, however, clear that the atmosphere of those early days was not altogether propitious for works on such broad national lines. In his brief autobiography, Tolstoy mentions that his play was bitterly attacked when staged in 1929—"The staging of the first version of *Peter* in the filial of the Arts Theatre was met hostilely by R.A.P.P., and it was saved by comrade Stalin when, already in 1929, he gave a correct historical interpretation of the age of Peter." Tolstoy goes on to say that he felt that the " hostile atmosphere " around him dissolved as soon as R.A.P.P. was suppressed (1932) and that he was only then able to give all his energy to literary and social work. The 1930's also produced another historical novel of the new type in Chapygin's *Stenka Razin.* Here the " rebel " was seen in the background of the 17th century Russia of his day. There was also Kostylev's *Minin and Pajarsky.* These were the chief novels up to the outbreak of the war, although historical subjects were being popularized in other ways, as, for example, in the films *Peter the Great, Alexander Nevsky* and *Suvorov.*

2

The Re-discovery of History

HISTORY as now taught in Soviet schools or presented in historical fiction does not differ so fundamentally from ours as it did in the 1920's. The difference is one of degree : of emphasis, selection, prejudice. The greatest difference lies perhaps in that the rulers of the Russian State have their own theory of historical development—that of "dialectical and historical materialism," and that this theory is enforced through the Ministry of Education in the schools, and through other organs in those spheres where a knowledge of history impinges upon the writer or the man in the street. The teaching of history and the use of appropriate textbooks was to some extent controlled in France before the war— in the schools at least. Fashion and selection as well as political motif play their part in most education. The Russian, who has worked out a way of life for himself and who now claims to know where he is going, is not unnaturally insistent that the past shall serve him as well. But he is, of course, more dogmatic, all-embracing and political about it all; and also more critical of "objective" history for which he has no understanding or use. But then, Russian society has not lost the motive-power of belief, and where belief is, there a measure of intolerance is bound to thrive.

The Soviet view of history to-day is less dissimilar in appearance at least from what we are accustomed to regard as normal, than it was twenty years ago when the Pokrovsky school of history was in its prime. Anyhow, to understand the new historical trend and indeed the atmosphere of the new Soviet Russia of to-day, it is essential to grasp the implications of the change brought about by the reform in the teaching of history in the middle 1930's and the suppression of the Pokrovsky school.

From 1919 to 1932, the historian M. N. Pokrovsky (1868-1932), once described as "the greatest marxist historian in the world," was the chairman of the State Learned Soviet (*Gus*), attached to the Commissariat of People's Education (*Narcompros*). As the leading marxist historian of his day, Pokrovsky was responsible for the educational programmes and textbooks in history, and his own book, *A Brief History of Russia, was the then classic on the subject.* Round Pokrovsky were grouped other historians and critics who shared his theories of historical evolution, and these indeed had the sanction of the government of the day.

In his book, Pokrovsky shows himself the champion of that trend of

47

marxist thought dominant in the 1920's, which analysed history in terms of economic determinism and class warfare only. His analysis is abstract and schematic : there are no living historical personalities; no local colour or chronological details; all profound social and political changes are explained in terms of economic factors, and these are valid for any age. Applied to literature, this theory produced statements like the following made by the critic, Pereverzev : " There is no individual in literature. To understand Byron, we must take a description of English aristocratic society, for the person of Byron does not exist. Neither does Pushkin."

The currency of this abstract and arid doctrine coincided with the notion, also popular in the 1920's, that the day of the school and the textbook was over, and that new radical methods of teaching should be tried and experimented with. The Dalton plan was given a trial and a system of " complexes " was instituted. These latter were a method of studying a series of rather wide subjects (throughout the ages) such as, for example, Nature and Man, Labour, Society. Pereverzev's statement above is a clue to the abstract treatment employed. At the same time, textbooks and lectures were discouraged. " History should be taught as an outline of the historical evolution of the different sides of human culture in their mutual relations and conditioning." That was the somewhat vague ideal. History in the sense of chronological data, concrete events and definite periods, statesmen and soldiers, poets and scientists, had ceased to exist. It was H. G. Wells's *History of the World* made still more abstract.

A reaction was inevitable; and politically it coincided with the purge of Trotskyist elements from the body of the new industrialized Russian State. By 1936 Pokrovsky and his historical school had been fairly thoroughly purged—but not entirely, for it was not easy to eliminate all the traces from all the textbooks or from all the minds that had been nurtured on these theories—and branded as " defeatist, anti-scientific, anti-Marxist, and anti-Leninist." The reform had obviously fundamental implications and involved a thorough reorganization of the national education in all spheres and it could not be effected in a single year. In 1943 one still came across echoes of the Pokrovsky controversy and the Soviet educational system is still in the process of overhaul.

The main battle, however, was won in the middle 1930's and its stages were as follows : in 1931, by a decree of the Central Committee, history was re-established as an independent subject in the schools of the U.S.S.R.; in 1934, a decree of the Central Committee and the Soviet of People's Commissars laid down the principles of the teaching of civil history in the schools of the U.S.S.R.; in 1934, too, Stalin, Zhdanov and Kirov published their *Commentary* on the projected textbooks on the History of the U.S.S.R.; in 1936, there was a decree of the Central Committee and the Soviet of People's Commissars on the teaching of history in higher educational establishments; and again, in 1936, a decree dealt with new history textbooks, drawing attention to Pokrovsky's "distortions" of history and to their prevalence still in the works of contemporary historians. Eventually, in 1936, a new history textbook, Shestakovich's *Short Course of History of the U.S.S.R.*, was produced; and finally, in 1938, there appeared the fundamental book of the new historical period, *A Short Course in the History of the All-Russian Communist Party (of bolsheviks)*, a section of which, *On Dialectical and Historical Materialism*, was written by Stalin himself. An accompanying decree pointed out, among other things, that " In historical studies until lately anti-Marxist distortions and vulgarizations were connected with the so-called school of Pokrovsky, which presented historical facts distorted, and contrary to historical materialism threw light on them from the standpoint of the present and not from the standpoint of those conditions in the environment of which the historical events took place, and in that way, distorted real history." In the same year was published the first volume of a collective work, entitled *Against the Anti-Marxist Conceptions of M. N. Pokrovsky*, in which Pokrovsky's errors were analysed under different historical headings such as "The Tartar Yoke as explained by Pokrovsky," "The Foreign Policy of the 19th century Autocracy in Pokrovsky's Distorting Mirror," and so on.

If we have dwelt at length on this reform, it is because we think it essential to the understanding of the new Soviet Russia of the 1940's, of the new national revolutionary outlook, and finally of the evolution of the Soviet historical novel, which takes on a new lease of life in this period.

3

The Historical Theme and the Historical Novel since 1941

THE revolution in the interpretation of history was but one aspect of the profound changes which affected the life of the U.S.S.R. and the outlook of its citizens during these years. The most important was the success achieved in building up a new industry and in collectivizing agriculture. This was the fundamental revolution and the source of future power. The reforms consequent upon the analysis of the new situation thus created were to be effected gradually over a span of years and are far from being terminated now. In the sphere of the historical theme, there was already the beginning of a renaissance in the later 1930's, as illustrated in Eisenstein's film, *Alexander Nevsky*, Simonov's poem on Suvorov, the institution of centenary celebrations such as that of Pushkin in 1937, and the work begun on a number of historical novels which were to make their mark during the war years. The war itself proved a stimulant and only quickened the process. The search after historical analogies became less artificial and more immediately fraught with emotional content. It was natural that patriotism in action should be reflected in " the glorious deeds of the past." A war such as this summoned into play forces and strata of the population which had previously been less considered or even adversely affected. A broad national policy was not only a sound policy but also a correct inter-pretation of the wishes of the majority. Thus, even the Orthodox Church gained progressive official recognition; and by 1944 the method advocated for fighting superstition was not the encouragement of anti-God societies but the popularization of scientific ideas. This is not very different from what happened in Great Britain in the later days of the Victorian age, when the science versus religion controversy was at its height.

On November 7th, 1941, when Moscow was hard pressed by the Germans, an army review was held in the Red Square and, in the course of it, the historical theme received a new consecration. In his historic speech, Stalin said : " Let the manly image of our great ancestors, Alexander Nevsky, Dimitry Donskoy, Minin and Pojarsky, Suvorov and Kutuzov, inspire us in this war." Thus, the bond between the national past and present was unmistakably and officially sealed.

The historical novel as it emerges during the war seems to serve three closely-knit purposes : national, patriotic and educational. On the one hand, it reflects a new awareness and pride in national unity and achievement, and seeks the support of notable predecessors or relevant traditions in all spheres of activity. On the other, it manifests an increasing desire to assess the national heritage and extract from it both moral principles and examples of meritorious conduct (loyalty, patriotism, heroism). The active rôle of the *people* and the imperative need for the leaders to base themselves on the people and to feel its pulse are stressed throughout. Another aspect, a political one, is also increasingly emphasized—that of the stages, principles and character of the development of the Russian State throughout the ages. A culmination of this development is implied in the present or near future. These trends are largely educative and are intended to stimulate national awareness. They are also inevitably political in the sense in which a particular image of history is being created. Historical situations, personalities and events, are presented anew as examples of actions to be studied and imitated or of mistakes to be avoided when fulfilling present-day aspirations. In the light of this re-illuminated past, the present course of history assumes a dynamic and inevitable logic, and the citizen is encouraged to become aware of his potentially active part in this process which has a purpose and aim. If he is sufficiently aware, he becomes a *maker* of history rather than its *agent*.

What are the main historical themes which emerge in these years? Broadly they may be divided into mediæval and modern. Among the former we have Russia in the days of the Tartar invasion and Russia of the Kiev age and her connection with Byzantium. Among the latter there are the ages of Ivan the Terrible and Peter the Great, Pugachev and Suvorov and the Napoleonic war of 1812, Alexander I and Pushkin, Admiral Nahimov and Sebastopol, General Brusilov and the War of 1914-18.

To what extent can these themes have a topical interest? In 1939, when the question arose of Polish Ukrainian relations following the collapse of Poland, the talented Ukrainian dramatist, A. Korneychuk, published a play about the 17th century Ukrainian leader, *Bogdan Khmelnitsky*. A film was also made on this subject. The topicality of a theme may be judged by the amount of publicity given to it. Sometimes the publicity is impressive and simultaneous projection is given to a theme through all the available media such as the novel, biography, poetry, the theatre, the cinema, painting and lectures.

The themes of Ivan the Terrible and Zoya Kosmodemyanskaya have been publicized in this intensive way. Not only has an older play, *Tsar Feodor* (son of Ivan) by A. K. Tolstoy (1817-75), been revived at the Arts Theatre, but two new plays on Ivan the Terrible have been written during the war by A. N. Tolstoy (1882-1945) and produced at the Malyi and the Arts Theatre respectively. The first of a series of films on this subject by Eisenstein appeared in 1944. There are also a number of paintings by Sokholov-Skalya, in particular one illustrating the surrender of a Livonian city to Ivan; there are the novels of Kostylev and the historical works of Vipper, Bakhrushin, and others. " The Karl Marx Factory in Leningrad has organized a cycle of lectures on ' Ivan the Terrible and his campaigns.' " This notice from *Trud*, the Trades Union paper, of the 2nd March, 1945, confirms the widespread nature of this publicity.

Whereas Alexander Nevsky is an " heroic ancestor," Ivan the Terrible is presented now as the image of a great statesman and the personification of the problem of the consolidation and expansion of the Russian State. This view represents a re-assessment of Ivan's life and work, which in the past has been distorted " due mainly to the Germans, our constant enemies, always ready to blacken what we hold dear " (Eisenstein). Ivan was not a cruel despot as depicted in romantic history but a great statesman who, in consolidating the Russian State, had to face and deal with dangerous internal and external enemies; Ivan's foreign policy was to get a necessary outlet to the sea; and Ivan actively encouraged cultural progress—the Russia of his day was not the barbarous country as sometimes painted by foreigners, but was rapidly becoming a cultured country of the Renaissance type under Ivan's guidance. Thus, in making the film, Eisenstein had in mind " to stress the power of the Russian State. . . . the magnificence of court life has been dwelt on with this end in view. . . . The main idea of the film is the might of Russia and the great struggle which took place to consolidate this might. . . ." This is undoubtedly also true of Tolstoy's plays and the other recent images of this period, such as Vladimir Solovyer's *The Great Sovereign.*

The theme of Zoya Kosmodemyanskaya is by contrast a contemporary one, but it has become historical almost over-night. Zoya is the nearest thing to a contemporary martyr-Saint—an eighteen-year-old girl steadfast in the face of torture and death; a shining moral example. Her memory is already enshrined in poetry, painting, biography, film and ballet. We may take it that these are examples of the concrete historical side of Socialist Realism and the very antithesis of the one-time Pokrovsky school which denied the importance of personalities and heroes in the historical process.

We have mentioned A. N. Tolstoy's new plays on Ivan the Terrible. They were his main wartime contribution, and, as he says, " written in answer to the humiliations which the Germans inflicted upon my country. I evoked the great passionate Russian soul of Ivan the Terrible, in order to arm my enraged conscience." These plays, *The Eagle and His Mate* and *The Difficult Years* (1943), treat of different periods of Ivan's reign : the first covers the conquest of Kazan from the Tartars and the Livonian war and the second the institution of the *oprichina,* internal plots and the raid on Moscow of the Crimean Tartars. Great importance was attached to the production of the first play in Moscow in the autumn of 1944 at the Malyi Theatre; the décor was by Sokholov-Skalya.

Some confusion may result for foreign students and readers in the future from the fact that two Tolstoys wrote plays on the same period. A. K. Tolstoy's plays, *Death of Ivan the Terrible, Tsar Feodor Ivanovich,* and *Tsar Boris,* were a trilogy in verse, and they pass beyond the reign of Ivan. Unfortunately, A. N. Tolstoy died (February, 1945) before completing Part III of his *Peter the Great* series of novels, but the opening chapters of this third volume were printed in *Novyi Mir.* The book was planned to cover events from 1702 to the Battle of Poltava (1709). From a statement by Madame Tolstoy, it appears that his method of work was such that very few notes have remained to indicate the detailed structure of this uncompleted novel. The earlier volumes are still the best that has been written in this *genre* in the Soviet Union. It is interesting to note that the theme of Peter the Great first attracted Tolstoy in 1917, on the outbreak of the Revolution, and that he was the pioneer of the novel of the broadly national theme.

With V. Kostylev, we are back again to the theme of Ivan the Terrible. This writer is engaged on a trilogy of that period. The first volume, *Moscow on the March*, begun in 1938, appeared in 1941, and involved the author in a controversy with S. Borodin, who accused him of " slandering the Russian people " and propagating descriptions of Russian types " insinuated by writers of Western orientation." The second volume will deal with the problem of the Russian outlet to the sea. Kostylev's approach to the historical novel is based on the notion that " the problem of the novelist is to express a useful truth in an interesting fable." The reign of Ivan is for him " also the beginning of the formation of a multi-national and most extensive State, shaking by its emergence the whole of Western Europe." Kostylev is also planning to start work on a novel about the Black Sea expeditions of the Kievan Princes, their relations with Byzantium and the Balkans.

The disasters and the national experience associated with the Tartar invasions of the thirteenth century are described by V. Yan in his trilogy, *Ghengiz Khan, Batu Khan* and *Alexander the Uneasy*. The heroes of the first two of these books are " the Russian people fearlessly defending their native land " rather than well-defined historical personalities. The third volume (1945) deals, of course, with the times of Alexander Nevsky. Yan has also lately published a volume of short stories, *Fires on the Mounds,* which touch on the times of Alexander the Great. It is interesting to reflect that Alexander the Great's expedition impinged upon territories such as Uzbekistan which are now part of the Soviet Union. In an article on *The Problem of the Historical Novel,* Yan agrees with Leo Tolstoy that the aim of all creative works should be " usefulness and virtue," and that the aim of such works should be a lofty one. He maintains that " the historical novel, besides being accurate and entertainingly written, should, above all, be a teacher of the heroic, of truth and goodness." As to the artistic form, " here the author should have complete freedom to seek and create new forms. Here we may recall Chekhov's words that only that which is new is talented and that which is talented is new."

Mediæval Russia is the background of S. Borodin's *Dimitry Donskoy* (1942), the story of the Prince who routed the Tartar Khan Mamai on the Field of Kulikovo in 1378. This theme has, of course, often recurred in Russian literature, and Dimitry Donskoy is one of the heroic ancestors mentioned by Stalin in 1941. Mediæval Kiev is the setting of *Prince Vladimir,* a play by Olga Forsh and G. Boyadjiv, while Antonovska's *The Great Mauravy* is a novel of the 17th century national hero of Georgia, George Saakadze. *Ghengiz Khan, Dimitry Donskoy* and *The Great Mauravy* were all awarded Stalin Prizes as outstanding historical novels in 1942.

The Napoleonic war of 1812 was naturally a favourite theme and had inspired a number of biographies and novels and stories, such as Golubov's *No Easy Victories (Bagration)*, 1943, Vsevolod Ivanov's *At Borodino*, 1943, and Bragin's *War-Leader Kutuzov*, 1944, but they are in no sense exceptional. Neither is *Suvorov*, by Ossipov. A more impressive novel is V. Shishkov's *Emelyan Pugachev* (Vol. I, 1943), a broad canvas of the reign of Catherine II and the days of that Cossack rebel. This novel is undoubtedly the best thing in this *genre* after the *Peter the Great* novels of A. N. Tolstoy. Part of the book was written in Leningrad during the siege. Like Tolstoy, the author also died in 1945 before completing the second volume of his work. Soviet historical fiction has suffered a great loss in these two writers.

Pushkin, the great Russian poet, who was killed in a duel in 1837, will always attract the biographer and the novelist. Two of the latest novels about him are Grossman's *The Death of a Poet* and Iugin's *Pushkin in the South*. Coming nearer to our day, the theme of the Russo-Japanese war was revived by A. Stepanov in his bulky *Port Arthur*, 1944. The book had been first published in the south of Russia in 1940, but the edition fell into the hands of the Germans, and its re-publication on the eve of the second Russo-Japanese war made it all the more topical. As a boy, Stepanov was himself a witness of the siege and afterwards he made it a hobby to collect eye-witness accounts and other documents of the siege. As a novel it suffers perhaps from too much detail, but the picture it paints is convincing enough. It brings out the devotion and self-sacrifice of the rank and file of the army during the siege and exposes the corruption and treachery on the higher commanding levels—a fact well enough authenticated. Another imposing three-volume novel of over a thousand pages is the *Sebastopol Ordeal* by Sergeyev-Tsensky (b. 1876) which was awarded the Stalin Prize in 1941. It is an ambitious panorama of the war year 1854-55, with the defenders of Sebastopol in the central plan. Though a writer of an older generation, Sergeyev-Tsensky is actively working on a whole cycle of novels to be known as *Transfiguration*. The cycle will comprise some ten novels. About half of them have already been published, and his historical novels, *The Brusilov Break Through*, 1943, and *The Guns Promote*, 1944, are part of this cycle.

Soviet writers are also turning to the theme of General Brusilov, the commander of the 1916 offensive. There are a play, *General Brusilov*, by Ilya Selvinsky, published in 1943 and later staged, and a novel, *Brusilov*, by Sleskin. Brusilov's own memoirs have also been published. Brusilov, although a Tsarist general, is now seen as a patriot and a capable commander, who was handicapped in his plans of offensive by the stupidity and corruption of the higher court circles;

and there is a great deal of truth in this thesis. This period is now attracting a number of other writers, and S. Golubov, the author of *No Easy Victories*, is working on a trilogy, *The Fiery Wall*, which will cover the years 1910-18. Olga Forsh is writing a trilogy, *The Deathless Town*, about Petersburg and Leningrad, embracing the early days, 1905-17, and the days of the siege.

4

The Historical Novel and the Future

SINCE the days in the early 1930's, when A. N. Tolstoy wrote his first tentative novel about Peter the Great, which Gorky called " the first real historical novel of the Soviet age," there has obviously been a great development in this *genre*, reaching its first climax during the war. This development is now well beyond the initial stage but it still has a long way to go to produce anything on the level of Leo Tolstoy's *War and Peace*. It is significant that during the war this book became a sort of writer's bible, and it is undoubtedly the ambition of many a mature or aspiring writer to write a similar epic about the men and events of the period we have just lived through. There can be no doubt that many attempts will be made; and their success or failure will depend above all on the degree of genius with which the writer is endowed. A Leo Tolstoy or his like are not born every day, not even in every age. The material is there and so is the awareness of the task to be performed; but the question also arises of the degree of objectivity and the perspective in time necessary for the accomplishment of such a work. If it is achieved, it will more likely be the work of a writer of a younger generation whom we have no means of envisaging yet, and he will be writing in different conditions and in a different historical atmosphere.

The Soviet historical novel has come to stay and its further development should be a matter of interest. Its quality so far has been uneven, and now that A. N. Tolstoy and V. Shishkov have gone, its leading exponents are comparatively few : Sergeyev-Tsensky, Yan, Borodin, and Olga Forsh. Two of these writers were born in the 1870's. But as Yan says, " The past of the peoples of our country, especially of the Great-Russian people, offers inexhaustible material for many historical novels. It serves as a source of understanding and perception of the historically formed character of the Soviet man of to-day. That is why the historical novel, created in our time and answering the strictest demands, does not divert us from actuality but on the contrary helps towards a deeper and more serious understanding of the present." If we examine the implications of this statement, it

55

will reveal a tendency in the Soviet writer to make actuality out of history, and history out of actuality. This tendency does exist and is no doubt the result of the dialectical analysis of reality. And in this sense every Soviet writer has become potentially a writer of historical plays or novels. There is, therefore, every sign that the *genre* will develop enormously, not only in Russia proper, but also eventually in the other Soviet Republics, European, Asiatic and Caucasian. Thus, besides *The Great Mauravy,* other Georgian historical novels have made their appearance. K. Gamsahurda, author of *The Right Arm of the Master* and *David the Builder,* treats of Georgian 11th century history and the Georgian kings of that time. King David (1089-1125) is portrayed as a national hero who also defeated the Seljuk Turks. There will also very likely be an increasing number of books devoted to Russian's relations with her Eastern and Western neighbours as well as about the history of other countries (Eugene Lann's *Old England* of the days of Marlborough is already one such example). In this connection, the educative importance of the historical novel should not be forgotten. Its national significance has already clearly emerged.

While it is true that a more critical attitude to historical problems is the order of the day since the end of the war, this must be taken to imply a change in emphasis rather than an abandonment of the historical heritage.

CHAPTER IV

THE IDEA OF THE HERO IN SOVIET FICTION

L IKE an advancing army, the Revolution at its first onset had destroyed many bridges; and there are still many people who have a more vivid impression of that destruction than of any constructive work since achieved. The lines of communication between Soviet Russia and the outside world have remained tenuous and uncertain; and the characters or types revealed in Soviet fiction have not yet been critically assessed. But communication was slow even before the bridges were blown up. It is true, we already find Matthew Arnold writing about *Anna Karenina,* but Carlyle had evidently not heard of Pushkin when he wrote that Russia had not produced a great national poet; and both Dostoieysky and Chekhov attracted more general attention only after 1918. For all their power, psychological interest and humanity, the characters of Dostoievsky and Chekhov created some consternation; their world was *so* strange. By comparison, Turgeniev's and Tolstoy's characters were more balanced and probable in the eyes of the western world. When it came to Soviet fiction, the reader had lost his bearings; and besides, there were no longer one or two great names of writers to be conjured with or one or two mountains to climb, but rather a plethora of smaller mounds and hills, a number of none-too-familiar names, and a distracting variety of trends and political arguments.

But not all the bridges were blown up; and some of the others were to be mended. There was Maxim Gorky, of whom no solid critical appreciation has yet appeared in English; and there was Alexei Tolstoy. Since the early days of the Revolution and in particular since the 1930's, many of the traditional threads have been picked up and a surprising number of bridges have been rebuilt. When we look at Soviet fiction to-day, we behold Russian fiction as it has developed since the Revolution, dressed in a different garb, clothed in the experience of a profound national transformation. The question naturally arises : Who is the hero of this fiction?

From Feodor Dostoievsky and Leo Tolstoy, Anton Chekhov and Maxim Gorky, to Alexei Tolstoy and Michael Sholokhov, Leonid

Leonov and Konstantin Fedin, and other Soviet novelists, is like stepping down from a higher range of mountains to a lower one. Some might be tempted to jump to conclusions and blame the Revolution or the political and social order that resulted from it for this absence of a "greater literature." But is this really the case? Like any great event which disturbs or alters the social order, such as the war of 1914-18 or the war of 1939-45, the Revolution had a tremendous repercussion not only on Russian life and the world at large, but also on Russian literature as it *found it.* Many threads were snapped and many writers disappeared in the whirlpool of events. New people, new facts, a new basis of life and a new vision of the world, emerged, and these were bound to condition literature anew. And then in the 1930's it was discovered that many of the leading ideas and theories of the first decade were "wrong," and not only the writer but the average Soviet citizen had to re-adapt himself mentally to a new but more traditionally Russian conception of his place in the scheme of things. Is it to all this that we must attribute the lack of greater mountain ranges, of a greater literature during this period? But in what state did the Revolution *find* Russian prose? If we look at the facts, we have to admit that, though Dostoievsky may have become popular in England in 1918, he really died in 1881. If we examine the writers of the great prose age, that is, Turgeniev (d. 1883), Dostoievsky (d. 1881), Saltykov-Schedrin (d. 1889), Lieskov (d. 1895), and Tolstoy (d. 1910), we are forced to conclude that the great prose came to an end in the eighties of the last century. By that time these great writers had either died or had already written their best works. Their chief successors were Chekhov (1860-1904) and Maxim Gorky (1869-1936). Of the others such as Korolenko (1851-1921) and Kuprin (1870-1938), Bunin (b. 1870) and Andreyev (1871-1919), Remizov (b. 1877) and Biely (1880-1934), it may be said that they were all eminent writers who had made valuable and sometimes original contributions to literature, but theirs was definitely not a great age of prose. A number of other writers born in the 1870's, such as Sergeyev-Tsensky, Alexei Tolstoy, Olga Forsh and Prishkin, survived into the new period and became leading Soviet writers.

On the eve of the Revolution, Russian prose was in a state of decline by comparison with the great age that had preceded it. Moreover, a trend had set in as in Western Europe—a trend particularly evident in the work of Andrei Biely—the implications of which were the disintegration of the novel in its narrative classical form. This disintegration was well on its way on the eve of the Revolution and the latter, in its early stages, only accelerated the process. In Biely's *Childhood of Kotik Letayev,* written in 1915-16 in Switzerland and published in 1922 in Petersburg, Pilnyak's *Naked Year,* 1922,

Vesioly's *Rivers of Fire* (1924) and *Homeland* (1926), Malyshkin's *The Fall of Dayir*, we can see the substitution of lyricism and rhythm, mass feeling and disjointed narration, for direct narrative, logical action and the description of character. In the West, we were of course afforded more monumental and far-reaching examples of this style in Joyce's *Ulysses* and *The Work in Progress*.

The new period of Soviet prose does not properly begin till after the end of the Civil War, in 1922-23, when with Gorky benevolently acting as midwife, a new generation of prose writers, many of them novices straight from the ranks of the Red Army or from Partisan detachments, begins to emerge; and the novel is given a new and tentatively realistic birth. This is not the place to examine the different literary theories of that time or the different forms which the novel assumed in the 1920's; but it is significant that, with Fadeyev's novel about the civil war in Siberia, *The Rout*, 1926, and Sholokhov's now well-known *And Quiet Flows the Don,* 1929, there was a conscious return to the style and method of Tolstoyan narration. (Only some fifteen years before, in their 1912 Manifesto, the Russian Futurists had urged that Tolstoy should be thrown out of "the boat of our age"; and the Andrei Biely school of prose writing had put this precept into practice.) Now the Tolstoyan method was vindicated in some of the better works of the new period, and Tolstoy's reputation as a master-writer and a model was to grow rather than diminish until, by the time of the war, it had become the ambition of many a writer to do for his own age what Tolstoy had done for his with *Sebastopol* and *War and Peace*. But by 1946 Tolstoy is not the only model or example that a budding writer may follow : most of the classical prose-writers have been or are being revived through new mass editions of their works. The satirical works of Saltykov-Schedrin and the short stories of Chekhov are being much publicized at present, while the works of Kuprin and Korolenko have also been re-published. Among foreign prose classics, Balzac and Maupassant, Dickens and Thackeray, seem to be the most popular.

This is but a brief background to the Soviet novel to-day; but its implications are significant. It is clear that since 1932 a synthesis has been taking place, at first gradually and then at an accelerated rate, between the young literature, founded in the 1920's, and the great traditions of Russian 19th century literature. The schism of 1918, which had made itself felt in various ways in the next two decades, now appears to have been finally healed in the tempering experience of the war, and to have resulted in a synthesis of *revolutionary* and *national* experience, of tradition and dialectical materialism. Thus by November, 1945, in a speech made to the Moscow Soviet, V. Molotov can say that "the rapid growth of the cultured life of our country and the fact that *the intelligentsia* as the most cultured section of the population, *has become fused with the people,* thus raising the moral and political unity of Soviet society to a still higher level. . . ."

This statement is but the official recognition of an accomplished fact, for which there is plenty of other evidence. The "fusion" affirmed by Molotov implies the disappearance of any serious antagonism that may have persisted either between the intellectuals or between some of them and the new order of things; and inversely it also connotes that a general agreement has been reached on the literary traditions to be defended and developed, as well as on the general direction in which Soviet literature is to evolve in the future. Broadly speaking, this direction is a national and classical one, with the principle of Socialist Realism and the dynamic method of dialectical materialism to serve the writer as a guide and to stimulate his *historical sense;* and this *consciousness of history* is also the link between him and the people in its national and revolutionary development.

As a result, the writer now finds himself within a much broader framework in which to produce his creative work, and if some writers are still slow to grasp this new charter of liberties, it is because such things are inevitable in a period of transition when a great deal of responsibility falls upon the critics. It may be argued that the Soviet writer is still limited, that he is still within a "framework." That is, of course, true, but only relatively so : the "framework" in question is approximating more and more to that of any strongly defined tradition. Europe has not been without such traditions in the past if we take only the rise and development of the classical tradition in 17th century France; in the drama it lasted long enough —until Victor Hugo's *Preface to Cromwell* in 1827. In Soviet Russia we are still in a period of transition when the traditions and foundations are being established in preparation for a new classical era; the conscious aim, and there appears to be one, is to create as far as possible conditions which will pave the way to a great new age of Russian letters. And this age is prophesied to follow the period of the Great Patriotic War just as the age of Pushkin followed upon that of the Napoleonic Wars.

All this has the closest bearing upon the conception of the hero in Soviet fiction. It would be a mistake to assume that the hero emerged all ready-made in the 1920's and has since been reproduced *ad infinitum.* On the contrary there was a succession of heroes and some of them were in conflict with each other. In the early days, the hero was the anonymous mass, as can be seen in Pilnyak's *The Naked Year,* and Serafimovich's *The Iron Torrent.* The following quotation from *The Iron Torrent* gives us an idea of this mass hero : " There go thousands, tens of thousands of people, already there are no units, detachments, battalions, no regiments—there is one anonymous vast unity. It goes forward with countless steps, it looks with endless eyes,

and its one boundless heart beats with the majority of hearts. . . ."
Mayakovsky's poem *150,000,000* expressed the same notion in verse.
At the same time, the image of the *bolshevik*, as the born leader in
action and the driving power of events, began to emerge in novels
like *Chapayev* 1923 by Furmanov (1891-1926), *The Week* and *The
Commissars* by Libedinsky, and *The Rout* by Fadeyev. But that is by
no means the whole scene. In Fibikh's *Intoxication*, we have a
" Darwinian " character who maintained that " It is the most intelligent, the strongest, those who are in authority, who lay down the
law. . . . For my part, I snap my fingers at the law. I make my own
laws. I do what I like; if anyone wants to oppose me, I knock him
down and sweep him out of the way."

Other writers like Fedin in *The Brothers*, Kaverin in *The Artist
is Anonymous*, and Olesha in *Envy*, were concerned with the intellectual's doubts and problems in the face of a world of changing values.
In the characters of the romantically subjective and frustrated
intellectual, Kavalerov and the grimly efficient bolshevik, Babich,
Olesha has confronted two diametrically opposed worlds : that of
sentiments and spiritual values, on the one hand, and that of inhuman
business efficiency on the other. The dramatic version of this novel
was significantly entitled *The Conspiracy of Sentiments*. Critics have
since noted a tendency at this time to portray the bolshevik as an
abstract and efficient type of American business man and no more;
and they attribute this tendency among other things to the abstract
and over-simplified character of some of the theories and the
criticism of that day, when Pokrovsky was the chief historian and
Pereverzev a leading critic.

In the early 1930's, in the background of the Five Year Plan and
the vast schemes of industrialization, a new type of industrial hero
appears, as in Gladkov's *Power* and other novels of the type. At the
same time, the birth of a newly collectivized countryside and its new
character, the *kholhoznik*, are excellently and realistically portrayed in
Sholokhov's *Virgin Soil Upturned*. In the later 1930's two other
types of hero, much quoted to-day, which appear to have exercised
a considerable moral influence in the war years, are personified in
Korchagin, hero of Ostrovsky's *How Steel Was Tempered*, 1937, and
Bassov, hero of Krymov's *Tanker Derbent*, 1939. In Korchagin it
is the will-power and self-discipline in difficult situations that are
admired, while Bassov is the new type of intelligent worker, bent on
rationalizing production, introducing new methods, and getting the
maximum use out of his machinery and the most out of his fellow-
workers by having the right idea of team-spirit. Bassov has his
difficulties—it was the days of the " wreckers " and he is himself
under suspicion and persecuted because he wishes to introduce
new methods but he eventually succeeds in applying his theories. He

is the prototype of the hero of initiative in industry, in the arts or on the field of battle—the type of man who may become a hero in real life by winning the title of Labour Hero of the Soviet Union, an order of some distinction and privilege.

In Korneychuk's much publicized play (it had the distinction of being serialized in *Pravda*) *Front*, 1942, we observe a similar situation in a topical wartime dress. Here the author confronts two schools of "military tactics," personified in the old-fashioned, civil war veteran, commander Gorlov, and the younger Stalinist-strategist Ognyev, who knows better how to beat the Germans. To this type of hero, the hero of initiative, engendered by pre-war Soviet fiction, we must add another, which was to become increasingly important in the later 1930's and during the war, and that is the *historical* hero as portrayed in Tolstoy's *Peter the Great,* Chapygin's *Stenka Razin,* and Kostylev's *Minin and Pojarsky.* These historical portraits were symbolical of the synthesis that was taking place between the historical traditions of Russia and the new-found revolutionary faith.

Such are the main hero types revealed in Soviet fiction up to 1942. No one hero type entirely fills the stage or dominates throughout the two decades except in so far as the traits of the positive bolshevik type tend to recur in different settings and faced with different problems. Zoshchenko's comic characters are, of course, always essentially human and often provide an amusing commentary on the popular mis-interpretation of official jargon, but they lack the positive and heroic qualities for which Soviet critics are looking. In Ostrovsky, however, this type is much more human and is enlarged to include ethical and spiritual problems. In general, the hero has evolved from the abstract to the concrete, from the mass to the people, from the type to the character, from the narrow revolutionary to the socially conscious person, from the class-bound theorist to the dialectical history-maker. In fact, the hero as now conceived was only barely outlined in the first two decades of Soviet fiction; and the time was spent *searching* for him. The hero's traits were dispersed here and there in the features of different types, more or less successful, but no one powerful image had as yet assembled them in a large-scale vivid personality—that of the "hero of our times," the Evgeny Onyegin or Pechorin of to-day.

It was the war that finally brought the realization of *who* this hero should be. In its sudden fury, the war had swept over a vast territory, bringing death and captivity to millions of men and women. But it also revealed a united people and a remarkable display and variety of personal valour. It was no longer a question of civil strife as in 1920, or of enforcing programmes such as the collectivization of the land which had met with opposition at the time. Here was national unity against the foreign invader; and that unity had been prepared and cemented by the final success of the industrial revolution and the collectivization of the land in the 1930's, as well as by a fundamental change in outlook resulting from the educational and social reforms of that time. Therefore, out of the war, the notion was born of a "heroic people" such as was expressed in Valery Grossman's *The People Immortal* and in Gorbatov's *The Taras Family*, but at the same time, the heroic individual becomes the concrete embodiment of the virtues of this people. From this to the revival of the idea of the human personality as the core and essence of the human being was but a step; and gradually this notion begins to make itself more and more felt among the critics when they are analysing the qualities of the heroes of wartime fiction. These latter are found often enough to be too narrowly conceived, and the demand now is for heroes who can combine social awareness with the expression of their inner thoughts and dreams, their emotional and spiritual world.

Parallel with this renewed emphasis on emotions and feelings, on the inner life of the personality that is not in rebellion against but in harmony with society, is the idea of a new humanism which lays fresh stress on the noble aspects of human nature such as love, loyalty, devotion, self-sacrifice, originality, creative genius and the discipline of harmonious human relations. Here again it may be said that Soviet writers have not so far succeeded in embodying these qualities in a great character of fiction. But in contrast to the researches of the preceding period, at least a more distinct and spacious image of the desired hero has at last been propounded and partially sketched. On analysis this hero turns out to be a blend of selected virtues displayed by the Russian character in history and the positive traits of the revolutionary or the conscious history-maker. In its outlines the image is a positive one; and in so far as it reacts to and reflects back on life, it is an open invitation for potential genius to come forward and in its turn mould the reality of the future.

What relation does this hero of 1946 bear to the heroes of Gogol and Turgeniev, Dostoievsky and Tolstoy, Goncharov and Chekhov? But who *was* the hero of that great literary period? All the evidence points to the "superfluous man," that frustrated intellectual who either turns into a philosopher of inertia like Goncharov's *Oblomov* (1849-59), or a nihilist like Bazarov in Turgeniev's *Fathers and Sons* (1862), or a petty Napoleon like Raskolnikov in Dostoievsky's *Crime and Punishment* (1866), or an eternal student like Trofimov in Chekhov's *Cherry Orchard* (1904). Gorky's vagabonds were also social misfits though no longer intellectuals; but they were more robust and had a greater animal greed of life. Frustration seemed to be the keynote of that world, into which minor characters of a more purposeful nature began to intrude and finally start cutting down the trees of mortgaged domains. This frustration was in itself a form of criticism of the social order of the day, which bottled up potential energies and gave little scope for the development of the majority of the illiterate population or few opportunities to the intellectual, who, if he did not stagnate, was only too conscious of his impotency. D. S. Mirsky's account of the writer Leonid Andreyev illustrates this point : " Like practically all Russian intelligentsia who were not absorbed by revolutionary ideas, Andreyev had no genuine interest in life. His life was only an effort somehow to fill up the void in his soul. This usually led to drunkenness, for they needed some sort of intoxication to keep them running. . . ."

Already in 1859, in his penetrating article *What Does Oblomov Represent?* the realist critic Dobroliubov analysed the social implications of this character, and affirmed that progress lay in the stimulation of a different positive type. The Soviet critic of to-day would have little to add to Dobroliubov's analysis; he would say that Oblomov and other negative characters of the 19th century fiction were " superfluous " types because the small upper or middle classes to which they belonged had become fundamentally isolated from the life of the mass of the people and were therefore left without any creative dynamic urge.

With the advent of the Revolution and of Soviet literature with its new problems, the " superfluous man " takes a back place but he does not disappear entirely; his traits can still be seen in Olesha's *Kavalerov* and in some of the characters, like Veshkin in *The Thief*, of Leonov's novels. He reappears again in Leonov's play, *Invasion* (1942), in the character of Feodor Talanov but only to suffer a moral regeneration in the end. The dominant characters in Soviet fiction are positive heroes who have some purpose in life, aim to accomplish, job to execute, social task to perform, or historic mission to fulfil. If many of them in the past have not been rounded human types or integrated characters, in whom the personal was harmoniously adjusted with the social life, or if they have been two-dimensional and erred in concealing their thoughts and emotions, this is a fault of which both writers and critics have become increasingly aware during the war years. Thus the critic Pertzov protests against " superficial characters in whom there is no image, no philosphy of the age," and he urges writers to see man as " a personality and not only as a master of his profession, military or otherwise." This emphasis on the importance of the personality is of comparatively recent origin and, if it makes headway, it can only broaden the writer's conception of human nature that is so essential to the complete portrayal of character. The objective world had long been dominant and now apparently the time has come for the inner life to begin unfolding, not in any revolt against objectivity but rather to complement it, and to enrich it with a deeper sense of reality. Here it is worth noting what Prishvin says about the *Personality* in his book *The Forest Drop*, 1943.

"Here is a flower," says Prishvin, "and there is another : they are so different but their roots resemble one another, and the earth, which each of them represents in its own way, is also one. Such are the creative personalities of men; each personality is the representative of all. But in addition, it is essential to define the personality. There is the individual ' I,' the ' I ' in retail : ' I am not like you.' And there is also the personal ' I,' the ' I ' as a particular representative of its kind of all men and the whole world. This ' I ' is the creative relation between men (culture). The individual ' I ' is at its best limited by its ' talent,' but in most cases it leads to men reproaching each other for the size of one another's nose or something of the sort. Tolstoy . . . . could not bear doctors because in their search for the cause they systematically ignored the human personality and its ethical world. Zamoshkin, the literary critic, once told me that when in the course of an operation the doctors thought that he would die, he knew that he would live. ' If they had only asked me,' Zamoshkin would say, ' but they did not ask me and merely called out to someone through the door—" He is still alive " '."

Arriving at Prishvin and Pertzov, we have travelled a long way from the time when the first hero in Soviet fiction was the lyrically conceived, featureless but dynamic mass—an abstraction of the notion of the proletariat in action. Then there was the intellectual hero of doubts and hesitations or the social misfit and outlaw. At the same time there was the portrait of a positive and socially-conscious character, usually with party associations, who was a militant type and whose life was passed in the thick of the struggle either against " intervention " or on the home front. This is the dominant type, having its ancestors in minor 19th century characters, who will gradually be transformed into the maker of history. But to begin with, because of its single-mindedness, this type tends to be one-sided and inhuman. In the later 1930's, this sort of hero begins to be criticized for his one-sidedness, " soulless optimism," and narrow or insincere political conventionality; and it is held by some critics, like Usievich, that a " man not capable of experiencing suffering, sorrow, anxiety, is not an optimist but a dummy."

With the war and the emergence into the arena of action and history of the whole people, with its great variety of character, the limitations of the conventional hero appeared narrower than ever. At such a time, when " there were hours and days when the whole character of the people was manifest, the whole of its long history from the legendary Ilya Murometz to the symbols of the greatness of to-day, Lenin and Stalin " (Pertzov); and when the writer was faced with the problem of recording and giving artistic expression to the variety of characters thus revealed; then the critics were obliged to reconsider the rôle and scope of character in fiction and to criticize the writers for their inadequacy. This leads Pertzov to conclude that " There is no path for our literature in the future except through the affirmation of the complete and precious personality of the hero, and, incidentally, of the personality of the writer himself."*

This is no doubt an important re-discovery, which, like so many others in the past decade, is already broadening and modifying the theoretical basis and the actual accomplishment of Soviet literature. We have the synthesis between the Revolution and Russian history as in Tolstoy's *Peter the Great* and *Ivan the Terrible;* between the Socialist Fatherland and the Russian people as in Simonov's play *The Russian Folk,* 1942; and now we are in process of a fusion between the inner world of this Russian man of to-day, his capacity for joy and sorrow, and the objective world in which it must find expression. The schism between the sentimental and the efficient man revealed in Olesha's *Envy* is now to all appearances healed and, as a result of the war, it is replaced by a new self-confidence, a more spacious optimism and the ideal of a new humanism.

This humanism can be defined as a belief in man's capacity and ability to conquer nature, solve the most difficult problems, and *make* or *create* history. It is an optimistic belief. It was confirmed and given a keener edge and added significance by the course of the war and the final victory. The wartime hero was first of all the " Russian people " and then the fighters of all types that it produced. But the personal deeds and exploits of individuals were only one side of the picture; the other was the superior direction and the strategy of the war. There were also the images of the historical ancestors. Thus in the potential hero of future fiction, as the critics see him, we have a combination of the best traits of the traditional Russian character, that of a Lomonosov or a Suvorov, with the firmness of the " bolshevik who," as the critics say, " inherited and developed these traits of the Russian character." Russian history now becomes "full of strong-willed characters who were formerly but little portrayed in our literature." In building up this image of a strong, purposeful character of genius, whether it be that of a soldier, statesman, scientist, inventor, traveller, or the like, recourse was had more to the examples of history and the present than to 19th century fiction with its negative types. It is built on legend, history and biography : on the early epics, on folk legends, like those of Ilya Murometz, Mikula Selyaninivich, and Olesha Popovich, the *Bogatyry* or champions of old Russia; on historical characters like Minin and Pojarsky, Peter the Great and Ivan the Terrible, Suvorov and Kutuzov; on the lives of great men like Lomonosov and Mendeleyev, Griboyedov and Pushkin; and, of

**Znamya No. 9, 1945.

course, upon more contemporary biographies such as Lenin's.

The image of this national hero, of this maker of history, is all pervading in suggestion. The unifying stimulus of the war and the new pride of achievement are its inspiration; but wartime literature has only produced the bare outlines of such a hero. In Simonov's Stalingrad novel *Days and Nights,* as in most other novels of the war period, the hero lacks breadth and depth, and is only a partial " hero of our time." This general failure may be due to war conditions or the still incomplete synthesis in the writer's mind between the inner world and the objective one; or simply to the absence of a really great novelist at this stage of Soviet literature. Whatever the reason, it need not be a lasting condition of this literature. There is every evidence that the critics are preoccupied with this very problem, and they wish to stimulate a post-war renaissance. If the fusion has been achieved and the notion of the personality revived, it would seem that the road was now wide open to the writer to create more important works, and make use of the abundant material, human and historical, at his disposal. Thus we find Tikhonov, in his directive capacity of President of the Writers' Union, saying in 1946: " If Shakespeare portrayed with such force human passion and tragedy, taking his heroes from among emperors, kings, queens, nobles, merchants and ministers, then now it is essential to portray with the same Shakespearean force these authentic heroes of our time, who surpass those of antiquity in their deeds and characters." It remains for us to see what harvest the next decade will bring. The renewed concentration on " current problems " may, of course, impede to some extent the lines of development that had taken shape during the war.

CHAPTER V

THE WRITER AND ACTUALITY: THE SHORT STORY AND THE DIARY

I

The Daily Press and the Wartime Pamphlet

IT is impossible to ignore the close connection during the war between a large number of writers and the daily Press. In Soviet eyes the Press is one of the sharpest weapons of propaganda at the disposal of the Party and the State; and it was only natural that, when the whole national effort was concentrated on the war, the Press should " play its part in the campaign " as distinct from just reporting news, and that a good many Soviet writers should contribute a daily or, at least, a frequent quota of pointed articles and reportage. Many of these writers were directly attached as correspondents to the central papers like *Pravda, Izvestya, Red Star, Red Fleet,* and *Trud.* If we take *Pravda,* for example, we find that its list of writers included Gorbatov, Kozhevnikov, Marshak, Leonov, Simonov, Sobolev, Tikhonov and Sholokhov, as regular correspondents, quite apart from other writers who contributed occasionally.

The two most important categories of wartime newspapers, which involved the collaboration of writers, were these central dailies and the front-line papers produced for the active armies. According to Alexei Tolstoy, nine hundred writers—novelists, dramatists, poets, reporters and journalists—were to be found in the ranks of the active army. There were a good many casualties, of course, and among them we must number Evgeny Petrov, Krymov, Stavsky and Joseph Utkin. The mobilization on the whole affected only the younger writers : they were assigned either military or political work in the army under the control of the Political Directorate of the Red Army, of which Scherbakov was the chief; or they were attached to the Soviet Information Bureau or again as correspondents to the leading dailies. The older writers were at one stage, 1941-42, evacuated from Moscow for the most part, and found themselves in places like Kazan, Kuibyshev, Sverdlovsk or Alma Ata.

The majority of the writers at the front were there in a professional capacity and they were expected to make the most of their experience not only by reporting immediate events but also by recording their impressions and notes which might serve them for more artistic productions in the near or distant future. Thus the reportage of the early days soon made way for the short story and then the novel, while the diary would serve as a basis for more comprehensive postwar works. The Soviet writer was therefore very much in the position of our war-artist, but we had no equivalent war-writers except professional correspondents.

Since reality is the chief criterion of Soviet literature, the war was conceived as a school of character and a panorama of contemporary history, from which the writer was expected to delineate the features of the hero of the day and to draw the moral of his time. In the confusion of the early war days little could be attempted beyond the article, pamphlet, sketch and reportage. But by 1942, the short story begins to appear and to multiply, and later in that year we have the first plays and novels of the period, which are henceforth to be published in greatly increasing numbers, though the shortage of paper doutbless delayed less topical publications. In this war, it must be remembered, Soviet life was organized on a rigorous system of priorities in all spheres of work. Less essential periodicals just ceased publication, while the shortage of paper was such that even *Pravda* missed one day a week.

The fact that so many writers were afforded ˙direct front-line experience, that they could question German prisoners or Russian traitors on the spot (as is clear from Simonov's *War Diary*), or that they could be systematically supplied, as Ehrenburg was, with German letters or other material from the field of battle; and the fact that there were no two opinions about the significance of the war; all helps to explain why and how the war produced such a direct impact upon Soviet prose and poetry. Another thing that touched the pride of every Russian and made writers react immediately was the avowed Nazi policy of exterminating all cultural values in the " East." This explains in great measure the enormously increased attention paid to the revival of Russian cultural traditions and values, and the new emotionally felt pride in past achievements and the qualities of the national character. It also partly explains the great impetus given to the study of Slav origins, which is now beginning to assume a more political complexion. The pamphlet-article in the hands of writers like Ilya Ehrenburg and Alexei Tolstoy proved a handy weapon with which to reply to Nazi cultural attacks and to defend Russian cultural values. Thus we have Tolstoy's *What We Defend, My Country, The Blood of the People, The National Character, The Brown Drug,* and other pamphlets of the sort, some of which were referred to in Shvernik's funeral oration. In these Tolstoy delves into history and attempts a brief cultural portrait of a nation that is not to be despised or lightly trampled upon.

Ilya Ehrenburg was undoubtedly the outstanding writer-journalist and pamphleteer of the war days. He harnessed himself to an enormous daily output of the most mordant, satirical and destructive pamphlet articles intended to undermine any illusion there may have been of German culture, values or formidable strength.* He did in prose what Marshak and the Kukriniksi did in the domain of the Tass Window posters, that is, make the German look ridiculous in the eyes of the average Soviet citizen. It has been said that by his ridicule and satire Ehrenburg helped to kill the fear of the Germans. His articles were especially popular in the Red Army, where they were always the last bits of newspaper to be used for rolling cigarettes, and he wrote steadily for *Red Star,* which circulates mainly among army people. Writing from the front, a Soviet artilleryman has compared these articles to a gun barrage and they do seem to have had a stimulating effect on the morale of the army. Ehrenburg went on in this vein inspiring hatred and contempt of the Germans until the spring of 1945, when suddenly *Pravda* published an article entitled *Comrade Ehrenburg Exaggerates.* The article was signed by G. F. Alexandrov, the Head of the Department of Agitation and Propaganda attached to the Central Committee. The result was that Ehrenburg stopped writing in that vein, in fact he published nothing for a month or so. Alexandrov's article had made a distinction between good and bad Germans : the reason was obvious; the war was being won, Soviet troops were entering German territory, and a practical policy of dealing with the German population would have to be applied. The reader will not help noticing with interest the procedure used in this case to put an end to Ehrenburg's line, which had been very popular for four years but which had now served its purpose; it gives us a glimpse of one of the control levers which are at work when necessary to start, stop, or modify the public expression of any line of policy.

Ehrenburg's preoccupation with the daily Press was the cause of an illuminating difference of opinion between him and the critic Pertzov. At a discussion at the Union of Soviet Writers on " How best to fulfil the great tasks set to Soviet literature," Ehrenburg suggested that writers were wasting their time delving into " history " or trying to produce " creative " works at such a time; they would be much better employed in day to day publicity and articles in the Press.

Pertzov attacked Ehrenburg's thesis and defended the right to creative activity during the war. He said : " Ilya Ehrenburg is not right to demand that a writer should speak daily. Not everyone can do so. And may not a writer be silent because he is writing? And he

---

*On occasion, he did not spare the Allies either.

may be engaged on a big novel embodying the philosophy of the war period and full of living characters. Would it be right, for example, to hurry Sholokhov, who is working on his novel, *They Fought for their Country,* when one knows his nature? . . . A writer should speak with his full voice whether in a feuilleton or a novel. Let each do what he can. . . ." (*October* 6-7, 1943).

2

Reportage and the Short Story

I N the light of this concentrated war effort and the mobilization of all resources, it is understandable that the writer should have become very largely a reporter in the first months of the war. The recording of facts and events remains indeed a dominant mode of expression throughout this period. But by 1942 writers were beginning to get their second wind and to attempt more ambitious works. The first plays were written and novels were planned. The short story, too, begins to develop out of reportage, but it remains closely linked to it and sometimes almost indistinguishable from it. This was in itself a problem, for the facts and human situations were many and varied but there was little time to digest the material under pressure of events. In Simonov's *War Diaries* we find an interesting passage where the author discusses this very point of how to treat the material and distinguish between the story and reportage. Here is the passage in question:

" I must say this reconnaissance operation was for me, as a correspondent, a touchstone: I became convinced that people relate their experiences an hour after the event and the day after . . . I questioned over thirty of the raiders . . . and wrote down some eighty to a hundred pages. Later, I used this material for my sketch *On the Road to Petsamo.* . . But I was able to establish that the accounts of men, who had just arrived with their reports, still frozen and shivering with excitement, differed from those they made after they had slept . . . and discussed the events amongst themselves as a result of which a common point of view emerged. . . . From then on, I attached much more value to accounts heard immediately after the event. They differ not only by their greater authenticity but also by their greater number of lively, uninvented details. When I hear such a first-hand account, I take it down verbatim for my reportage. I only have to think out the arrangement of the material. But when I hear of an interesting event a week or a month later, I make use only of the theme and think myself in the right to invent a lot myself, and to make up the details I like, for I have become deeply convinced that in relating his experiences months later, a man will inevitably invent some of the details though fundamentally speaking the truth. And if he does it, I can often do it better, and in any case I think I have the right to do so."

Despite the abundance of material and the exceptional opportunities for documentation given to writers, there was a tendency to turn out "standard" stories which had all the necessary ingredients in them but little character or originality. It is to these that K. Paustovsky refers when he says: "We talk a lot about the paths of our war literature. The heat of these discussions is to be explained by the fact that together with authentic works there is a lot of rubbish. In the two years of war there has already been worked out a standard type of 'front-line' and 'home front' stories. Their danger lies in that superficially they have all that is required with the exception of the principal—artistic truth, emotion and individuality. . . . Some writers have fallen for naturalism and photography . . . forgetting that art is above all generalization."*

The wartime crop of short stories is in the end a fairly large one but it is uneven in quality, and much of it is thinly veiled reportage. As in the novel, the home front is on the whole neglected and the main attention is centred on the front-line and the occupied territories. There are few traces of humour. Zoshchenko did write satirical and humorous sketches in *Crocodile* but he appears to have produced nothing very distinctive in the style of his earlier short stories and no volume of his stories was published during the war. There is, indeed, a pleasing touch of humour and a lyrical note in V. Ilyenkov's stories, *Home, Spring, Sorrow, The Second Breath, The Pink Rabbit, The Letter, The Spark, Sukhopluyev and Faust.* In Lev Kassil's *There Are Such People,* there is a combination of adventure and artificial plot with the war theme, but in most other writers there is a straightforward realistic approach based largely on reportage. Tikhonov in his Leningrad sketches, *The Traits of Soviet Man,* is a pamphleteer and reporter, while Fadeyev's *Leningrad in the Days of the Blockade* is pure reportage. Of some of the earlier stories we may single out Gabrilovich's *Under Moscow,* Stavsky's *Cossacks,* and some of Sholokhov's stories. Those of Kozhevnikov and Dovzhenko, Platonov and Paustovsky, Simonov and Kaverin, are worth noting, and show us a variety of mood, style and approach. Pavlenko in his *The Path of Bravery* writes about the ordinary soldier hero. Leonid Sobolev has chosen the navy as his theme in his *Soul of the Sea,* 1943. This collection of stories deals with the war only in part, for some of the stories date from the 1930's. Sobolev had previously written a novel about the navy, *Capital Refitting,* 1937, and he has largely specialized in naval themes. In his stories he is concerned with the

Literature and Art, of February 23rd, 1944.

character and distinct qualities of the sailor as a human being and fighter. Russian sailors had to do a lot of fighting on land and we do not have any accounts of important naval engagements as we would in British stories of this type. In a later book of stories, *The Road to Victory,* 1945, Sobolev covers the last stages of the liberation of the South of Russia, that of Sebastopol and the road to Bucharest. The accounts of the liberated towns are intermingled with memories of the earlier days when they were besieged and lost. His style is factual and restrained, and he endows his characters with a simple dignity. But when he looks at Bucharest, he tends to be satirical—a common enough tendency among Soviet writers when summing up " foreigners " of a " capitalist " vintage.

A number of reactions from soldiers at the front, in letters written by them to editors, show that many of them were interested in stories about the war rather than escapist literature, and they seemed to have wished to see themselves reflected in literature. In one such letter, a soldier writes : " We are especially interested in stories, the heroes of which act in the same conditions as we do. We see the front all the time, but . . . such a story shows us an example." Here we are back to that direct educative importance which seems to attach to Soviet literature. Another soldier writes, " After reading Ehrenburg or Dovzhenko, I have more strength and aim more surely, and if a German comes into sight, he is certain to be killed." The direct impact exercised by literature on minds such as these is a factor we have constantly to bear in mind when considering the tasks and character of Soviet literature. The war has undoubtedly revived the popularity of the short story and, if from the point of view of wider and more permanent interest little was produced in this period, it has nevertheless stimulated a debate as to what is a good short story and the classics are now being seriously studied to provide examples for the future.

3

The Wartime Diary

IN a time of events and records such as this was, it is not surprising that a number of diaries were kept and that some of them should already have been published. The earliest was that of Polyakov, *With a Unit Through Enemy Lines,* 1941, which described the experience of a unit which had been cut off and fought in the enemy rear. This book, however, was one of the first Soviet war books to be translated into English and should be familiar enough to the reader. A number of other diaries published more recently present, perhaps, a greater interest. They are not many in number and chief amongst them are Vera Inber's *Almost Three Years: A Leningrad Diary*, 1945*; P. Ignatov's *The Diary of a Partisan*, 1944; Major-General P. Vershigora's *Men With A Clean Conscience*, 1945†; and Konstantin Simonov's *War Diaries*, 1945.

We have already had occasion to refer to and quote from Vera Inber's diary. It is one of the more interesting documents of the Leningrad blockade and gives us an insight into the life of a Soviet intellectual under those conditions. The diary covers the years August, 1941, to June, 1944, and is full of interesting details of the life of those years—the sort of details that are usually lacking to make up our picture of Soviet life. There are, of course, many glimpses of the besieged city and at the same time the thread of intellectual activities that the author attempts to carry on despite the physical hardships and the very low rations. There is a vivid description of a visit to the front-line over the frozen Lake Ladoga to give a poetry reading to the troops. This inter-relation of the intellectual and the army of which we have constant evidence is a striking feature of Soviet life : the Red Army man seems to enjoy a poetry reading as much as a concert. In one place Vera Inber mentions a talk she gave in which she referred to "the 'evil' inertia which at times grows amongst us with the rapidity of weeds and drives us to write about that which has already been mastered. And in the meantime the reader is ahead of us and waiting for something else. The discussion turned on the purity of language, on composition, on the selection of theme, on editing and on the knowledge of how to revise what needs revising. It was not said in vain that ' Apollo is the god of corrections.' Rarely, too rarely, do we feel the presence of this god in a whole lot of things. . . . In the end I said : ' We have convinced ourselves in the force of our verses, in their *effectiveness* : the proof is in the letters we get from our readers. Our books are taken to the front, carried in the soldiers' rucksacks, and read before they go into attack.' . . ." It is to be hoped that this diary will be eventually translated into English, for it is more revealing of Soviet life than many of the other works that are being translated.

P. Ignatov's diary has been translated into English under the title of *The Partisans of the Kuban*. It covers the war period of 1941 to May, 1943, and the activities of a partisan detachment in the Krasnodar area—the foothills of the Caucasus. It is interesting in showing what type of people made up such partisan detachments and how whole families could live, do their sabotage and survive, in a region occupied by the Germans. Ignatov had his family with him and in one of the passages we are given an account of his son, Genya's, aspirations : " On such a night I particularly want to dream. I love dreaming. At first it seemed shameful to dream when others are dying and fighting. But then I noticed that the more I dreamt the better I fought. . . . When the war is over I shall throw up everything . . . and become an engineer. . . . I shall construct a machine. A go-everywhere. Shaped like a bomb . . . it will travel on earth like a car, in the water like a submarine, in the air like an aeroplane. But above all it will travel through the earth. . . . I shall fly in it to the Far East. Landing near Jakutsk, I shall burrow into the earth . . . I shall see all that lies hidden in the earth. . . . The earth shall show me all its precious stores. . . ."

This passage is characteristic of the enthusiasm of Soviet youth, for whom engineering is not a routine job but an ideal combining a retarded Faustian enthusiasm for dominating nature with a romantic and mechanical Jules Verne strain.

General Vershigora is an Ukrainian, and he was a film producer when the war broke out. Joining the ranks, he went through all the peripetias of the early fighting. Later he dropped by parachute to join the famous partisan division of a legendary leader, Kovpak, who operated in the German rear, not only in the forests of Bryansk but for hundreds of miles around. Kovpak's force was literally a division and it made some extraordinary sorties behind the German lines. One of these marches covered some thousand miles, and the division finally ended up in the Carpathians. Vershigora's and Ignatov's books are the best and the most detailed that have appeared so far about partisan activity, and give us a more realistic account of the organization of these movements than does the romantic notion of " guerillas." The fact emerges, especially from Vershigora's book, how organized these units were and how closely some of them, at least, kept in touch with Moscow all the time.

Simonov's *War Diaries*, which were published in *Znamya*, Nos. 5-6-7-8, 1945, are another interesting document recording the experiences of a writer-correspondent during the war. In the course of his duties, Simonov travelled from one end of the Soviet Union to the other, from the Arctic regions to the Black Sea. He certainly saw the war from most of its angles. It is astonishing that he has been able to write so much in that time. Lack of space prevents us from quoting a prolonged and agonized description of how he had a tooth pulled out in the Arctic by an inexperienced girl-dentist.

CHAPTER VI

SOVIET FICTION IN THE WAR AND AFTER

I

The Background of the Novel

WE have dealt with the revival of the historical novel and have sketched the image of the potential hero of Soviet fiction. And now we come to the fiction published during the war and in the period immediately succeeding. It cannot be said that the war was marked by an abundance of first-class fiction or the work of great novelists anywhere; and it is too early yet to assess the possibilities of the post-war decade in England, for example. It is likewise impossible to foresee what new talent this decade will reveal in post-war Russia, and we are therefore restricted to the authors we have known, and the authors who made a name for themselves during the war but whose future is still uncertain. Statistically we know that in the first year of the war (1941-42), there were published in the Soviet Union one thousand and twenty-seven non-scientific or non-technical works, and that in the following years the number progressively increased. Of these one thousand and twenty-seven works, one third were reportage stories, one eighth were short stories, one fifth were books of poems, and the novels, full length and short, numbered some seventy. Four years of the war must then have produced at least three hundred such novels, if we include what the Russians call *povest*, a tale or narration usually of about forty thousand words, in fact, a short novel or, alternatively, a long short story, a popular literary form with Russian writers. Leonov's *The Taking of Velikoshumsk* is representative of this literary *genre* which we propose to treat here together with the novel. The seventy and the three hundred novels we have mentioned must include regional and national publications, not always of a high quality, so that the works of literary significance, which we have to consider, are proportionally smaller in number.

To an English reader accustomed to a variety of well-developed *genres,* not only of the novel itself but of its specialized subsidiaries such as detective and adventure fiction, and other forms of fiction catering for different tastes and for " amusement " only, the realm of Soviet fiction must at first glance appear unusually restricted, monotonous and thematic. To begin at one extreme, *boulevard* fiction is completely non-existent : here the moral puritan nature of the new State has fully asserted itself. The detective story and thriller, long held in contempt, have begun to find favour again and are to be revived as we shall see later, but for the purposes of our survey no concrete example of this *genre* exists. The novel of adventure has been sadly neglected and only a few specimens are to be found, but this *genre* also is now to be revived. Of the novel itself, it can be said that, since the inception of the Soviet era, and, of course, apart from the historical *genre,* it has treated mainly of the emergent Soviet man in relation to a series of problems confronting him, such as the schism and the civil war, the beginnings of a new industry and the social confusion of the Nep period, the doubts of the intellectual and the criminal activity of the social misfit, the collectivization of the land and the industrial revolution of the early 1930's, the rise of a new industrial type and of the innovator in all branches of social life, the struggle against the " enemies of the people " and the appearance of a new, more solidly and traditionally based citizen. There were, indeed, a few novels like Lidin's *The Unknown Soldier,* Fedin's *Rape of Europe,* and a number of Ehrenburg's novels, written in Paris and of which the *Fall of Paris* (1941) was the last, that dealt with European themes, but they have a distinct satirical bias that would strike us as somewhat forced. That, in brief, is the panorama of Soviet fiction until June, 1941. After that date, apart again from the historical novel, Soviet fiction is almost exclusively dominated by the war theme.

An English reader may pertinently enquire : where is the romantic novel of love? Or the sophisticated novel of human relationships? Or the history-of-a-family novel? Or even where is the Russian Mr. Bunting? He will be disappointed, for they do not appear to exist as such. The elements of the love theme and family relations do indeed figure in many of the works but they are very often only subsidiary, almost as in a detective story, to other problems to be solved. Human relations cannot, of course, be avoided, and indeed they must play an essential part in the development of a novel, but even here there was a tendency to abstract and to produce types rather than characters. The soul of man, the humanity on which Russians like to pride themselves, seemed to be lacking in many of these novels of the first two decades. In the latter thirties, there is a return to the notion that man is a more complex being and needs fuller expression than that hitherto given him, and this notion is further and more emphatically affirmed during the war years and since. In Gorbatov's *The Taras Family*, we do find a more human background, but judging by many works still and the criticisms of others, the human butterfly is not over-quick to emerge from its present chrysalis stage.

In approaching the Soviet novel, therefore, we need not expect to discover a great variety of types and characters, although the war has undoubtedly enriched the novel both actually and potentially with a great reservoir of human characters and new problems. During the war, the war theme itself, either in the form of front-line fighting experience or in that of the population under German occupation, took precedence above all other themes and certainly to the detriment of that of the Home Front. The Russian people, having been stirred and having donned khaki, was re-discovered with all its native traits at the front or in civilian garb resisting the Germans in the zone of occupation. It is a remarkable fact that about a third of the population suddenly found itself for the time being under foreign rule and, as it were, abroad. In its broad outlines, before and during the war, Soviet fiction appears to be concentrated on a number of well-defined themes. It is this compactness and single-mindedness that makes it seem strange and a little unnatural to us. There are a great many works, not the best of course, that are much of a pattern, but to their credit, Soviet critics are now very severe on such " pot-boilers " as they call them. It seems that they are now doing their best to stimulate greater variety, a more human approach and more discussion. And if one examines the scene more closely, there is more variety than might have been expected at first.

2

Novels About the Home Front, Industry and the Urals

OUTSIDE Russia the ordinary reader is very anxious, when he comes across a Soviet novel, to discover how the ordinary Soviet man or woman lives, works, enjoys life or faces misfortune. He would like to know what sort of a person the Soviet Russian is. This interest is well-founded, for whatever the political differences may be, the new Russia of to-day has shown herself capable of great achievements in industry and in war; and these things do not happen without men to carry them out; and it is their spiritual world and background that interests us. But it must be confessed that no very clear image of such a more universal Russian or Soviet man has yet been created in fiction or made accessible to readers outside the Soviet Union. By contrast, the characters of Russian 19th century fiction impress themselves on the mind and are not to be forgotten, although to the Englishmen, at least, some of them may seem very "queer." That is why the reverse, the 20th century side, of this medal would be so valuable. But it is not only a major work that can help to enlighten us : minor novels too have their uses and charms. A wartime novel of the life of a Moscow family, for example, with the proximity of the front at one time, the unheated winter, the work and the tribulations, and a complex of human relationships, might be very illuminating. It should be remembered that we know very little of Moscow, the new capital; most of the 19th century novels depicted Petersburg or the countryside. But there is no such novel as yet—Emilyanova's *The Surgeon* does indeed treat of a Moscow hospital in the early war days, but her attention is centred on the hospital staff in the execution of their duties and on the technique of operations. The war did not produce it; and we have seen no sign of one since, although Moscow is now the home and certainly a visiting centre of most of the leading writers.

Behind Moscow lie three vast regions full of potential stories : the Urals, Siberia and Central Asia. But these themes have hardly been touched upon. The Urals in themselves, one might have thought, would have exerted a triple attraction because of the local traditions, a great industry built there, and the wartime experiment of evacuating industries and factories from the occupied regions and re-starting them there. Moreover, the Urals were the workshop of victory for the Soviet front. True, the Urals theme was better illustrated than that of Siberia or Central Asia, in the novels of Shaginyan, Gladkov, Karavayeva, Perventzev, Panferov and Vassilieva; but their performance, though varied in quality, can hardly be called impressive. Nor are they as interesting as some of the Five Year Plan novels such as Katayev's *Speed Up, Time,* which were written about the beginnings of the industrial revolution in that region.

We mentioned Shaginyan, although her book, *The Urals in Defence,* is not a novel but a series of reportage on subjects such as the "intelligentsia," "the housewife," and so forth; a background book about the Urals in wartime, in fact. Karavayeva, also a woman writer, is more ambitious. In *The Stalin Foremen,* 1943, she deals with the types of workers who are forging victory, while in *The Lights,* 1944, the first big novel on the subject, she treats the theme of wartime Urals industry in a broader way, showing us the reaction of older workers to new methods of work and increased importance of women in industry. This novel is the first of a trilogy : the second volume, *Hot Spring,* will deal with a new generation of workers in the years 1942-3, while the third, *Two Years Later,* will show the Urals as they were in the days of the Kursk-Orlov battles. Perventzev's *The Test* tells the story of how an evacuated aircraft factory was set up again in the Urals. Feodor Gladkov, author of *Cement,* 1926, the first important industrial novel and of the Five Year Plan novel, *Power,* 1932, also writes of an evacuated Leningrad factory this time. His hero, Sharonov, an advanced worker of the Leningrad type, sets about to revolutionize Urals methods of production, to make them quicker and more efficient in fact. The story is based on the real achievements of a Leningrad worker, Dimitry Bosoy. Panferov's *War for Peace,*1945, from what we have seen of it in serial form, does not promise to be a revelation; for although the author gained fame over ten years ago with his collectivization novel *Brusski,* it is clumsily written and the characterization is poor.

These are the main novels on the theme of industry and the Urals, and they also happen to be the only novels, or very nearly, of any standing on the subject of the Home Front as distinct from that of the occupied regions or the front-line. It is true, there are, apart from the five writers mentioned above and who are really visiting writers, a number of regional Urals writers, of whom Bajov, the author of *The Malachite Casket,* is the most prominent. The region has certain traditions, and in Mamin Sibiryak (1852-1912), author of *The Privalov Millions,* it had a notable 19th century minor novelist, who as far as we know, has not yet been translated into English. There is no doubt that this region has characteristics and " Siberian " qualities of its own, and is capable of great development. One day, perhaps, Sverdlovsk, the local capital, will become a thriving literary as well as industrial centre.

3

A Novel of the Schism

ALEXEI TOLSTOY'S novel, *A Path of Torments,* which was translated into English as *The Road to Calvary,* takes the reader back to the earlier days of Soviet fiction when the theme of the civil war and the schism was dominant in literature. It falls outside the main current of the fiction of this time and has its own " history." The novel is a trilogy, the first part of which, *The Sisters,* was begun in 1919, finished in 1921, and published shortly after. At the time of writing *The Sisters,* the author was in emigration whence he returned to the Soviet Union in 1923. Parts two and three, *1918* and *Cloudy Morning,* appear to have been written throughout the thirties, and *Cloudy Morning,* as the author says, was finished on June 22nd, 1941, the day the Germans invaded the Soviet Union. The trilogy as it stands was first published in 1943. In *The Sisters,* we are shown Petersburg as it was, in its intellectual circles, in 1914 on the eve of the war and later. This is the most vivid and concentrated part of the trilogy, and we are given character portraits of the two sisters, Dasha and Ekaterina; Bessonov, the decadent poet, whose features bear a distant and distorted resemblance to the famous Russian poet, Alexander Blok, or some of his imitators; Telegin, the socially-conscious intellectual; and Roschin, the officer, who first sides with the " Whites " and then makes good with the " Reds " like not a few of the old Tsarist officers who eventually held prominent ranks in the Red Army during the war of 1941-45. The Petersburg of this book is one in which a premonition of future events was in the air : " There was a spirit of destruction in the air; with its deadly poison it penetrated into the grandiose Stock Exchange machinations of Sakelman, into the gloomy spite of the worker in the steel-smelting works, and into the distorted dreams of the fashionable poetess who sat up till five in the morning in the artistic cellar, ' The Red Bells ' —and even those, whose duty it was to fight this destructiveness, unconsciously did everything to increase and sharpen its force. . . ." It was the early days of modernist art : " The mouth, set crookedly; no nose, its place a triangular hole; a square head, and on it stuck a rag of real material. Legs like logs on rollers. . . ." These echoes of the artistic battles of thirty years ago have their reverberation in the Picasso controversy of to-day. There were the Futurists too (shades of the young Mayakovsky!), marching through Petersburg : " The Futurists were dressed in short, unbelted blouses of orange colour with black zig-zags on them, and in top hats. Each of them sported a monocle, and had painted on his cheeks a fish, an arrow and the letter ' R.' About five o'clock a police inspector held them up and took them in a cab to the police station to establish their identity."

The war and then events of even greater magnitude scatter Tolstoy's characters to their different fates throughout the length and breadth of Russia which was enduring its transformation along the " paths of torments " into the Soviet Union. In *1918* and *The Gloomy Morning,* we are shown the peripetias of personal fortunes against the vast background of anarchy, disorder and civil war, out of which a new order was finally established. In the later volumes of the trilogy, the sisters, Roschin and Telegin, are somewhat dwarfed by the events (the decadent poet was killed off in the 1914 war), but they painfully work out a place for themselves in the new society. The author is also obviously preoccupied with giving a " correct " 1940 perspective on the historical figures and course of the civil war, that is, one in keeping with the changes in the historical outlook and other events of the middle thirties. The author has clearly revised his historical appreciation of events and that explains perhaps why this trilogy took so long to write (1919-41). This trilogy has one feature rare in contemporary Soviet fiction, and that is the absence of consciously striving heroes such as we have described in our chapter on *The Hero in Soviet*

Fiction. This fact was remarked on by Fadeyev, the then President-Secretary of the Union of Soviet Writers, when at a writers' and critics' discussion of the trilogy, he remarked : " As a reader, I find it a pity that there are no heroes, conscious makers of history, running through this novel. . . ."* Fadeyev's criticism is an added illustration of the present-day trend in Soviet fiction.

The Road to Calvary is Tolstoy's chief prose work published in these years. As we have seen, his principal contribution during the war was in his two plays on Ivan the Terrible, and in his pamphlets, reportage and stories, which are slight in bulk, as well as in his unfinished historical novel, Part Three of *Peter the Great.* It does not look as if there will be many new works of his published posthumously. There are the five volumes of *Russian Folk Tales,* which he was editing and of which only two volumes had appeared, one in 1940 and the other in 1943. His collected works, which will be published shortly, will reveal any gaps in our knowledge of his work and will permit us to assess it as a whole. In his unexpected death at the age of sixty-four in 1945, Soviet fiction has lost one of its leading exponents and the Soviet Union one of its most prominent literary figures who formed a bridge between pre-revolutionary and post-revolutionary literature. His style, which owed much to the traditions of the Russian folk tale and the Russian historical documents, was certainly richer and more flavoured with historical associations than that of the majority of Soviet writers of to-day, except perhaps Leonov. Sholokhov, Leonov, or Sergeyev-Tsensky, another writer of the older and bridging generation, are among those who may now fill the gap left by Tolstoy as the doyen of Soviet literature.

4

The War in Fiction (I)—The Tolstoyan Approach

THE war, the participation in it of Soviet citizens either at the front or as partisans or again as heroes reacting to German oppression in the occupied territories, is the dominant theme of Soviet fiction. The potential material for character, plot and invention is plentiful and rich, for the war had involved tens of millions of people in direct adventure or misadventure. There were many new problems, including that of the study of an alien psychology at first hand—that of the German and the Nazi. But the greatest revelation of all appears to have been the character of the Russian people as it trod this new path of torment—that of the simple and hitherto undistinguished folk who previously had no particular axe to

---

**Literature and Art,* of 22nd May, 1943.

grind but who now emerge in the light of history with all the attributes of heroic self-sacrifice. There were, of course, traitors amongst them local quislings, and others who were not sure of themselves until " regenerated." It was a time when, as in the case of Feodor Talanov in Leonov's play, *Invasion*, " astonished eyes for the first time opened on the world and on one's self." The material is indeed so varied and full of possibilities that even long after this war Soviet literature is likely to allow much paper and ink for this theme. The war in the Far East was, of course, of the briefest as far as the Soviet Union was concerned and most of the writers, like Pavlenko, who had previously written novels about the Far East, did not get there in time for the actual fighting phase; but no doubt something will eventually be written about these regions which can now be looked at in different historical perspective from the Soviet point of view.

The novelists themselves, who have treated of these events and the impact they have had on people, may be divided roughly into two categories : those who embarked upon longer and weightier works that are just beginning to see the light of day; and those who, pedalling at various but rapid tempos, produced either their daily super-quotas, like Ehrenburg, of articles and reportages, short stories and, finally, novels while the pace was good and fast. We must put M. Sholokhov and A. Fadeyev as well as Fedin in the first category. Their war novels, of which extracts only have so far been published, lead one to assume that they will be larger and more solid works than the bulk of what has so far appeared. Sholokhov and Fadeyev are exponents of Tolstoyan realism, a method they applied in their first novels away back in the twenties, and they like to paint on broad canvas. Alexei Tolstoy, too, if he had lived, would no doubt have written his war novel *post facto*.

Michael Sholokhov (b. 1905) is already well-known outside Russia for his novels *And Quiet Flows the Don* and *Virgin Soil Upturned*. We have already quoted Pertzov's remark that Sholokhov likes to take his time over his work. During the war he published a few stories but he has concentrated mainly on a big novel, *They Fought for Their Country*, extracts of which have appeared in *Pravda*—some indication of the importance attached to it. It is, unfortunately, impossible to discuss this novel at greater length here, but it deals with the early and most difficult part of the war, the days of retreat, and judging by his previous works, this should certainly be an outstanding Soviet novel of its kind.

Alexander Fadeyev (b. 1901) is not given to over-writing. Since his first novel, *The Rout*, in 1926, he has published the first part of *The Last of the Udegheyans*, 1928, which was to have been a very broad canvas of characters and actions set in the Far East, and involving a remnant of an Asiatic tribe. The complete novel has not yet been published. Like Sholokhov, Fadeyev peoples his novels with a multitude of characters, who are all portrayed as individuals with their own ways of thinking and behaving, in contrast to some of the conventional types of Soviet fiction. It is, in fact, the Tolstoyan method, compounded of realism and psychology, which we see practised in his novels. During the war, Fadeyev has held an executive post with the Union of Soviet Writers and has not appeared much in print. He has, however, published his reportage impressions of besieged Leningrad, and has also written a novel, *The Young Guard*, which began publication serially in *Znamya*, No. 2, 1945. As in the case of Sholokhov's new novel, it is too early to assess the import of *The Young Guard*, which has already provoked the following reaction from a Soviet critic : " I feel only as if the fiery lava of a new content had broadened the literary tradition in which Fadeyev has worked, thus creating a new form "* (Pertzov). What we have read of the novel reveals a mastery of character drawing and the ability to create and move independently living personages, young and old. The canvas is a broad one, linking occupied territory with the Soviet mainland. The story is that of the underground movement in the occupied Krasnodon industrial area and the fortunes and fortitude of various underground workers, some of whom, like Shulga, fall into the hands of the Germans. A leading part is also played by a number of young Komsomol girls, who are smuggled through the German lines to assist in the underground activities. The portraits of the Germans involved and of Russians working for them are, from what we have seen, in the best detached Tolstoyan manner. This novel, varied in incident, situation and character, has all the features of a solid and spacious work reflecting a section of contemporary history.

5

The War in Fiction (2)—The Psychological Approach

LIKE Sholokhov and Fadeyev, Leonid Leonov (b. 1899) is a novelist of some weight, and in some ways perhaps the most original of Soviet prose writers. Since *The End of a Petty Man*, published in 1924, all his novels, including *The Badgers*, 1925, *The Thief*, 1927, *Sotj*, 1931, *Skutarevsky*, 1932, and *The Road Beyond The Ocean*, contained the elements of one and the same problem which the author has been re-stating in different situations without seemingly arriving at any fundamental solution. The problem is of a spiritual nature, the dualism of the old and the new, which the author had probably inherited from Dostoievsky, of whom he appears

---

* *Znamya*, No. 9, 1945.

to be the only revealed literary descendant in the Soviet era. His style, too, is distinct, weighty, and salted with proverbs, with much of old Russia and an almost biblical flavour and fervour in it at times. His natural predisposition leads him to a psychological interpretation of character and events, and his characters have a soulful aura about them, but they are incomplete as if they had not expressed to the end what was on their mind and they pass through the novel creating a vivid but somewhat mysterious atmosphere.

During the course of the war, Leonov had not produced any large-scale prose work, and his big war novel, on which he is working, is still to appear. He has, however, written *Invasion*, 1942, one of the three most staged war plays; the others are Simonov's *Russian Folk* and Korneychuk's *Front*. This play undoubtedly has great psychological tension and many of the elements that recur in his novels. The hero, Feodor Talanov, is again one of those seemingly "superfluous men" and a most enigmatic character until he is regenerated and dies through patriotic action in the end. Leonov did, however, write a *povest* or short novel of the war, *The Taking of Velikoshumsk*, published in 1944, and it is with this novel that we are concerned here.

The Taking of Velikoshumsk is worth a detailed examination. The title would indicate that this novel has to do with a battle episode. But this is true only in a sense. Fundamentally it is again a psychological study centred round three characters : General Litovchenko, the commander of a Guards' Tank Corps, a tank driver also named Litovchenko, and finally Tank No. 203. A tank is not a normal character of even modern fiction, but by the time Leonov's tank has gone through its battle experience, other experiences and met its death, it has assumed almost human characteristics. Perhaps because we are gradually given the "biography" of the tank from its birth in a Urals factory, and to the "medical" attention it received before joining in its last battle, its life and death leave a vivid impression in the mind. In its structure the novel falls naturally into two very distinct parts, almost making it seem as if it contained two episodes from a larger work. In the first, we are with the General, who is making the rounds of the Tank Corps, just arrived at this strategic spot near Velikoshumsk preparatory to a planned break through. The general's psychological ruminations and encounters with various types of his tank men, officers and a number of civilians, who had just been liberated in this section of the front, make up the first part. The General has some features resembling the characters of Leonov's earlier novels. The region in which he finds himself now turns out to be that of his native childhood home, and he is inclined to be reminiscent. The landscape, too, at one point, is not unlike the background of *Sotj* : "Here his childhood had been passed. . . . The first fourteen years had flowed cloudlessly under the wing of his grandmother, a famed healer of the region. . . . In the little town, in the midst of the cherry-tree jungles, ancient monasteries were living their last days; from all sides streams of pilgrims flowed towards them. And those to whom the ostentatious sacred places afforded no help, wandered to the outskirts towards the neat little house of the old woman Litovchenko. The uncomplaining ailments of the simple folk were always to be found at her porch. The old woman made no charges—the people left what they could by stealth, often enough generous gifts : flowers, even if they were withered, must be paid for according to the hopes and joys they afford the soul."

The evocation of an old landscape, of an old way of life, as a contrasting background to a dynamically transforming reality, is typical of Leonov. In this case, the contrast is not sharpened by the confrontation of two antagonistic characters but is bridged and mellowed in a sort of spiritual unity, that of the character of General Litovchenko, who is at once a symbol of modern technique, a spearhead of mechanized warfare, and a Russian, who in the process of recovering national territory, re-discovers a portion of his patrimony.

The second part of this novel is really a distinct episode, with only a spiritual thread connecting it with the first. Here we are with a younger generation of men, with the tank crew of Tank 203, and young Litovchenko—no relation but from the same parts—is both the tank driver and central figure. He is still immature, an emotional type whose force and conviction eventually find expression in action rather than words or reflection. His inner world is not clearly or logically explained by himself; we are only given a few hints by his fellow-soldiers; and his growth seems to be accomplished by an identity which he seems to achieve with his tank in action. This identity, the story of the tank in battle, and its final epic thrust, when it bursts upon and crushes a column of enemy reinforcements on the road before it is itself knocked out, assume the proportions of monumental symbolism, for when the General learns the story of action, he orders the tank to be converted into a monument : " ' Such as it is, I shall set the tank up on a high stone pedestal. Let the ages see who saved them from the knout and slavery. . . .' And here it occurred to him that anyone travelling by train towards the warm shores of the Black Sea, would be able to see the lofty grave of No. 203 standing out like a lighthouse."

The Taking of Velikoshumsk is both characteristic of Leonov's original style and an example of the psychological approach in Soviet fiction. This manner is to be met with more rarely than either that of the straightforward realistic narrative or that of the more balanced Tolstoyan narration favoured by Sholokhov and Fadeyev. In itself, this short novel suggests a fragment of a larger work rather than a completed story; it has depth but no great breadth. Its interest lies principally in its being the first serious study of tank warfare in Soviet fiction and as an example of Leonov's approach to reality, that of an undoubtedly talented writer.

6

The War in Fiction (3)—Boris Gorbatov and Valery Grossman

BORIS GORBATOV'S *The Unconquered* or *The Taras Family* and Valery Grossman's *The People Immortal*, both published in 1943, were among the first novels to deal directly with the war and its impact on the Russian people. Prior to their publication, the authors were known rather as writers of short stories and did not occupy a very prominent position in the hierarchy of Soviet letters. These novels were, however, to bring them very much into the foreground.

In *The Taras Family*, Gorbatov reveals himself a competent, straightforward narrator with a good eye for human situations. He has, however, to some extent deliberately borrowed the general outlines of his story from Gogol's famous Cossack tale, *Taras Bulba*. The story is centred in the Kuban region which was overrun by the Germans and is later linked with some of the battles resulting from the Stalingrad operation and which were to liberate that region. In this modern parallel there is a rough resemblance in the relations of the old father and the two sons, one of whom in the beginning is not a very convinced patriot, as in Gogol's tale where the youngest is led through his love of a Polish girl to fight for the Poles against the Cossacks. The novel combines a study of family relations and the patriotic motifs of those years with descriptions of the war situation as a whole in that region and the development of local resistance to the Germans in which the young sister Valya plays a prominent and tragic part. When compared to many other novels of that time, Gorbatov's stands out by virtue of its human portraits and the traditionally simple background and situation. As a novel, it is certainly more accessible in its human message than a great many other examples of Soviet fiction to the reader outside Russia, who is often puzzled to know what sort of people the Russians are.

In his *Letters from Stalingrad*, Valery Grossman had already sketched a vivid reportage description of some of the defenders of Stalingrad. In his novel, *The People Immortal*, he is concerned, as the title indicates, to portray the Russian people as he sees them in the ranks of the Red Army battling with the invader. His problem is different from Gorbatov's; he tries to delineate and contrast various types of Soviet commanders and fighters, like Bogarev and Merzalov, and explain why one is a better all round fighter than the other. This particular problem tends to recur in the Soviet fiction of this period and can be explained by the lessons learned from the first year's fighting and the preoccupation to improve technique and master the principles of broad strategy. The palm goes to the commander who reaches out beyond the circumference of mere local tactics. Awareness is the keynote. In the atmosphere of Soviet Russia, where education and example are so all-important, literature also plays its part in illuminating topical problems; and the formation and character of the Soviet officer is one of the problems that was constantly discussed.

7

The War in Fiction (4)—A Novel of Stalingrad

KONSTANTIN SIMONOV is an ubiquitous character. He is first of all a poet, but he is also a reporter, diarist, playwright, film scenario writer, short story writer and finally novelist. He is a new type in Soviet literature and has been called a " representative of the rising generation." During the war he has managed to do all these things while spending a fair amount of time on the various fronts—one of his books is called *From the Barents Sea to the Black Sea*. He usually strikes first when a new theme is in the air : he is the pioneer of the revived love lyric; he was the first to bring " Russian Folk " on the stage; one of the first to touch the theme of homecoming; and he is the first to have written a novel on the defence of Stalingrad.

His *Days and Nights*, published in 1944, is the story of that defence as seen on a narrow sector and as personified in the action of his hero, Saburov, and his immediate companions in the battle. Here it should be recalled that the battle of Stalingrad involved two distinct operations which were nevertheless linked by a main strategic plan. One was to tie down and exhaust the Germans in the battle for the town itself; the other, when this was accomplished, was to strike at the German flanks with other armies, and so break through, surround and destroy the enemy forces. The army defending Stalingrad itself was a distinct group with a limited objective in view and was not, contrary to what might be thought, over-supplied with reinforcements. This is the phase of the operation shown in Simonov's novel : in fact, it comes to an end as soon as the guns of the general offensive on the flanks are heard. Simonov's heroes live, fight and adventure either in the rubble of the city streets or in the immediate vicinity of the city itself. His is not a novel of Tolstoyan proportions wherein all the threads of a vast action are woven into a broad pattern; rather it is the story of the nightmare period of street fighting, when days and

nights became almost indistinguishable, and the fighters had little or
no sleep.

For a poet, Simonov's prose style is austere, unornamental and not
at all lyrical. It is the style of his diaries that have covered many
fronts. His hero, Captain Saburov, is likewise an austere character,
almost wholly engrossed in the battle, and it is in action that we
observe him and his relationships with his fellow-officers and men.
There are, however, a few moments of relief, such as when he is
wounded and temporarily evacuated, for example. There are also the
beginnings and slight development of a love affair, made possible in
these surroundings by the fact that Russian women did act as stretcher
bearers in the front line. We thus have the portrait of Anya, but this
theme is not pursued very far. But her presence and the feelings she
evokes in Saburov do give rise to some brief but nevertheless revealing
reflections on his part. These reflections are valuable not only as a
guide to Saburov's character, but also for the light they cast on Soviet
men of his generation, who had started out in life in the early thirties
at the time of the first Five Year Plan and were now facing this
stupendous war. Here is a passage that gives us some idea of this
character :—

"The war . . . Of late, remembering his former life, he
involuntarily reduced it to this common factor and divided his
former actions into good or bad, not in a general way but in their
relation to the war. Some of his habits and inclinations impeded
him now that he was fighting, others helped. There were more
of the second sort, no doubt because men like him, who had started
out in life in the years of the first Five Year Plan, had gone through
such a school of life, full of self-sacrifice and self-discipline, that
the war with its daily difficulties, could not surprise him. Saburov
was a man of his generation. Like his contemporaries, he had
started working when he was but a lad, tossed here and there, from
one plant in construction to another. He had started his education
more than once, first in Komsomol and then in Party circles, and
not finishing, had gone off again to work. When his time came, he
had served his two years in the army and had left with the rank of
first lieutenant. Returning again to his job as professional worker,
he had once more taken to spending his days and nights in the
boiler plant and in the forests of Magnitogorsk. The years of the
Five Year Plan had carried him along, as they had many others, by
their rage for construction, and had thrust him into a different profession from that he had dreamt of as a boy. Nevertheless, like
many others, he had found in himself sufficient strength to give up
his customary work, income, and way of life, and, though no longer
a youth, to exchange all that for a student's desk, a bed in a
dormitory, and a hundred roubles a month grant. A year before

the war, he had come up to Moscow and had joined the History Faculty. On June 21st, 1941, he had with unexpected brilliance passed his first University exams, and on the morning of the following day he had heard Molotov's speech. There had occurred that which everyone had expected but in which in the depth of their souls nobody had believed. The war had started, which had brought him within fifteen months—after thrice escaping encirclement, with two decorations, and five times wounded and shell-shocked—here to Stalingrad. . . ."

". . . . So they sat in silence, for perhaps five or ten minutes. Then Maslenikov spoke again, this time of love. At first with boyish seriousness he related his school-boy infatuations; then he spoke of love in general and ended by suddenly asking Saburov : 'And you? Weren't you ever in love?' . . . 'In love?' . . . Saburov thought for a moment, pulled at his cigarette, and shut his eyes. Love. . . . Had there really been no love in his life? He remembered two or three women who had passed casually through his life just as he had apparently passed casually through their life. In this they had no doubts been quits; he had not been disillusioned in anyone and had not hurt anyone. Perhaps that was not a good thing—who knows? Probably that had happened in this way, easily and briefly, not because he had not wanted love, but just because he had wanted it too much. And the women he had happened to meet and the way it had all happened, all that was so unlike love as he imagined it, that he made no attempt to force a resemblance. Incidentally, he could only admit these particulars to himself, and when Maslenikov, after a long pause, asked him again : 'And weren't you ever in love?' He replied : 'I don't know. I don't know. It looks as if not. . . .' He got up and walked about the room. . . . 'No, it cannot be that there was no love,' he thought. 'It would be more exact to say that there was none, but it will come.' And he suddenly remembered the words the girl had uttered on the boat (as they were crossing the Volga) when she said that she was more afraid of death because she had not loved, whereas he should not be afraid because he was more mature and had probably experienced everything. . . . 'No, not everything,' he thought, 'not everything. My God, how much and how little there has been of everything and how boring and impossible it would probably be for a man to go on living if he could imagine even for a minute that he had experienced everything. . . .' He walked the length of the room once again and then going up to Maslenikov, he put his hand on his shoulder. 'Listen, Misha,' he said, 'listen, Misha, you and I, must not die. We simply mustn't.' 'Why?' 'I don't know. But I do know that we mustn't.' . . . At this moment the orderly entered and uttered only one phrase : 'They're attacking'

. . . . 'Well, we've missed our sleep,' said Saburov, fastening on his belt. And Maslenikov felt in the captain's words a sad and kindly irony about all they had been remembering with such emotion and which now meant so very little when confronted with the brief phrase now filling the whole of their life: 'They're attacking. . . .'"

8

The War in Fiction (5)—Other Writers

VALENTIN KATAYEV (b. 1897), author of that charming story of childhood reminiscences, *The Lonely White Sail*, 1937, and of those novels so characteristic of the .time as *The Embezzlers*, 1926, and *Speed Up, Time*, 1933, has not so far contributed anything so outstanding to wartime fiction. He has devoted more time to the stage and has written two plays, *The Blue Scarf*, 1942-43, and *The Paternal Home*, 1943. The first is a slight, humorous but somewhat conventional comedy based on a love intrigue and cases of mistaken identity arising out of gifts received by soldiers at the front. It was amusing enough and brought the relief of laughter in those dark days, but it was severely criticized as a " pot-boiler," and disappeared from the stage. The second play was one of the first on the theme of reconstruction—the return to a reoccupied town, and it was produced in Moscow. In fiction, however, besides a book of short stories, *The Wife*, 1944, some of which were written before the war, Katayev has published only *The Son of a Regiment*, 1945, a short novel which might appeal either to youths or grown ups, and which tells the story and adventures of a boy who was adopted by a front-line regiment. The novel is no doubt based on fact for there were many such boys, orphans or others, who were stranded in the line of battle and got adopted. We have seen not a few such, aged about twelve, in uniform and with decorations, enjoying a well-earned visit to a Moscow theatre. Many of them have since been sent to the Suvorov military schools. This novel has since been awarded the Stalin Prize.

A writer who has attracted much attention is Wanda Wassilewska. She is really a Polish writer and her earlier novels depicted Polish life and the oppression exercised by Polish landlords. During the war, however, she found herself in the Soviet Union and the themes of her novels, *Rainbow*, 1942, and *Just Love*, 1945, are closely connected with the reality of the war and wartime domestic problems. *Rainbow*, which has been filmed, is a concentrated picture of Soviet folk under German occupation, where the sufferings of the local inhabitants and the brutality of the Germans are vividly enough portrayed. In *Just Love*, a slighter and less vivid work, the author broaches the theme of a war-maimed husband returned and a wife's decision to stand by him. The emotional situation here is greatly over-simplified and the novel adds less than nothing to our knowledge of character. Another novel of hers, *Song Over the Waters*, has lately been announced. Wanda Wassilewska is obviously a writer much concerned with social problems and she has a knack of choosing the right social theme at the right moment. In this sense her novels are almost like posters in another medium. In her method she differs from most Soviet writers and might claim descent from the naturalist school, which, however, is not in favour with Soviet critics, who hold that "Naturalism is irreconcilable with the heightened ethical purpose of art."

Consideration of Wanda Wassilewska prompts a digression on Soviet women novelists or rather the lack of them. It is indeed surprising that there should be so few; there are far more prominent women poets, as we shall see in a later chapter. Of women novelists, there are, of course, Olga Forsh and Anna Karavayeva. Lydia Seifullina, who was to the fore in the 1920's, is little heard of these days. We cannot think of anyone else except perhaps Nina Emilyanovna, author of *The Surgeon*, and Gerassimova, author of *The Baydar Gates*. This compares rather strangely with the number and variety of British women writers in the past twenty years. But then, there were hardly any women writers in 19th century Russia either, although Russian women both then and now have done the most astonishing things in social life and even in military action. It almost looks as if novel writing were a man's job in the Soviet Union; but it is to be hoped that there will be a blossoming of feminine talent in the post-war era.

Of the fiction directly concerned with the war and published during the war years, there is little left to consider. Libedinsky's *Guardsmen* and Beck's *The Volokolamsk Road*, reflect mainly the problem of the character, behaviour and military science of Soviet officers and men at the front. Beck's short book, which was translated into English under the title *On the Fringe*, has certain points of interest : one of its chief officer characters is a Kazakh; it deals with an early stage of the war when General Panfilov's division were trained and then took part in the defence of Moscow; and it is very much preoccupied with the technique of being a successful commander. Ovechkin is a new writer, and in his *Greetings from the Front*, 1944, he links the army with the theme of the Home Front. Another young writer, Anatoly Kalinin, attempts a novel of more ambitious scope in his *In the South*, 1945. This is also a novel of the battle of Stalingrad, but seen from an altogether different angle from that of Simonov's *Days and Nights*. Kalinin, who was a correspondent attached to the mounted Cossack armies, which had been driven back to the Terek, describes the advance of these armies to the Don to cut off the German relief forces rushing to von Paulus's rescue. His characters are Don and

Kuban Cossacks of various generations—one of the contrasts is that between an old Cossack, Chakan, and his son, who is now his commander. But this work is hardly more than a promising first novel. A first novel, which was published in America and Great Britain but not in the Soviet Union, is Boris Voytekhov's *The Last Days of Sebastopol*. The title provides the clue to the subject-matter. This is a documentary novel; but it is distinguished by its terse realism and vivid description.

9

Other Writers of Fiction. Konstantin Fedin and Venyamin Kaverin

WE appear to have exhausted the war theme and with it the bulk of current Soviet fiction. Is there anything besides, the reader will ask, sighing for a change? It would have been strange if we had had to omit Konstantin Fedin (b. 1892) from among the authors here reviewed. Since his first novel, *Cities and Years*, published in 1924, Fedin has gained himself the reputation as one of the most finished Soviet novelists. As a writer he has great finesse and is an austere and meticulous stylist. Since 1924, he has published *The Brothers*, 1928, *The Rape of Europe*, 1934, *Sanatorium Arctur*, 1936. He has not been extrovertly very active during the war, but the fact that he was quietly working was disclosed when he published his two volumes of reminiscences, *Gorky Amongst Us*, in 1943 and 1944 respectively; and more will be said about these hereafter. The first intimations of a new novel were when *Novyi Mir*, No. 4, 1945, began serial publication of his *The First Joys*. But it appears that this novel is but the first volume of a trilogy, which, as the author says, " has been planned as a series of pictures of human destinies in our time. Independent in themselves, the three books will be linked by leading characters and an inner unity of theme. The action will develop over some thirty years, not in consecutive chronological order, but in confrontation of three historically and thematically closed periods. The events, described in the first novel, take place in 1910 in a large Volga town. The second novel brings us to 1919. Its plot is threaded with episodes of the civil war on the Volga. The third novel will carry the action into the years of the Patriotic War, as lived in Moscow and at the front.

" In 1910 we see the early youth of the hero of the trilogy, who is a revolutionary, the childhood and youth of the heroines, one of whom later becomes an actress. These characters are Cyril Izevkov, Liza Meshkova, and Anochka. Their families together with a great number of other characters will, I hope, afford the possibility of describing various circles of society and characters such as actors, teachers, workers, traders, navvies, and among army people, soldiers, red army men and officers.

"Time is the acting personage of the trilogy: events develop, children grow up, old people go their way. Time changes people, and men change time. I am therefore endeavouring to fill the novels with movement, to endow them with an energetic but natural subject-matter. These should be novels of manners in which the realistic pictures of everyday life will blend with history and the romance of heroism."

Such is the author's own description of his trilogy-in-progress. It would seem to reflect a trend we have already observed, of wishing to bridge the chasm between past and present. The plan of this work is also another indication that the post-war world of Soviet fiction is going to be a more solid one.

A different note is struck by Venyamin Kaverin (b. 1902) in his novel, *The Two Captains*, published in 1945. Here we have a note of adventure and boyishness as well as of psychological fantasy. The story is that of the adventures of a boy, Sanya Grigoriev, who finally becomes a sea captain and takes part in the search for a lost polar expedition. The search is unsuccessful owing to some subtle sabotage, but during the war Grigoriev discovers and unmasks the saboteur, so that he can now go ahead and pursue the lost trail. Kaverin is undoubtedly an interesting and talented writer if we recall his *The Artist is Anonymous*, 1931, his *Room With a Larger View*, and some of his stories. From his début as a writer in the 1920's he has shown himself possessed of a vein of fantasy. He has been writing in a more realistic manner of late, but a Hoffmanesque fantasy still peeps through occasionally, as in the scene where the villain is finally unmasked. During the war he spent a lot of time in the arctic regions writing reportages and stories. His long novel is really a completed and revised version of a shorter book published in Leningrad in 1940. Since *The Two Captains* has brought us to mention adventure, we shall now pass to consider this *genre* and also that of the detective novel.

10

The Revival of the Adventure and the Detective Novel

A VISITOR to the Soviet Union might be surprised by the demand among his Russian friends for detective fiction and by the apparent complete absence of it as a current literary commodity. There is no doubt that this *genre* fell into disuse after the Revolution and that translations, say, of Edgar Wallace were not on the whole encouraged. At one time the *genre* was probably regarded as an unnecessary and harmful manifestation of corrupt bourgeois society. If we examine the history of Russian literature, we shall perceive that this dearth of detective fiction is not an indigenous feature of the Soviet period only. The *genre* does not appear to have taken strong root in Russian literature and had produced no Russian classics of its kind. But some of the elements are to be found transmuted in psychological novels of the type of Dostoievsky's *Crime and Punishment*. Otherwise there was not much to be found in between the penny dreadful of the Nat Pinkerton type and the translations of foreign models such as Conan Doyle; and these latter enjoyed large sales and popularity.

The same is roughly true of adventure fiction in its various forms, such as travel, discovery and scientific fantasy. Here the most popular authors were also foreigners : Jules Verne, Mayne Reid, Fennimore Cooper, Robert Louis Stevenson, H. G. Wells, Jack London, Louis Bousenar. The latter, a Frenchman, is not very well known in Great Britain, possibly because of his late nineteenth century anti-English bias, but his tales of travel and discovery all over the world were much read by Russian children before the Revolution.

Until recently in the Soviet Union, there has been very little development in this field and, as far as I know, very little translation and publication of the classics. There was, of course, Alexander Green (A. S. Grinevsky, d. 1932), a talented writer who wrote adventure stories of the sea and sometimes fairy tales, and who was for long much neglected and is certainly little known outside Russia. His fame has lately been revived when the Bolshoy Theatre produced *Crimson Sails*, 1942, a ballet version of one of his fairy tales. Alexei Tolstoy also tried his hand at the story of Wellsian scientific fantasy; and his *Aelita*, 1922, and *The Hyperbolid of Engineer Garin*, 1926, bear witness to this attempt to launch this *genre* which did not prosper. There is nothing much else of this kind or, indeed, of the more straightforward type of adventure story on the horizon of the 1920's and the 1930's. There was a slight stirring just before the war : in 1939 there appeared a story, *The First Blow*, by Nicolai Shpanov—a topical fantasy on the first days of an imaginary war between Germany and the U.S.S.R.—and the interest was concentrated on aerial warfare. While in the Soviet Union, we came across another book by the author, *The Adventures of Professor Burago*, published in four short volumes, in which we found momentary relaxation from the social life of Moscow on the occasion of a weekend at a country *dacha*. We cannot now remember all the adventures of Professor Burago. Suffice it to say, there was an invention involved, something very atomic in its consequence, as well as Russians, British and Germans, all in Norway.

That was in 1944 and by that time the revival of the adventure story was being openly discussed by critics. In reviewing *The War Secret* by Sheynin and *The Golden Star* by Lev Niculin, both attempts at adventure stories based on the war, the critic Anataly Glebov* greets them as "the first swallows, announcing a post-war flowering in this domain of our literature, especially important for the young reader." He goes on to say that "The literature of adventure is rich in many possibilities. There is history, travel, war, scientific and technical fantasy. There is the detective story, which centres upon the struggle with the criminal and the solution of mysteries. In all these varieties of the *genre,* action is the chief ingredient. In this specific characteristic of the literature of adventure lies the secret of its enormous success with the mass reader and especially young people, *as well as its educative and activizing significance.* It is the literature of action. In this lies its right to existence."

In Anataly Glebov's criticism we can observe an emphasis on the educational value of this literature. This is not accidental. As we have pointed out before, education is still one of the main problems of the Soviet State and, as a result of the reforms of the 1930's, the broad lines of the new education policy are still in practice being laid down. It would seem that detective and adventure fiction, in the form in which it is now being revived, is going to be made to fit into the framework of the new policy. This is understandable in so far as this sort of fiction will be largely read by the youth of the country and the State has an immediate interest in the shaping of the outlook of the younger generation. The Soviet detective novel as it will now be written will have a definite patriotic and moral bias; it is intended for edification as well as amusement. As another critic pointed out in 1945, "The educational significance of the Soviet detective literature must express itself not only *in stimulating the watchfulness of the reader,* sharpening his ability for logical analysis and observation, but also *in exposing the intolerability and abomination of all crime against Soviet society,* thus portraying artistically the foredoomed nature of every such criminal and the inevitability of the discovery of every crime, however artfully and cunningly it may be performed. . . ." The Soviet detective, then, would seem to become a personification of the all-watchful State rather than a detached observer of human nature like Sherlock Holmes.

A somewhat similar purpose is present in the revival of the adventure story. The latter is "to help an appreciation of heroic character." It is obviously intended to encourage the growth of an adventurously-minded generation which believes it has a world of great possibilities before it. The revival of these *genres* is not artificial;

Literature and Art, of 28th October, 1944.

it answers a genuine demand, but at the same time the State is evidently exercising a controlling influence by laying down specific principles for its development.

To encourage these *genres,* a special Section was set up in the Writers' Union. We learn that at its first session " a Commission was formed under the chairmanship of L. Sheynin, the Public Investigator, who recently published a detective story in *Pravda.* Among others who attended the discussion were M. Shaginyan, I. Papanin, the arctic explorer, and S. Eisenstein, the film producer."

II

Men and Officers, or Naval and Army Traditions in Fiction

JUST as there is a new demand for adventure stories, so increasing attention is being paid to the theme of the sea in literature. Broadly speaking there are two main reasons for this interest : the wish to record and reflect the actions of Soviet sailors during the war and the desire to work out a basis for Soviet naval traditions in view of the apparent intention to expand the Soviet fleets and shipping generally after the war. As the writer Vsevolod Vishnevsky, author of *At the Walls of Leningrad,* says, " We stand on the eve of the creation of a Big Fleet—a Fleet of two Oceans, for which communal efforts will be necessary." This theme has become a topical one and has led to a great deal of discussion. Of actual literature on the subject there is so far not a great deal, and most of that is dispersed in short stories. We have already noted Leonid Sobolov's collection of short stories, *The Soul of the Sea.*

It is characteristic of any revival that it should seek support in certain past traditions. In this case, we observe that the personalities and deeds of historic admirals like Ushakov and Nahimov have been revived both by institution of orders named after them and by the publication of their biographies. History is also being combed for sea adventures, travellers and explorers. It is recalled that Goncharov, author of *Oblomov,* took part in a sea voyage of the Frigate " Pallada " and kept a diary, and that a 19th century writer, Staniukovich, wrote much about Russian sailors. In his *Sebastopol Tales,* too, Leo Tolstoy has descriptions of sailors who were defending the town. In Soviet days there was Novikov-Priboy (d. 1944), who in *Tsushima,* 1934, evoked the memory of Russian sailors and of the Fleet as it was in the days of the Russo-Japanese war. His *Captain of the First Rank,* published in 1943, is also about the old Fleet, but he did write some stories of contemporary Soviet sailors. M. Solovyev's *Ivan Niculin, the Russian Sailor,* 1943, and A. Zonin's *Brotherhood of the Sea,*

1945, are the only wartime novels on the subject. Solovyev's is a simplified heroic image, while Zonin's is a more documentary and technically-minded work. Neither is comparable to Forester's *The Ship*, which has incidentally been translated in *Krasnoflotetz*, the magazine published for circulation among the men of the Soviet navy. Many of the wartime stories, like Sobolev's, which depict Soviet sailors in action, are concerned with land fighting rather than action at sea, but here it is the special character and traditions of the sailors as distinct from that of the soldiers that is dwelt on. Iury Herman, who has spent most of the war in the arctic regions, has also written a number of reportages, stories and a book, *The Frosted Sea*, on this theme, but it is difficult to assess his work since it does not seem to circulate in Moscow.

But the problem that has been most discussed in this connection, is how to depict the sailor as a *Soviet* sailor and how to portray the *Soviet* naval officer. It is pointed out that works about the Fleet should not be over-technical and should not deal mainly with ships and mechanisms, but should portray the kind of people who are in charge of them. And these in their turn should not be made to talk in conventional sea-jargon since they are, after all, cultured Soviet citizens. Another point is how to make a clear distinction between the sailor of to-day and the sailor of the Tsarist Fleet, who may have been a good fellow but lacked specific Soviet characteristics. And finally there is the problem of depicting a human being—" each man has his biography "—instead of a professional type.

The discussion centring round the image of the Soviet naval officer was brought to a head by the publication and staging of A. Kron's play, *The Officer of the Fleet*, 1944. Here in the person of its hero, Captain Gorbunov, the question of an officer's honour, general outlook and relations to fellow-officers, is raised. The play itself is not a very outstanding work, although it was produced by the Arts Theatre, and its merit lies rather in ventilating these topical questions. The theme in brief is that Gorbunov disagrees with a fellow-officer about a line of conduct in a particular case and makes an issue of honour about it. In its broader aspects, this situation reflects what is in fact happening—the re-birth of a tradition which has become inevitable as a result of the reappearance of an officer class and of the whole trend of the past ten or fifteen years. The same pre-occupation with the correct portrait of the officer is now shown by writers when dealing with the army.

Three days, December 7th, 8th, and 9th, of 1944, were devoted by writers to the discussion of " The Image of the Soviet Officer in the Literature of 1944." The discussion was organized by the War Commission of the Union of Soviet Writers. General Ignatiev, author of *Fifty Years in the Ranks*, took part in it. A lot of time was devoted to the criticism of Simonov's Saburov, whose "inner thoughts" and reasonings were found not to have been sufficiently expressed, and of Beck's Momysh Ula, who was discovered to be "too dominating over his subordinates, and often crushing their initiative." The main point of all these discussions is how to portray a type of officer, who has inherited the best Russian traditions and a distinct Soviet moral outlook. In this connection, we may recall Simonov's brochure, *A Serious Conversation,* 1945, written in the form of a conversation between Red Army officers and a visiting foreign correspondent, "Mr. Leslie." Its purpose is to bring out some distinctions between the Red Army and the old Russian army, and to deny that old traditions have just been taken over wholesale. A few quotations will illustrate the thesis : "I am a materialist," said Pankratov, smiling, "and because of that, I know the part played in war by spiritual education and the soldier's spiritual strength. If I am not mistaken, it was not with us, but with you in the West that the theory of robots and mechanical armies was advanced. We in Russia never put them forward. . . . It seems to me that if we are speaking of the qualities of the Russian character, then one of its chief qualities is that of being critically disposed towards all that was bad in the past. We are continuing the good traditions and we never bow before the bad ones. . . ."

12

Michael Prishvin or The Poetry of Nature

TO read the work of Michael Prishvin is to enter a different domain; it is to fling open the windows of a country house upon a natural landscape full of quiet beauty and poetry. It is to forget the town and the machinery of civilization and to lose one's self in a forest where each detail of natural life, the trees, the birds and the animals, are all clearly noted and harmoniously expressed. Prishvin is a poet of nature, writing in subtly shaded and musical prose. He can convey barely perceptible impressions and enchant with the slightest modulations of the simplest and most tenuous natural manifestations. He is an observer and psychologist of nature, which for him is peopled with "personalities." He is descriptive and evocative. But there is more than that in his art. He seems to penetrate into the very essence of any natural thing, whether it be an insect, a flower or a bird, feel its inner pulse and re-create a living image of it. He is a philosopher, too, and can reflect on human nature, but he sees it as part of the greater world in which his trees, and flowers, and birds also dwell. If his men have their immediately recognizable personalities, his fauna and flora are as distinct.

This transition into a world of nature may appear sudden after the terrifying and topical world of wartime reality in which we have been travelling, but we are now in the domain of Prishvin. He is, of course, a writer of the older generation, born in 1873. His literary career dates from 1907, when his first book, *Where Birds Have Not Been Frightened,* appeared. As the title indicates, Prishvin knows those remote regions where nature is still virgin; and he has specialized in nature lore and scenes from provincial life ever since. All his works cannot be considered here, but we may note that in 1924 he published *Kurymushka,* the story of the unfolding of a childhood life—probably his own; and he has since published many other tales, stories and prose-poems.

His wartime book, *The Forest Drop,* 1943, consists of a series of brief notations, each one a perfectly wrought prose-poem, bearing titles such as *Autumn Leaves, Trees Imprisoned, The Dark Wood, The Mole, The Badger, The Belated Stream, Natural Barometers, The Workshop of the Woodpecker,* and so forth. Here are subtle notations of the very movements of nature, finely-drawn descriptions and unobtrusive comment, all blending into a clear poetic image.

One of the notations, *Complex Simplicity,* deals with the writer's own method. It is as follows : " We must put great store on our meetings with animals, and make notes even without lyrical reactions. Ordinarily I seek such a reaction in myself—it serves as a stimulating motive to writing. But sometimes it happens that one simply notes down, for example, how a squirrel crossed over on a log, one notes this down without any relation to one's inner self—and the result, one does not know why, also turns out to be good. One should practice this more, because that is already not naturalism, but something very complex in its simplicity." In *Goethe's Mistake,* Prishvin gives us his view of the personal and the impersonal : " I noticed for the first time that yellow thrushes sing in different ways, and remembered Goethe's thought that nature creates the impersonal while only man is personal. No, I think, only man is capable of creating side by side with spiritual values entirely featureless mechanisms, while it is precisely in nature that everything is personal, including the laws of nature : for in living nature even these laws are mutable. So even Goethe was not always right." A quiet humour is discernible in *My Mushroom* : " In the mushroom forest one clearing shakes hands with another over the hedgerows, and when you step over these hedgerows, your mushroom greets you in the clearing. There is no need to search here : your mushroom always looks you in the face."

We have quoted here only some of the briefest of these notations and we must resist the very real temptation to go on indefinitely until not a drop of forest has been left out of this book. In 1945, Prishvin published another book, *The Storehouse of the Sun.* This is a tale, with a simple plot, and tells of the forest experiences of a boy and girl. It is curious to think that Prishvin has been writing for some forty years now and that his work has received little or no appreciation outside Russia, though he is undoubtedly a classic of his kind.

13

"When the Sun Rises" or A Study in Conditioned Reflexes

MICHAEL ZOSHCHENKO is one of the best known of Soviet writers outside of the Soviet Union and one of the most popular in England. This fame he owes to his short, humorous and colloquial stories of everyday life. Born in 1895, he first became prominent as a writer in the early 1920's, and has since published many volumes of his typical stories. But in 1933, he suddenly tried new ground with a short novel, *Youth Restored,* to which he gave a certain scientific or psychological basis. The author's own description of this novel is as follows : " It was an ordinary novel, one of those of which many are written, but it had additional comments—studies of a psychological nature. These studies explained the behaviour of the heroes of the novel and gave the reader certain information about human physiology and psychology. I did not write *Youth Restored* for men of science, but nevertheless, it was they in particular who paid special attention to this work. There were many discussions. Quarrels, too. I heard many sharp things said. But there were friendly words spoken also. I was abashed when scientists argued with me so seriously and hotly. That can only mean, I thought, that it is not I who know much, but it seems that science has not sufficiently considered those questions which, through my inexperience, I had the boldness to raise. In any case, scientists treated me almost as an equal. I even began to receive invitations to sessions of ' The Brain Institute.' And Ivan Petrovich Pavlov used to invite me to his ' Wednesdays.' But I repeat. I did not write my work for science. It was a literary work, and the scientific material was but a component part."*

In publishing his *When the Sun Rises* in 1943, Zoshchenko had clearly made another attempt to develop a work on somewhat similar lines. According to the author, it is a book " about how I got rid of many unnecessary disappointments and became happy." It is largely autobiographical and treats of the first thirty years of the author's life when his spiritual-physical state was such as apparently to make him constantly unhappy and depressed. In this thirtieth year, however, a change had taken place, " a new life began, altogether different from

*October, No. 6-7, 1943.

the previous one." This was not the result of psycho-analysis and Freud, but according to the author, "It was Pavlov. I made use of his principle. It was his idea. . . . I did essentially a very simple thing : I swept away that which was impeding me—the wrong conditioned reflexes which had mistakenly formed themselves in my consciousness. I destroyed the false connection between them. I broke the ' temporary connections ' as Pavlov called them."

In the published parts of *When the Sun Rises*, Zoshchenko deals with his search after the root and cause of his " unhappiness." This search leads him in the first part of the book to examine his life from the age of sixteen to thirty. He does so in a series of sixty-three incidents that had once " excited him," and these are described under separate headings. That is, indeed, his method throughout the books : generalizations, comments and analysis are treated separately. Thus, the first part consists of a Foreword, a Prologue (1), a section *I Am Unhappy, I do not know why* (2), *Fallen Leaves* (3), in which occur the sixty-three incidents covering the years 1912 to 1926, and a *Conclusion*, in which the author confesses that he is discouraged : " It seems I set myself a task beyond my power in trying to discover the cause of my anguish, the unfortunate event which had made of me a pitiful grain of dust swept along by any wind of life." But then he asks himself if the cause does not lie in earlier childhood years and recalling some incidents of that time, he finds that they move him even more. He is thus led to examine his early life, first from the age of five to fifteen, in a section entitled *The Terrifying World* (4), where there are thirty-eight incidents; and then from the age of two to five, and further from birth up to the age of two, in another section *Before the Sun Rises* (5). Here there is some discussion of the systems of Freud and Pavlov. In the final section of this part, *Black Water* (6), as a result of a visit to a village where he has spent his childhood, Zoshchenko begins to see light and comes to the conclusion that " the unfortunate event had taken place at my first acquaintance with the surrounding world. It had occurred in the pre-luminous twilight before the sunrise. It was not even an event. It was a mistake, an unfortunate occurrence, an astonishing combination of accidents. This accident gave rise to false pathological conceptions of certain things, water among them. This was a drama in which my guilt was not greater than my sufferings. . . . It was not necessary to find the conditioned nervous reflexes which led from the water to something which was, perhaps, even more terrifying. Without that, the water would not have inspired such fear. And so, sure of myself, I proceeded further. in search of my unfortunate occurrence."

Thus ends the last published instalment* of *When the Sun Rises*. We were, however, deprived of the final instalment and the discovery

*October, No. 8-9, 1943.

of the cause of the " unfortunate occurrence," because at this stage a heavy storm of criticism broke around the work. In the ensuing flashes of lightning and peals of thunder, Zoshchenko changed his place of residence from Moscow to Leningrad, and the final chapters of the book appear to have been put away in a drawer. In any case, they did not grace the pages of any future issues of *October*. This incident affords an interesting example of the frontiers of possibilities open or closed to Soviet writers, and we shall treat more fully of the criticism levelled at Zoshchenko in our next chapter. In the West of Europe where literature has passed through its freudian and psycho-analytical stages, Zoshchenko's book might excite interest, but it certainly would not cause such a commotion. The book has some resemblance to Andrei Biely's *The Childhood of Kotik Letayev*, but it is more realistically written and purports to have a scientific basis in place of Biely's mystical approach. A typical, but not one of the more " depressing " Zoshchenko childhood incidents is *I am Not Guilty*:

" We are sitting at the table and eating pancakes. Suddenly father takes my plate and begins to eat my pancakes. I howl. Father wears glasses. He looks very serious. He has a beard. Nevertheless he is laughing. He says :

'You see what a greedy chap he is. He is sorry to let his father have one pancake.'

'One pancake, please, eat it,' I say. 'I thought you were going to eat them all.'

The soup is brought in.

'Papa, would you like my soup?' I say.

'No, I shall wait until the sweet is brought,' says Papa. 'If you let me have your sweet, then indeed you are a kind-hearted boy.'

Thinking that the sweet was going to be cranberry jelly with milk, I say :

'Please. You can eat my sweet.'

But suddenly cream is brought in, to which I am not indifferent. Moving my saucer of cream towards my father, I say :

'Please eat it, if you are so greedy.'

Father frowns and leaves the table. Mother says :

'Go to father and beg his pardon.'

'I shan't go,' I say. 'It's not my fault.'

I leave the table, not having touched the sweet. In the evening, when I am in bed, father comes up. In his hands he holds my saucer of cream. He says :

'Well, why didn't you eat your cream?'

'Papa, let's take half of it each,' I say. 'Why should we quarrel over it.'

Father kisses me and gives me spoonfuls of cream."

CHAPTER VII

THE WRITER AND THE CRITIC

I

The Foundations of Present-Day Criticism

THE relations between critics and writers, and the pronouncements critics make on works of art, are inevitably a reflection of the taste, the critical standards and the interests prevailing at any given stage of literary development. Similarly, they may also reflect the lack of taste or the confusion of critical standards. Or, again, they may be evidence of a more pointed conflict between a traditional concept and a new theory. A critic like Matthew Arnold, for example, deplored the lack of a more centralized tradition and of more authoritative principles in English literature. He also defined literature as " the criticism of life."

It can certainly be said that since the 1840's Russian literature has been increasingly and predominantly concerned with the criticism of life. There were, of course, special conditions attaching to 19th century Russian literature, of which the attempted control of thought by the autocracy was one, and the chasm between the illiterate peasant masses (serfs until 1861) and the small ruling or cultured minority was another, that made Russian literature a vehicle of the more advanced and reforming ideas of the time. The Russian writer by virtue of his awareness of social issues was liable to find himself between the two grind-stones of popular up-surge and autocratic tyranny. The conflict, however, was not a cut and dried one, as we can see from the case of Dostoievsky who, for all his great national pathos and popular appeal, started out as Petrashevsky reformist in 1848 but ended as a champion of Orthodoxy in 1881. There were not many writers of this age up to 1905 who had not been in conflict with authority and who had not been either imprisoned or exiled at one time or another. The list of such cases is too long to recapitulate here. The most striking case, though it is an earlier one, is perhaps that of Chaadayev, who, in 1836, published his *Letters on the Philo-*

sophy of History. An officer of the Napoleonic campaign, he had travelled in Europe and had been influenced by the theories of Joseph Le Maistre, and in his *Letters* he propounded the view that Russia had suffered and missed a great deal because of her Byzantine associations and lack of communication with the Western Catholic tradition. His view was that "hostile circumstances have alienated us from the general trend in which the social idea of Christianity grew up; thus we ought to revise our faith, and begin our education over again on another basis." The expression of these views led to the exile of the editor of the periodical, *Telescope,* in which they were printed, and to Chaadayev's being declared insane; he was put under medical supervision for a time.

The atmosphere of Russian literature throughout the 19th century was not a healthy one. The censor was constantly in the background, but looking back on it, it is remarkable how much " dynamite " was nevertheless allowed to appear in print or how much of it got through in various forms, often camouflaged. Chaadayev was an exception in his views. The majority of writers who came into conflict with authority were either critics or reformers on revolutionary lines of another sort; and there was a constant war between the main schools of reformers, the Westerners and the Slavophils. To be a writer or critic in those days, and to have the strength of one's convictions, was almost tantamount to asking for a term of exile or penal servitude. Criticism was, therefore, not a matter of critics and writers alone : first and foremost there was the censor with the paternal State behind him. This being so, it is remarkable how many Russian writers of the time were civil servants or censors themselves. No doubt the organization of the Russian State since the days of Peter the Great made of the civil service one of the few openings for a gentleman's career.

But if the censor was the most difficult 'critic' to circumvent, the critics themselves were far from a harmonious family. This, perhaps, is as it should be; but it is noticeable even from the early days that political and social considerations tend to predominate, and that a work of art is judged by its social or political message in the first place and for its formal qualities only later or not at all. The only times in Russian literature since 1850 when an æsthetic trend was at all dominant or at least flourished, was in the 1860's when the Parnassian poets sang in political isolation or when, at the turn of the century, the Symbolists, or one section of them, at least, looked at the world æsthetically from their ivory towers. It is perhaps significant that both these schools had their roots in European literary movements and drew their inspirations, in the one case, from Théophile Gautier and Théodore Bainville and, in the other, from Mallarmé and Verlaine. Another instance of a political criticism occurred strangely enough in the 1920's when the Formalist school of criticism was enjoying its brief heyday. But, taken as a whole, throughout the 19th century and after, Russian criticism is fundamentally a politically-social one; it pronounces judgment on a work on the basis of its success or failure to realize the hopes and strivings of an advanced intelligentsia towards a better life and ideal or a new social order.

Speaking of Bielinsky, one of the first outstanding Russian critics, in a book published in 1914, Maurice Baring says : " The didactic stamp which he gave to Russian æsthetic and literary criticism has remained on it ever since, and differentiates it from the literary and æsthetic criticism of the rest of Europe, not only from that school of criticism which wrote and writes exclusively under the banner of ' Art for Art's Sake,' but from those Western critics who championed the importance of moral ideas in literature, just as ardently as he did himself. . . ." Baring goes on to say that *" a truly objective criticism scarcely exists in Russian literature."* That was written in 1914, that is to say, before the Revolution, and it is well to bear this fact in mind when discussing Soviet criticism and literature, for otherwise we shall get our perspective wrong as so many people do when faced with Soviet reality at second hand or what appears to be peculiarly Soviet propaganda. The fact of the matter is that the Revolution is an experiment which is being tried out, not in an abstract void, but in a particular sort of laboratory, in a given atmosphere and temperature, with specific instruments, materials and assistants at hand. It would be foolish to suppose that the *new* is born without a revived admixture of the old. Scratch a Soviet citizen, one might say, and find a Russian. But it would be untrue to argue that it is just the same old Russian again. There are new traits but they are becoming blended with others we recognize in the 19th century or earlier.

What then are the features of Soviet criticism? Here again, as in all things Soviet, there is a main division into two periods—prior to the early 1930's and after. In the case of criticism the dividing line is April, 1932-34, when the Union of Soviet Writers came into being and the principle of Socialist Realism was worked out and made into a canon. Prior to that and until 1928, at least, it was very much of a free-for-all, a mass of conflicting theories and schools of thought. It is no wonder, for example, that an *On Guard* editorial of 1923 said : " The most inexcusable muddle reigns in our own ranks (i.e. communist ranks) upon all questions of literature. This must come to an end. We must stand for a consistent proletarian line in literature. . . . We shall engage in merciless battle both against the stagnation and self-repetition current among several groups of proletarian writers and against the excessive research in form. . . ." Another group, *The Serapion Brothers,* out of which some of the leading novelists were to emerge, held in 1922 that : " We think that present day Russian literature is amazingly decorous, conceited and monotonous. We are allowed to write stories, novels and obligatory dramas in both the old and new styles, but only as long as their content is social or concerned with topical themes. We ask but one thing : that a work of art should be organic and real, and that it should live its own peculiar life." These differences of opinion current at the time, could be multiplied many times over; but perhaps the most interesting and unusual development of this period was the Formalist school of criticism. Victor Shklovsky, O. Brik and Eichenbaum, were the leading exponents. Their credo can be briefly summed up in the following quotation from Brik : " There are neither *poets* nor *writers,* but only *poetry* and *literature.* . . . A poet is master of his craft and no more. . . . A general investigation into the devices of the poetic craft is essential. . . . The history of poetry is the history of the development of the devices which constitute its literary formation. . . . We will help proletarian creation not by vague discussions about the proletarian spirit and communist consciousness, but by precise and technical demonstration of the devices underlying contemporary poetical creative work." These, then, were critics whose method was to analyse the structure of a work of art by splitting it up like a mechanism into its component parts; they were not interested in its content or idea as such. Little wonder that " Formalism " later became a term of abuse and a synonym for any modernism or other undesirable trend, including Fascism.

Opposed to Formalism but later also to be condemned, is the main marxist school of criticism of that time, the school of Pereverzev, which is later referred to as the school of " vulgar or sociological marxism." It was this school which reflected most closely the historical conceptions of Pokrovsky whose theories and downfall we have described in the chapter on the *Re-discovery of History.* Its exponents maintained that " a literary work is a social and not individual phenomenon. It originates according to laws of inevitable necessity. To look for an author of an artistic work is to look for secondary things. . . ." It was against this dominant but mechanistic theory that the critics of the later 1930's were to wage a relentless war. But before that stage was reached, there was another interlude which was to prove a transition between two very different worlds, and that was the period of R.A.P.P. dictatorship, coinciding with the first Five Year Plan. This was the phase of the " Social Command," when writers of all groups were mobilized under proletarian leadership and given their orders by the proletarian critic Averbakh. This interlude was over by April, 1932, when in the Central Committee Resolution of that date, it was pointed out that " the framework of the existing proletarian organizations was becoming too confined and impeded the development of artistic creation."

Thus the dictatorship of a minority body was succeeded by the organization of a comprehensive Writers' Union, in which fellow travellers and communists met on equal footing. This and the proclamation of the principles of Socialist Realism were most important steps determining the future background of the relations between Soviet writers and critics. From 1932 until 1941, the critics may be said to have performed two main functions : on the one hand, they were disentangling themselves from the web of " vulgar or sociological marxism " and, at the same time, in fits of excessive zeal, they were staging heresy hunts among their *confrères*; on the other hand, they were helping to build up the positive sides of the new era (interpreting Socialist Realism, discovering history and literary ancestors, etc.) and re-discovering all sorts of simple, but none the less refreshing truths.

As a principle, Socialist Realism has the advantage of being a supple and comprehensive term depending a great deal on intelligent interpretation. It implies quite a different world from that of " sociological marxism " which simply said : " You belong to this class or category." The very term Socialist Realism implies the notion of change as distinct from mechanistic analogy : first, because reality, which is the subject of contemplation, is a different reality each time it is contemplated—not different in essence but in combination of potentialities (thus, in a writer's vision, the Russian hero of 1946 would be a much more expanded person than the hero of 1940, because his whole view of the world or his relationship to it had changed); second, because Socialist when linked with Realism in this context is not an abstract notion but refers to a given state of an existing and, in this case, rapidly evolving society (the Russia of 1940 is industrially and educationally very different from that of 1930; the Russia of 1946 or 1950 will be very different again). Thus, Socialist Realism is a principle allowing for growth and development, and the appearance of new elements as part of the reality contemplated. It allows the critic considerable range and freedom if he is subtle and dialectical enough to take advantage and not afraid to provoke reactions.

As an example of some of trends in 1935-36, we may cite the case of critics like M. Lifchitz and V. Kemenev, who re-introduced the epithet *narodny* (or " national " or " of the people ") and applied it to an increasing number of writers where formerly they would have been " classified." Thus, Kemenev apparently discovered that Shakespeare was a " national poet " rather than a " class poet," while Lifchitz went so far as almost to doubt the existence of classes altogether. This trend was criticized by Gurstein* who, in 1941, deplored what he called another form of " vulgarization " in this indiscriminate " nationalization " of the writers of the past. It is, however, true that class analysis as such has practically disappeared

Problems of Socialist Realism by A. Gurstein. " Soviet Writer," Moscow, 1941.

from Soviet criticism and that during the war it was hardly to be met with, while the epithet *Narodny* was in almost invariable use. Although Gurstein criticized Lifchitz and Kemenev, he was equally opposed to any return to the " class " notions of the school of vulgar sociology which he described as follows : " It had no room for the conception of *people* and *of the people;* these words were taboo and their very sound called forth indignation. . . . For, in all that is connected with the people and with national trends, there is a living breath of life, but it was of life above all that these ascetic and melancholy schematicians of the breed of *sociologus vulgaris* were most afraid. They regarded themselves as the champions of class analysis, but to the authentic marxist-leninist class analysis of literary manifestations, with all its living wealth, variety, complexity and often contradictory content, they preferred an over-simplified classification of pre-conceived class groups and groupings. Class analysis requires an effort of thought, a knowledge of life and history, a dialectical approach to phenomena. . . ." To the outsider this discussion may appear scholastic like so much of Soviet controversy, but it is nevertheless a clear indication of a new and more supple orientation in Soviet criticism. By the end of the war its basis was to become even broader, but since there have been signs that critics may have strayed too far from the path of dialectical interpretation and that they must be reminded from time to time of its existence.

Soviet criticism as we find it in 1946 has, on the one hand, adopted a broad national approach to literature; on the other, it is still guided by the principle of Socialist Realism and by the science of the dialectical method which can always be called in to correct any divagation from the main purpose. This latter can be defined in Gurstein's words as : " To reflect profoundly the content of the life of the people means not only to give a broad and truthful picture of reality, but also to illumine it from the standpoint of the people's interests properly understood, to illumine the deep processes taking place within it— processes which are sometimes hidden from the unexperienced eye, and to express the people's needs and strivings." This is the dialectical analysis of Socialist reality. But in addition to this contemporary method of analysis, Soviet criticism has also built up for itself of late a national tradition, the pivots of which are the 19th century philosopher-critics Bielinsky (1810-48), Chernyshevsky (1828-89) and Dobroliubov (1836-60). With Herzen, these now are the Russian classics not only in the sphere of philosophy but also in that of criticism. To them may be also added Pisarev (1840-88).

Let us briefly analyse their message and contribution to the *credo* of present day criticism. Bielinsky was the pioneer of social criticism : he arrived at this conception gradually after passing through phases of romanticism and Hegelian philosophy. In the end, he reacted against Hegelianism and its implied indifference to social problems, became a publicist preoccupied with social analysis and then applied his social theories to literature. Turning against metaphysics and idealist philosophy, he laid the foundations of the theory of organic criticism and of the notion of the critic as a publicist. Among his essays we find *The General Meaning of the Word Literature* (1840), *The Works of Pushkin* (1843-46), *Russian Literature in 1846*. In his *Speech about the Critics*, 1842, he says : " What is the art itself of our day? The judgment, the analysis of society and, consequently, criticism. The element of thought has now blended with the artistic element, and for our time an artistic work is dead if it portrays life only for the sake of portraying life, without any mighty subjective conviction deriving its principle from the predominant thought of the age, if it is not the cry of suffering or the dithyrambo of enthusiasm, if it is not a question or an answer to a question." One could go on quoting appropriate passages from his works to demonstrate that he was the originator of the socially-analytical, ethical, educative, and realist trend in Russian criticism. Chernyshevsky carried his doctrine a step further in his essay on *The Aesthetic Relations of Art to Reality*, 1855. In this anti-Hegelian work, Chernyshevsky boldly concludes that the manifestations of life itself are more beautiful than art. Inversely, according to him, " the sphere of art is not limited by the beautiful alone to its so-called ' moments,' but comprehends everything that interests man, not as a scientist, but as a human being in reality (in nature and life); the content of art is therefore what is of common interest in life." Chernyshevsky put his theory into practice by writing a novel, *What Shall We Do?* (1862), in which he portrays a new positive type of hero and a new order of human relationships based on reason as distinct from the traditionally-conditioned types of characters currently described in the literature of that day.

Dobroliubov was another critic of this type who especially stressed the qualities of the Russian people or simple folk, and contrasted them with the purposeless life of the higher strata; he was a critic of Turgeniev, Dostoievsky and Ostrovsky and many other contemporary writers, but it was his analytical study, *What Does Oblomov Represent?* that caused the greatest stir. In this study he drew a striking contrast between Oblomov and Stoltz, the superfluous man and the man of more wilful character whom Dobroliubov wished to see playing a more positive part in Russian life. Stoltz was not yet the man destined for this rôle, for, as the author says, " It should not be forgotten that beneath him is a bog, in his vicinity are to be found the elements that make up Oblomov, and that it is still necessary to clear the forest in order to find the main road and escape from all that Oblomov stands for. . . ." Pisarev was an even more austere social critic and had little use for the greater part of literature. One of his principal critical essays was first published in a periodical in 1865 under the title of *The New Type,* and it was then reprinted in his collected works in 1867 under the new title of *The Thinking Proletariat.* It is a critical analysis of Chernyshevsky's novel, *What Shall We Do?* His moral and utilitarian approach can be judged from the following quotation from this work : " I know very well that the majority of contemporary people, who consider themselves to be quite decent, contradict themselves at each step, both in their words and acts. A man who avoids the most obvious contradictions is proclaimed in our time to be almost a genius in mind and, in any case, a hero in character. But this only proves that in our contemporaries the capacity to reason is almost never used. The brain is considered to be the least useful part of the human body. It grows and develops according to immutable laws of nature just as if it were wormwood or mugwort; all kinds of filth is poured and thrown upon it; no one pays any attention to what may be harmful or useful to it, and because of this, it withers of course and becomes deformed, with the result that a strong and healthy brain is regarded as a rare exception and inspires the deepest respect for itself. . . ." Leo Tolstoy's later revulsion against Shakespeare and art had a similar puritan basis.

Such are the pre-marxist classics of present-day philosophy and criticism. They may be described as Utopian socialists who had reacted against idealism and Hegelian philosophy, and who were tending towards the positions later defined in the doctrine of historic materialism. In the tenets of the critical positivism, which they had worked out, they were clearly on the side of that hitherto neglected source of energy, the mass of the people. And it is not surprising that, at this stage in the development of Soviet criticism when the notion of " the rôle of the Russian people " is again in favour, they should have been reintegrated into the body of that criticism as a traditional element.

2

Soviet Criticism in Practice To-day. The Various Types of Critics

THIS does not purport to be an exhaustive study of the ins and outs of Soviet criticism even at this stage of its evolution, for which a separate book would be required. It is rather an attempt to sketch the general picture as the author sees it, and to provide some concrete examples of this criticism in action. A difficulty which arises, and which will have to be faced, is that owing to the compactness of Soviet literature, it is sometimes hard to distinguish between the criticism and the literature itself, between a literary personality and the critic, between a political trend and a literary one. In fact, such distinctions have largely to be abandoned, and this is appropriate enough in dealing with a literature which claims to have established an identity between content and form, between ideology and art. Since this claim is made, it would be critically false to approach this literature or criticism from a purely formal or æsthetic point of view. On the other hand, Soviet literature and criticism at its best is not a series of reproduced slogans or schemes, although these are common enough to a number of literary works and critical statements.

For the sake of convenience, we may divide the personages of the critical scene into lawgivers, pontiffs, interpreters and occasional literary critics. There is also the choir that takes up the pontiffs' irate chant. Among the literary critics we may include the poet, Antokolsky, some of whose criticisms have recently been collected and published in book form in his *Trial by Time*, 1945. In this we find a series of essays on Lermontov, Derzhavin, Lesya Ukrainka, Bagritzky, Tikhonov, Pasternak, Bajan, Surkov, Pervomaysky, and others. These are a poet's criticism, adhering, it is true, to the principle of Socialist Realism, but at the same time evidencing a wider range of literary appreciation. Victor Shklovsky, one of the former leaders of the Formalist school, is not now very prominent as a literary critic (he has been writing more about the cinema) but he affords occasional interesting sidelights in his very short book, *Meetings*, 1944, which in its turn came in for some criticism. Both Chukovsky and Pasternak have published interesting and valuable views on the art of translation. Whereas Pasternak's have been articles connected with the problems arising out of his translations of Shakespeare, Chukovsky's book, *The High Art*, is well worth studying in relation to the problem of translation in general. There are other writers, too, who have in occasional pieces demonstrated a more purely literary approach to their subject, but they are usually poets or novelists rather than professional critics. On the other hand, Chukovsky's *Chekhov: The Artist and the Man*, which stresses the positive side of Chekhov as a man and published for wide consumption, is far from congenial to a British critic, like Desmond MacCarthy, who has his own æsthetic appreciation of Chekhov.

Of the first category, the lawgivers, it may be said that they are among the highest in the land, and they are the guardians of the Party interest and the fundamental doctrines, such as Socialist Realism and the method of dialectical materialism. Their open pronouncements are few and far between, and are generally made to lay down or consecrate a new line of policy. Moves such as the dissolution of R.A.P.P. and its affiliated organizations, and the foundation of a single Union of Soviet Writers in 1932, as well as the laying down of the principle of Socialist Realism at that time, were quite obviously decisions taken on a higher level. Statements such as those that "the writer is the engineer of human souls," the evocation of the "heroic ancestors" made by Stalin on November 7th, 1941, and Molotov's pronouncement on November 6th, 1945, that "the intelligentsia has now fused with the people," are further examples of the guiding rôle assumed by the political leaders. Such policies when they are announced usually reflect a careful analysis of the realities of the moment rather than a desire just to lay down the law; but, of course, any modification of policy is carefully related to the interests of the fundamental objectives as well as the fundamental theories. In the current application of the policies thus established, and to ensure a close correspondence between policy, execution and interpretation, these lawgivers have an efficient instrument in the Department of Propaganda and Agitation attached to the Central Committee. This body has wide ramifications and, as we have already shown, direct ties with the Union of Writers itself as well as with similar bodies in other spheres of artistic activity. It seems to have, too, a number of critics, some of whom are not normally manifest in print, who will make *ex cathedra* pronouncements when something goes wrong or is not as it should be. These are what we chose to call the pontiffs. They may sometimes write under *nom-de-plumes,* or sometimes their articles may appear unsigned, but they usually cause a slight flutter and, depending on the seriousness of the offence, they may stimulate a controversy, a choir of condemnation or drastic revision. Some examples of the pontiff in action are afforded by S. Borodin's criticisms of Kostylev's historical novel on Ivan the Terrible and of Chukovsky's poem, *Barmalay* (children's verse), by the *Pravda* critique of the Malyi Theatre production of Alexei Tolstoy's *The Eagle and His Mate,* and by the organized onslaught on Zoshchenko's *When the Sun Rises,* and several similar cases which we shall touch upon in more detail.

In the instance of Borodin's criticism* of Kostylev, the point at issue was the accusation levelled that some of Kostylev's characters gave the impression that "Russia was a country of savages" and that in this respect Kostylev is reminiscent of "certain writers of western orientation" whereas he should have been aware "whence emanated this tendency of slander." More important, however, were those parts of the criticism which dealt with Kostylev's interpretation of the historic figures of Ivan. Here Kostylev is accused of over-simplifying or "popularizing" the image of Ivan, of making him too ordinary and insufficiently dignified. Borodin reminds the reader that Ivan "fortified and strengthened the Russian State and in that way helped to broaden the basis of the development of the people,

Literature and Art, No. 20, 1943.

of Russian culture and the State." At this stage, Borodin recalls the double-headed eagle of Byzantium and the court ritual inherited from Byzantium. Ivan, therefore, was not as "approachable" as Kostylev painted him and the scene where he is made to walk along the walls of the Kremlin in the company of a foreigner, a German who had recorded "the fact" in his diary, is declared to be improbable since "in the eyes of the people, the Tsar was a sacred personage and could not be seen in such proximity to an outlander." There are more references to etiquette and ritual and the insistence on this aspect of history may strike us as strange, but its high importance in the presentation of the image of Ivan is further confirmed by a somewhat similar and even more surprising criticism made a year after the production of Tolstoy's play (1944). On this occasion a weighty article in *Pravda* attacked not the play itself, but the production, alleging that in one or two instances, in particular, the interpretation of the Tsar's rôle was not sufficiently dignified and did not reflect the due majesty of the personage. Whereas Kostylev's book was on the whole approved as a "first attempt to understand and illuminate the image of Ivan from a marxist point of view," and whereas Kostylev himself replied in a letter published in *October*, No. 8-9, of 1943, to the criticisms levelled against him, the first production of the *Eagle and His Mate* was stopped and the play was withdrawn for revision (the producer incidentally changed his theatre). It re-appeared eventually at the Malyi Theatre within a month or two without any effects of *lèse majesté*.

Such are the pontiffs whose intervention is to be frequently encountered. Now we come to the critic-interpreters, a large class more or less equivalent to our critics and reviewers. They differ from our critics in that they have a more definite doctrine to interpret and to apply, and they range in quality from the rigid and simple executioner of the law to more thoughtful and dialectically equipped practitioners. Thus, while in any article one is likely to find a repetition of the same commonplace propositions or the same type of traditional quotations and references to authority, there is yet observable quite a variety of interpretation, personal discrimination and breadth or narrowness of view point. Whether a critic has anything to say or not, can usually be judged by the proportion of the commonplace in his article in relation to the rest of his text. Not infrequently a too-great reliance on quotable authority is a sign that either the critic is not very sure of himself or that he has improperly assimilated the principle of dialectic, for which he tends to substitute rhetorical passages. There are, indeed, to be found critics who express different views and who come to different conclusions about the same works. Thus, Marietta Shaginyan disagrees with the critical estimates made by Pertzov and two other critics of a number of Home Front Ural

Novels, and such cases are frequent enough; and from what one can gather, more discussion and a more critical attitude is being actively encouraged. The encouragement of satire and, more recently, parody, is another aspect of this.

The position of the critic is to some extent a delicate one, for he is not always sure how far he can go; he may suddenly rouse the pontiffs. And the memories of the reforms of the 1930's, when the widespread positions of "vulgar sociology" and "formalism" were blown up, appear to haunt not a few budding critics and make them tongue-tied. An attempt is being made to encourage them and to loosen their tongues. In an article entitled *Towards a New Flowering*, by Professor A. Beletzky,* which is principally concerned with the training of new critics and literary research students, we have the direct statement that "The fear of the formalistic disease has led many to impotency in their views of literature. The fear of being suspected of vulgar sociology has led to such care being exercised in relation to sociology that the sociological method is present in many works only in the forms of quotations from the classics of marxism-leninism. . . ." The professor goes on to say : "If boldness is the character and feature of Soviet science, then in literary criticism such examples of boldness are not to be met with. Instead, there is an obvious fear to express thought that may appear to be unacceptable to all and which does not, as it were, agree with the supposed ' canons,' and may thus lead to controversy. . . . As if the advance of science can take place without disputes and there is a ready-made answer to all questions. . . ." The Professor further argues that Classical Realism, such is the new synonym of Socialist Realism, needs its trained defenders in the battle between the new and old. Thus, the budding critic is being stimulated; but he is reminded at the same time that he must not forget the sociological aspects of art and that he must give them a new dialectical interpretation.

Another aspect of critical activity, which is less common outside Russia, is the critical debate organized round newly-written and so far unpublished works, or indeed published works, in the various sections or the Praesidium of the Writers' Union. In debates of this type, writers and critics meet and give their appreciations of particular works, and in most cases these debates are very much what one might expect anywhere in similar circumstances. Sometimes, however, they may lead an author to revise some portion of his work, also a thing that might happen anywhere, but there is also the possibility revealed as a result of the·post-mortem debate on Zoshchenko's *When The Sun Rises* that such a debate in the Praesidium might lead to a veto on the publication of a given work. But it is obvious that many works

Literary Gazette, of 24th November, 1945.

are also published without prior discussion and one frequently comes across the criticism that it would have been better if a work had been so discussed or if the editors or publishers had paid more attention to it. A criticism of this kind is not necessarily made on political grounds alone but often refers to the bad literary quality of the work. This is often the case when provincial publications are reviewed. There is the instance of an anthology of patriotic poetry published in the provinces where the compiler had taken great liberties with the texts. There is also the Almanack to which the writers of the Ivanovo region had contributed and which was criticized for the poor quality of some of its material. Here Moscow serves as the critical clearing house for the rest of the Soviet Union, and the Writers' Union has also its Regional and Republican Commissions or Sections to keep in touch with and centralize the information about the periphery.

Having described the background in which writers and critics meet and sometimes quarrel, we shall proceed to give a few salient examples of pontifical and other criticism.

3

Some Examples of Present-Day Criticism—(1) The Pontiff in Action (i) Pontiff versus Poet

WE have already referred to an example of pontificial intervention involving a discussion of how the times and figure of Ivan the Terrible should be interpreted. There are several other notable examples of such intervention during the war years. Let us begin with poetry. Here we have the cases of the Pontiff versus Korney Chukovsky, Selvinsky and Asseyev.

In 1943 Chukovsky published a long poem, *We Shall Vanquish Barmalay,* intended for children. Chukovsky is a leading children's writer as well as a notable critic and a specialist in problems of translation. His poem is a fantasy, in which an imaginary country, Aebolita, is portrayed, living a peaceful and cultured life and inhabited by nice animals and insects, such as elephants, hares, sparrows, bears, seals and bees. This happy land is attacked by a fascist-like gorilla, Barmalay, supported by savage animals—rhinoceroses, wolves and hippopotamuses. To the aid of the attacked from the land of Wonderfame comes a symbolically Russian character, Nanya Vasil-chikov. And the gorilla, Barmalay, is finally defeated and slain.

At first sight this appears to be a harmless enough children's tale with an appropriate moral. And yet it was severely criticized by S. Borodin in an article entitled *Facts and Zoology.** Let us examine

*Literature and Art, of March 4th, 1944.

116

this criticism and see what it portends. To begin with, Borodin quotes some examples from a poem, *Facts for Children*, by S. Mihalkov, praising this author for his "concreteness and simplicity." Borodin goes on to say that *Facts for Children*, which was printed in the pages of a daily newspaper, is equally understandable to children and grown-ups—to the old man and the child, to the academician and the ploughman. In it there is that truth of our days, which is easily expressed in a clear and simple form; the most complex theme, if it is clearly stated, is 'of the people,' that is, of course, if it is felt by the people. The 'people' cannot bear either the vulgar simplification of serious questions or confused and twisted forms of expression—the signs of an author's lack of thinking, non-understanding of the theme, its immaturity in the .author's consciousness; a transparent statement is achieved by an author only when an important theme is definedly clear and familiar to him. . . ." Thus, according to Borodin, Mihalkov found precise and compact lines in which to express his thought, whereas Chukovsky stated his theme in such a way as "to spoil and soil it." The conception of the poem leaves Borodin in no doubt that "the author had in mind the concrete war as his basis" and that the publication of his work proved that the "author ignored the most elementary notions of the duties and responsibilities of a writer in the days of the Great War. . . . Literally, on every page one can find a clownish interpretation of reality. . . ." And Borodin concludes : "Mihalkov addresses himself to millions of concrete Soviet children in order to consider once more the significance of the war for the life of the Soviet people. Chukovsky, on the other hand, propounds the image of 'the famous hero,' before whom enemies give way without any resistance, and, thus, he denigrates the significance of the war in the consciousness of the children, and in this way diminishes the measure of heroism and bravery displayed by the fathers and brothers of these children in the struggle with a by no means easy and dangerous opponent. The trivial distortions of Chukovsky excite a feeling of disgust. They raise the perplexing question : what is his 'poem'—the fruit of monstrous lack of thought or a conscious lampoon on the great exploit of our people, a caricature on the participants of the war camouflaged in the form of a children's book?"

This criticism of a children's book illustrates three points : the political importance attached to the printed word; the educative significance attached to writing; and the domination exercised by the principle of Socialist Realism. The violence of the judgment expressed is the hall-mark of the pontiff.

Asseyev, a well-known poet and friend of Mayakovsky's, was also taken to task in 1943 for "slandering the Home Front." These slanders consisted of some references in his poem to "uterine existence," "Asiatic primitiveness," and "want of culture," when describing some aspects of everyday life behind the front. Similarly, Selvinsky's poem, *Whom Russia Cradled*, was described as frivolous and unseemly. Later, in a general survey of Soviet wartime literature, these three poems were branded as " ideologically empty and harmful works which the people cannot accept " (A. Egolin : *Propagandist*, No. 6, 1944). It is clear that, in the case of Asseyev and Selvinsky in particular, the writers' interpretation ran counter to the official line of " the great rôle of Russia and the high destiny of her people."

4

Some Examples of Present-Day Soviet Criticism—(2) The Pontiff in Action. (ii) When the Sun Rises or When Zoshchenko is Eclipsed

OF all the critical " incidents " of this period, that associated with the condemnation of Zoshchenko's *When the Sun Rises* seems to have roused the most fury, noise and general expressions of indignation. The nature of this work has already been described in a previous chapter, and we can therefore pass straight on to the critical reactions which it provoked.

In an article *About Zoshchenko's New Novel*,* L. Dmitriev says that " It would be difficult to name a work which is so remote from the life of the people or so alien to it." He continues : " Tediously delving in his own intimate world, intentionally picking on the pettiest, most commonplace and deformed facts of his biography, the author endows all men and the whole world with these features. . . He willingly describes his love affairs. And in this there is no poetry, no romanticism, no humour. Everything lofty and noble, with which the conception of youthful love is associated, lies outside the bounds of this novel. . . . Under his brush, as if as a result of black magic, all men become crooked, hunchbacked and dirty; friendship turns into hypocrisy, joy into spite, love into the atrophy of that emotion or into sensuality. . . ." Then the critic explains Zoshchenko's limitations by the absence of any social element in this work : " It is unthinkable to explain the behaviour of man relying only on physiological data. ' To live in society and to be free of society is impossible,' said Lenin. We cannot find man outside the living social ties, outside his social life and struggle . . . Zoshchenko ignores the fundamental —*the social factors which form the consciousness of man and his relations to life*. . . That is why he sees the world ' bereft of logic and reason ' . . ." The critic then draws a comparison with Gorky, who " himself saw and taught others to see the fine qualities of the

Literature and Art, of December 4th, 1943.

human soul, to value and develop these qualities—*the buds of the imminent flowering of the human personality in the new social order . . . Such is the tradition of all Russian literature, which long ago had anticipated the great historic predestination of its people.* Pushkin and Gogol, Turgeniev and Nekrasov, Chehov and Leon Tolstoy, preserved and continued it, each in his own way. That was a literature illumined by love for man and belief in him. It did not shamefully hide its eyes from the dark sides of life. But in its very approach to phenomena it was always based on an active humanist principle. And if Saltykov-Schedrin or Dostoievsky describe with unsurpassed force the sores of human psychology and social life, was this not dictated by the same *active striving to purify the world* from filth? Was it not for the good of their native people that they put their fingers on its wounds? Only decadent art saw its chief aim in the depiction of suffering, dirt, and all kinds of deformity. . . ." The critic concludes : " Zoshchenko in fact pays no heed to the heritage of these giants of Russian literature from whom he must learn and continue to learn. . . His pseudo-scientific discussions remain on his conscience, while the world of men he portrays exists in the novel separately and gives a crudely distorted image of reality. . . . *It remains to express our surprise that the editors of a solid literary periodical did not understand this in thus hastening to print this trivial and harmful work.*"

Dmitriev's criticism was by no means the end of the Zoshchenko affair. It called into play the choir, by which in this context we mean the need for wider unanimous condemnation. On December 6th, 1943, at an expanded session of the Praesidium of the Union of Soviet Writers, a discussion took place on the work of the periodical, *October,* which had published Zoshchenko's novel; in other words, the editors were put on the carpet. As it turned out, *When the Sun Rises* became the chief topic of debate. It was found that there was " an absence of solidarity in the authors' group and in the work of the editorial board." This latter was also blamed for having published Katayev's play, *The Blue Scarf,* which had earlier been called a " pot-boiler " by *Pravda.* As to Zoshchenko, it was pointed out that it would be incorrect to make a distinction between the author's design and the result : both were " vicious." A. Fadeyev, as the then President-Secretary of the Writers' Union, gave a detailed analysis of the novel as an " anti-popular and anti-artistic work." In his opinion, " Zoshchenko's harmful book *would probably not have appeared in print if it had been previously discussed in all its aspects,* seriously and deeply, and without any reticences. That such a discussion did not take place was the fault not only of the periodical but also of the Praesidium of the Writer's Union which had not organized such a discussion in time."

What is remarkable, however, is that the writers and critics present at the discussion should have been so unanimous in their negative judgment—with the sole exception of Olga Forsh who tried to palliate the error by drawing a parallel with Rousseau's *Confessions*. In substance, the criticisms now put forward were on the lines of Dmitriev's article. One of the critics, P. Iudin, maintained that, despite the war, this novel " affirmed the right of man to feel despondent and spiritually soft.", He goes on to say : " Zoshchenko's novel is *amoral,* the most elementary forms of social behaviour are undermined in it, and *cynicism in relation to women is preached. All this contradicts the fine traditions of Russian literature."*

There were, of course, other criticisms of Zoshchenko; and there are several references to him in some of Tikhonov's surveys where he speaks scathingly of the author's " petty subjective feelings." But nothing new of a critical nature comes to light; and we may take it that Zoshchenko's novel was condemned mainly because it proved extremely subjective and non-social, and his inner world and characters were isolated from the " spirit and events of the time." It was its extreme individualism that excited such a violent reaction, although it is also true that Zoshchenko's bare and sometimes sordid documentation might very well have shocked the romantically inclined Russians of to-day just as it would have shocked Victorian taste some seventy years ago.

5

Some Examples of Present-Day Soviet Criticism—(3) The Pontiff in Action. (iii) When the Literary Past Should Be Forgotten

KONSTANTIN FEDIN is a distinguished novelist whose work we have already described. In the early 1920's, when Soviet literature was in its cradle, he met Gorky, was helped by him, and for a number of years kept up a correspondence with him when Gorky was living in Sorrento. Fedin conceived the idea of a book, *Gorky Amongst Us,* based on these letters and his reminiscences. Although Gorky is the central figure, and is seen in relation to the budding literature of the time, Fedin's book is in intention more than just a portrait of Gorky; it is at the same time a literary memoir of the period, although not an exhaustive one. The book was planned in three volumes of which the first was published in 1943 and the second in 1944. The third volume is still due to appear, but in view of what happened to the second it may not see the light of day. The first volume deals with Fedin's acquaintance with Gorky and their meetings during 1920-21, and also touches upon " the life of the writers at the time and the movements of literary thought." The second volume covers the years 1923-28, and contains Fedin's correspondence with Gorky and a description of his return to the Soviet Union in 1928. The final part was planned to deal with Gorky's later visits to Sorrento and his work in the Soviet Union from 1930 to his death in 1936.

The first volume, as we have noted, appeared in 1943. And on the occasion of Fedin's thirtieth anniversary of literary activity, celebrated on the 31st of October of the same year, the Praesidium of the Writers' Union sent Fedin a letter in which, among other flattering things, was said: " You are an example of that eternal restlessness which is the quality of great artists and men of action. Your last book about Gorky, whom you knew well and intimately, is undoubtedly one of the best books written about the great writer on the basis of personal reminiscences. . . ." That was in 1943. The summer of the following year saw the publication of the second volume. Here, however, something went wrong, for the big pontifical guns started up in *Pravda* and *Literature and Art*,* and these were followed by the usual discussion in the Praesidium of the Writers' Union.

What was the cause of this incident? In his second volume, Fedin had devoted several pages to the description and characterisation of Alexei Remizov, Feodor Sologub, and Volynski, a novelist, poet and a critic, who were all prominent literary figures in pre-Revolutionary literature and also in the early 1920's. Sologub and Volynski died in those years, while Remizov emigrated to Paris, where he still lives. It would appear natural to refer to these writers in a memoir, like Fedin's, which was treating of a transition period when things had not sorted themselves out, and Berdyaev was still lecturing at Moscow University. Besides, whatever might be said of Remizov now, and however little he may influence contemporary Soviet literature, he undoubtedly exercised a considerable influence in the first twenty years of the century—an influence acknowledged by Alexei Tolstoy in his brief autobiography and by many other writers. However, the three writers referred to have not been re-admitted so far into the Pantheon of Russian literary tradition and, as the discussion round Fedin's book will show, there is no immediate intention of doing so.

Another point arising from the discussion,† is the general criticism of Fedin's more purely literary approach to his subject, now denigratingly labelled as " objective " and " dispassionate." But let us look more closely at the criticisms. One of the critics, V. Vishnevsky,

---

*L. Dmitriev's article, *Contrary to History*, in *Literature and Art*, of 5th August, 1944.

†Reported in *Literature and Art*, of 9th September, 1944.

sees the matter thus: "The writer has come forth with a book about Gorky, about the stormy years of the Revolution. But there is no storm in the book. Only the quiet of salons and literary cabinets. The author fences himself off from battles, political passions and the great seekings. . . . You see each gesture of these diseased persons— Sologub, Volynski, etc. You see how they are dressed, but you hear no word of how these gentry conducted themselves politically. . . *Astonishing is the almost complete absence in this book of the historical-political background.* Somewhere outside the frame of the literary world a great struggle is taking place, but it is not introduced into the book. . . . Fedin's book is a sort of *defence of a displaced literature that knows no right or wrong, and accepts manifestations* ' *quietly*,' ' *objectively*,' and in the fashion of a chronicle. . . How can one be outside politics in the time of the Patriotic War? What will that lead to?"

Another critic, I. Lezhnev, speaks of those, who "not having freed themselves from the burden of old conceptions and among whom are to be found such as, not putting two and two together, have begun to delve into the heritage in the wrong place. . . . In their enthusiasm they have lost their sense of proportion. . . . Hence *their readiness to submit to revision the very foundations of our world outlook.* This tendency towards a re-valuation of values, so fashionable in the circles of people who are cut off from life, has been clearly expressed in Fedin's book. . . ." This critic concludes that the cause of Fedin's " crude mistakes " is his " toleration, dispassionate relation to the reactionary ideas of the past, and disintegrating scepticism."

There were other criticisms. M. Shaginyan made the point that *" Truth is always concrete and historical. . . .* The atmosphere of soft benevolence in which Fedin presents his memoirs disorientates the reader and distorts the past." Tikhonov goes further and accuses Fedin of giving a wrong interpretation of Gorky's fundamental thoughts, and he concludes : " If we speak of the heritage of Gorky, then the whole simplicity and boldness of Gorky's relationships lies especially *in the further transformation of the world,* and not in that chaotic self-wilfulness, which will only confuse all manifestations and lead us far away from the important questions of the present moment. *The artist, who attempts to restore individualism in general, will have nothing in common with the growth of socialist individuality, and the manifestations of life will lose for him that completeness and truth, which is being consolidated in art for a long time to come."*

L. Dmitriev's criticism had accused Fedin above all of "defending and justifying his false point of view regarding the place of the artist in relation to reality and the purpose and significance of art." Dmitriev also says that *" Fedin's book is an obstinate, thought out defence of the position of the contemplative artist, the defence of apolitical art.* . . . Fedin has clearly taken up a position contradicting the testament of Gorky."

These criticisms of Fedin's book are in many respects similar to those of Zoshchenko's, and this similitude is inevitable, since the values defended are very precise, while the errors condemned are also circumscribed. They throw, however, some light on the limitations of a Soviet critic and literary historian. A dispassionate critic is obviously a *persona non grata,* for literature, and the criticism that goes with it, are conceived of as *an instrument to help in transforming the world,* not as an orchard where fruits may be picked and tasted at leisure. It is the duty of the pontiff to remind the erring brotherhood of writers when they have sinned too grievously or strayed from this dynamic conception.

The truth is collective as of old in Russia, and the choir must join in chanting condemnation, so that the truth is reasserted and made clear to everyone. These castigations are now purely verbal and in this they differ notably from the 1930's, when a writer's personal position was less secure. Their effect on some writers must be depressing, for a time at least; for others it may be stimulating. But it is obvious that a certain amount of literature that would otherwise be written is bottled up or transmuted into other forms. But the same sort of thing for different reasons tends to happen in the rest of the world where poets may be asked to write novels or detective fiction under assumed names. Or again the contents of their poems may receive no notice at all from the critics. But when all is said and done, the Russian literary atmosphere is peculiarly different from the British, as is the conception of the rôle of the writer in society. And now we shall pass to another set of critics, the critic-interpreters, who are not pontiffs but more like ordinary mortals.

6

Some Examples of Present-Day Criticism—(4) Miscellaneous

SOVIET society has its elements of inertia, self-satisfaction and complacency. It is in a moment of outspoken revolt against these that Vassily Grossman exclaims in his article, *The Work of the Writers,* published in June, 1945 : " But is our literary work worthy of the great literature of the past? Can it serve as a model for the future? To-day we must reply to this question negatively. *And it is particularly painful to observe in our literary circles the now apparent conceit, self-assurance and well-fed satisfaction with the poor results of hurried and superficial works.* . . . Our writers are well received abroad, but this is a tribute to the Red Army and not to their works—this we must understand. The Red Army has done its job. It is now the turn of the writers. . . ." We may contrast this criticism with the frequently-made and not over-modest claim that Soviet iterature is " the best and most advanced " in the world. Grossman's statement is rather sweeping but it is indicative of a revived critical attitude and of a wish to re-assess current achievement both in the light of the past and of the future; and it implies a desire to prepare the way for a greater creative effort. As the war drew to its close, there was a tendency to hold a *post-mortem* on the literary contribution of the period and to contrast literary achievement with the historical one of the Red Army. A distinctly nostalgic note is sounded by some critics when they ask, " When are we going to produce our Iliad?"

In another article, *Be Not Afraid to Dare,* published on May 1st, 1945, the dramatist, K. Treniev, says : " In wartime literature there are to be found many vivid pictures, many pages full of fire, anger and love. But in these four years much that is stereotyped has also collected, and in some things *a primitive approach is revealed towards big and complex problems in prose, poetry and drama.* At the Theatrical Conference of 1943, it was said that more than ten plays had been written about the defence of Stalingrad, but we regret to say that none of them has survived. . . . Is there any need to explain the reason? They were not works of authentic literature, they were not artistic or poetic works. But the reader, *who has matured so much during the war,* will justly demand of us a greater and more authentic mastery. . . . The tragic has every right to exist in our post-war literature, as has the comic—not only the entertaining comic but also the serious revealing comedy-satire, for which a substitute is now often found in some hotch-potch devoid of any conflict or ' harm.' With us heroic deeds are a mass manifestation. This is so obvious and grandiose, and we are so strong, that *there is no need for us to shut our eyes to our failings . . . and the exposure of the vices of individuals or groups cannot do any harm.* It will only help to clear the way. Soviet literature should laugh at vices with the laughter it has inherited from our great literature." Treniev's criticism, though it refers more immediately to the drama, has also a wider bearing, and it points to at least two major failings that have proved an obstacle to the fuller development of Soviet literature : the *primitive approach* and the *fear of criticism.*

The question of quality arises most frequently in cases of provincial publications or first books by younger authors, in reviewing which the critic is usually on purely literary ground, drawing attention to faults of style and language, plot and construction. We have already cited the case of the Ivanovo writers, some of whose efforts were rather illiterate. The number of such cases is too large to be dealt with here.

Another sample of criticism is that of a book of short stories, *The Moral Coefficient,* by a young writer, George Solovyev. The critic, Boris Solovyev, says, " We see nothing ' moral ' in this Coefficient. On the contrary, the tirade we have quoted has little in common with the morality of Soviet man, who went through the war not at all in order to throw aside all anxiety about his wife and family, but, on the contrary, in a state of alarm for their fate and that of his country. Ermihin's relationship with his wife is a strange one. Perhaps he loves her, but he expresses that love in extremely sottish and awkward thoughts. . . . We are little moved by a hero, whose thoughts for his family are engendered not out of the fullness of living sensations but are ' wilfully twisted in the form of a protocol or a brief auto-biographical report.' . . . The ability to act automatically seems such a positive quality to the author, that he forgives his hero the absence of all others, including that of normal reflection. . . . In place of morality, we are confronted in this book with a ' moralization ' with which we cannot at all agree. . . . Heroes, who in real life confront us with the richness and uniqueness of their character . . . *with all the complexity of their inner life,* on the pages of books like this are transformed into lean abstractions, geometrical schemata or into mere shadows of themselves. . . ."

The contributors of the Leningrad periodical *Zvezda* have on several occasions come in for criticisms of another sort. Their faults seem to lie in being æsthetic, formalist and academic. There is perhaps something in the Leningrad air that still nourishes a tender shoot of æstheticism even despite the war. But it would appear that an inclination to æstheticism is not such a rare thing and is not confined to Leningrad. In an article *How to Fight Scholasticism,** T. Motyleva, a well-known woman critic, cites the following incident : " I recall a conversation I happened to overhear recently. *A student of the literary faculty, with the manifest support of some of his comrades, was hotly defending æstheticism in poetry, the right of the poet to create or to keep silent,* without any regard for what our age, our country and people, may require of him. . . ." Having recorded this, Motyleva goes on to express her surprise that " These youths and girls had read Lenin's article on the rôle of the Party in literature, they had read Bielinsky, Chernyshevsky, and Gorky's critical articles. How is it that *the fundamental principle of Russian classical æstheticism* and, at the same time, of *Socialist æstheticism*—that of the social service of art, how is it that this principle had not been assimilated by them? . . ." Motyleva's astonishment is rather naïve : surely it is a very healthy sign that the young, even in the U.S.S.R., can " hotly " defend the right of the poet to creative independence—the only path within any framework to a great literature. This incident suggests

Literature and Art of 8th April, 1944.

that it is not at all improbable that a strong æsthetic revival may take place if its immediate expression is not thwarted or diluted. On the face of it, an " æsthetic " trend would be a very natural consequence of an overdose of critical realism.

A difference of opinion between two critics, Makarov and Chetunova, about the probability of the heroine of Gerassimova's *The Baidar Gates,* is revealed in Chetunova's article *Models and People.** Makarov finds the heroine unreal and improbable because her behaviour is inconsistent, while Chetunova thinks that Makarov lives on a " critical Olympus " and that the heroine is inconsistent because she is young and human. The champion ends by saying : " Alas, life can never be crushed into a single, even the most model type. In this precisely lies the difference between the best model made in Olympian cabinets and the real human ideal, to which art guides people, that the ideal concentrates in itself the *principles* of human conduct, the relations with men and the world, whereas the model canonizes a definite *form,* thus inevitably arriving at a dead abstraction. For there is in nature no general form appropriate for any content."

Nor are established writers exempt from criticism of their literary style or for being occasionally stereotyped. Thus Panferov's recent novel, *War For Peace,* 1945, was very severely reviewed both for its style and its crude delineation of character. A moral shock is also provided by one of the leading characters, who when apparently disturbed at the sight of a woman bathing in a river, mutters puritanically : " She's teasing me. We'd better have her sent off to a timber camp (i.e., one of the Siberian labour camps)." But the critics were obviously not putting up with that sort of thing.

Alexei Surkov is a well-established and talented poet, and in a critical review of his collected war poetry a discriminating critic, N. Vengrov, while showing due appreciation of the poet, points out that : " Surkov's hero, that ' unbowed man in a tin hat ' and soldier's greatcoat, is inwardly collected, modest, and close worded. From his book we get to know little of the dreams and thoughts of his hero. We have the right to wish for more. The poet should have found the required words for him. . . . The gist of the matter is in the intellectual world of the Soviet man, which is *considerably richer and more complex* than that now portrayed by Surkov. . . . His creative work creates the impression of a certain unevenness and occasional incompleteness. At times, it seems that if an extra line were removed, another word or rhythm found, the poem might gain and take on a fuller life. . . ."

From some of these examples of criticism we gather that there is a distinct emphasis among Soviet critics to-day on the " fuller inner

*_____
**Znamya,* No. 7, 1945.

life " of man and its complexity—aspects of reality that for various reasons have been shelved or forgotten by Soviet writers. This emphasis is the result of greater self-confidence and awareness consequent upon the war. These have led also to a renewed interest in the personality as the kernel of the human problem. One of the most representative of the new critics, V. Pertzov, is constantly harping on this theme. We find him saying : " *If man was and remains the deciding factor in the war, then he does so precisely as a human being, as a personality,* and not only as a master of the military profession. . . . For an artist the age and the system are disclosed in concrete human characters. *Outside character there is no image, no philosophy of the age,* because in art character is generalization even when drawn directly from nature, from a living person really existing or known to all. . . ."* Pertzov, it will be seen, is a critic who generalizes and who is building up a dialectic of the personality in society.

Here is another quotation providing a clue to his approach : " Yes, man is the measure of all things, but this ancient truth is too diluted to serve as a lighthouse for the contemporary artist in his work. There is another, new ' measure ' of man, which did not exist and could not exist before, and which brought about an upheaval in the whole of his inner world. It came into being as soon as the possibility was created of speaking of Socialist man—the hero of our time. *This new ' measure ' is the conscious participation of the masses in the historical process, that is, man as the subject of history.* . . . In 1918, Lenin noted down the following in his ' Diary of a Publicist.' as a theme to be worked out : ' To raise the lowest levels to historical creativeness ' . . ." A great deal of this criticism may strike us as a re-discovery of the obvious, but in the light of past history and many anterior pronouncements the tone of some critics is, by comparison, almost refreshing. And while in many cases the language is ponderous and too much like jargon, we are no longer confronted with the class-bound terminology of an earlier epoch. The attempted integration, on a dialectical basis, is more broadly " historical " than before, although by 1946 the terms " imperialist," " capitalist " and " bourgeois," reappear.

7

The Fundamentals of Present-Day Soviet Criticism

THE examples we have quoted are not very numerous or in any way exhaustive, but it is hoped that they will give some insight into the ways and means of Soviet criticism, and into the relations existing between critics and writers; and, thus, into the possibilities

---

*Znamya, No. 9, 1945.

and limitations of Soviet literature in its present evolution. We have seen that this literature has its schoolmen and sinners, its controls and exceptions, its single-mindedness and variety, its Russianness and dialectic, its frictions and human comedy. The rôle of the pontiff is apparent in his sometimes mysterious but ultimately explicable interventions on occasions when the seriousness of purpose or the fundamental doctrines are in some way threatened or by-passed. It is clear that such by-passing does occasionally occur in print and is not entirely stifled at birth; and it is also apparent that more of it would occur if the pontiffs were less eagle-eyed and less concerned with the fundamental appraisal of a work according to their canons. It is, likewise, clear that the immediate appreciations of critic-interpreters and the final judgments of pontiffs may differ widely : on its first appearance a work may be favourably received and prove popular enough in print or on the stage, but may later be condemned from on high in the pages of *Pravda* and then be relegated to oblivion or withdrawn from the boards. It should be obvious from this that the initial censorship through which books and reviews have to pass before publication is concerned with other issues rather than the finer points of literary dogma. It is also clear that the critic-interpreters have a fairly wide range of operation and potentially even a wider one, if they can discard any inhibitions they may have and speak out their minds. They may run foul of the pontiff or they may strike a new vein and get every support. But quite often the inhibition may be in the mind of the editors rather than in that of the critics; and the editors may not risk publication or they may do some blue pencilling without the writer's or critic's approval, and alter the sense of an article to the writer's professional detriment. In such cases, a writer may feel hurt but no corrective letter of his seems to grace the pages of the *Literary Gazette*. These are some of the elements that make up the background of the critic's work and his published views of art and literature. It must, however, be impressed that until 1946 the atmosphere of this scene was incomparably less rigid, tense and thorny than it was a decade ago, and there was a perceptible draught of air blowing about in this hothouse.

And now let us consider the fundamental premises revealed in both the pontiff's judgments and the interpreters' criticisms. In Dmitriev's analysis of Zoshchenko's novel, we have a re-statement of some of these present-day canons, such as the touchstone of *Social-reality*, the *humanist* approach or the notion of man as a noble and positive force in life, the belief in the renaissance of the *personality* in a new social order and the revival of the idea of *romantic love*. In Pertzov, we find a constant stress also on the notion of the personality and that of *man as the maker of history*. Both these ideas are present in Tikhonov's criticism of Fedin. Borodin and others contribute the idea of *historical reality,* which emphasizes the complexity of historical phenomena, the precision required in their description and the perspective necessary to relate them to our own time. Professor Beletzky points to the need of trained champions of the theory of *classical realism,* a literary version of the principle of Socialist Realism as it is now interpreted. He also claims that *sociological criticism* is in need of revival and revision. This latter claim may be a pointer to a new trend. It may have been found that criticism has gone too far in the direction of broad dialectical interpretation and that it requires an added pinch of salt in the form of a revised class analysis. The renewed post-war concentration on a series of Five Year Plans, the ultimate objective of which is to achieve Communism within some twenty years would support this view. The next few years will show whether this is the case. The apparently widening antithesis between American "capitalism" and the Soviet system would also help to explain this trend to some extent, if its development should become marked. But above all the key to Soviet literature and criticism lies in their being regarded as agents of the theory and practice of the *dialectical interpretation of history;* by virtue of this, they are expected to be aware of and to reflect, in its broad outlines, the evolution of Soviet policy at any of its principal stages. They are, likewise, expected to have some perspective of the goal to be attained either immediately or in the more distant future. In this sense, the theory of *historical materialism* and the revival of the historical *genres* serve their purpose too. How far Soviet criticism and literature succeed in living up to the demands made on them, is another question; and a great deal of Soviet criticism is concerned precisely with this problem. And fundamentally, it is this complex of particular awareness that produces this often seemingly unbridgeable dividing line between two worlds when Soviet and Western thought are confronted.

CHAPTER VIII

WAR, POETRY AND OPTIMISM

I

The Background and Character of Present-Day Poetry

THERE is nothing comparable in Soviet poetry to-day to the situation of the 1900's, when æstheticism and symbolism were the gods of the day, and the " ivory tower " attitude was fashionable among some while others, like Alexander Blok, were tranced mediums for apocalyptic visions; or to the rivalry of the 1910's, when Acmeists, Futurists and Imaginists were shouldering Symbolism out of the way and proclaiming the superiority of the poet's craft and form, of the dynamic and revolutionary word, or of the image as the foundation of poetry; or the vociferous polemics of the 1920's, when proletarian poets, the *Left Futurism* of Mayakovsky, the Constructivism of Selvinsky, the poets of the Smithy and the new school of ballad poetry, were fighting for a place in the sun in an atmosphere of exalted enthusiasm and revolutionary romanticism; or to the period of group dictatorship in the early 1930's, when the Association of Proletarian Writers attempted to lay down the law and force poetry and prose into the narrow channels of " constructive " or Five Year Plan reportage.

From 1932 onwards the atmosphere gradually changed and a new trend set in. All poets were now members of one and the same Union of Soviet Writers, and distinctive groups and movements had ceased to exist. Socialist Realism became the guiding principle for all writers whether novelists or poets. This did not at first affect the mannerism of individual poets and in many cases the modification, if there was one, was gradual. To this day the constructivist principle of composition is still evident in the work of Selvinsky, while poets like Asseyev and others still write in the freer Mayakovsky style, though it may be said that in general the poet of to-day writes in classical stanzas.

Socialist Realism can be a broad enough platform; it all depends on the interpretation. At its broadest, it simply means that a poet should base himself on the classics, be simple and concrete, and draw his inspiration from the reality of the world around him, that is, the particular and *historically evolving* world of Socialism. Granted that this world is limited or self-limited by the antithesis which it creates in relation to the rest of the world outside its sphere, it still remains a complex and evolving rather than a simple and static world, a world of a distinctive culture, and as such, and within these limitations, it does permit of variety and the exercise of the imagination. As has happened not infrequently, it is when a too-narrow interpretation is given of this reality that a creative work or poem may prove shallow and merely rhetorical.

This realism of the 1930's, though in a sense induced by the official approval it received to the exclusion of other theories, is not as artificial as it may appear at first sight, for it has its roots deep in the Russian literature of the past, which has always tended to stress " truth " above " beauty." A recent statement of this proposition may be found in Prishvin when he says : " In a work of art beauty is beauty, but its force lies in truth : there can be impotent beauty (æstheticism), but truth is never impotent. There have been strong and daring men, and great artists as well as great painters, but the essence of the Russian man is in truth. . . . Great artists drew strength for their great works not in beauty, but only in truth, and this naïvely child-like worship of truth, this endless humility of the artist before the greatness of truth has created the realism of our literature. . . ." (from *The Forest Drop,* 1943). This distinction and attitude are essentially Russian and by now traditional, and they may be contrasted with Keats's affirmation that " Beauty *is* truth, truth beauty."

The return to the realist tradition in the 1930's was no doubt dictated by the need felt for a synthesis with the national past and for building up a more imposing tradition than should reflect in art the power acquired as a result of the industrial revolution, which was in full and successful swing. The 1930's were largely spent in building up these traditions and their significance became fully apparent when Pushkin was restored to a place of pre-eminence as " the father of Russian literature " during the centenary celebrations of 1937. On the reverse side, we witness the discouragement and suppression of such trends as may hamper or disturb the authority of the new tradition. Such are the movements of the Russian mind and such the force of the conviction that theory and practice are identical, that opposites appear irreconcilable and intolerable. According to this dialectic, once a new fundamental development is approved, man actively intervenes to encourage its growth and to discourage or eliminate whatever stands in its way. In this conception politics and life are inseparable, and it is little wonder then that the "formalist" or "international" trends in art were often identified with the arch-heresy of Trotskyism. A good part of the 1930's were passed in the atmosphere of this struggle, and it is not surprising that there was more debate and polemical discussion than artistic creation; nevertheless the foundations had been laid for a new period of poetic activity during the war.

The Soviet poetry of to-day has its national heritage. In the main line of descent, Krylov and Pushkin, Lermontov and Nekrasov, are the respected ancestors. During the war many other minor ancestors were discovered, such as Derzhavin and Batyushkov, and in fact any poet of the past who was a realist and had shown himself a patriot was now welcomed into the fold. Of more recent ancestral lineage, we find homage paid to Blok (d. 1921), Essenin (d. 1925), Mayakovsky (d. 1930) and Bagritzky (d. 1934). Lately, there has also been a revival of Bryusov (d. 1924). The work of Essenin had been officially neglected since his suicide, but he was a poet of too powerful an appeal and too broadly Russian to be left out for long in spite of the "demoralizing" influence which some of his almost Dostoievskian poems might have had. In the *Anthology of Soviet Poetry* published in 1943, he was represented by twenty-one poems—the same number as Mayakovsky. In the past few years there have been occasional poetic evenings devoted to his work and the twentieth anniversary of his death was duly celebrated on December 28th, 1945.

Of an older living generation, two very dissimilar poets, Nicolai Tikhonov (b. 1896) and Boris Pasternak (b. 1890) are the main figures and source of inspiration. Among the younger poets who made their mark during the war, we may single out Konstantin Simonov (b. 1915), Arcady Kuleshov (b. 1914), and Margarita Aliger (b. 1915). A still younger generation of poets has come forward but it is as yet difficult to assess their work. Of the three younger poets, Konstantin Simonov stands out in many ways as "the voice of the rising generation," as he has been called. He is the Soviet Rupert Brooke and he made a lasting impression during the war days. He is representative of the new generation that was made in the middle 1930's and that differed in outlook from the preceding one; and in him we have a return to many of those lyrical themes, such as love, which were despised by an earlier generation.

In considering the influences helping to shape Soviet poetry to-day, we must bear in mind the classics, foreign as well as Russian; for although the modernistic western influences have been exorcised, great attention is paid to foreign classics. Among these English poets are well but not fully represented. To begin with, our Ballad literature and nursery rhymes are very popular and have been excellently translated by Samuel Marshak. The ballad is a form which has influenced a number of poets, including Tikhonov. Thus we find that Kipling of the ballads is well-known, often translated, popular and not without his influence. His "positive" attitude to life seems to be in the spirit of Soviet literature and his "imperialist" implications are ignored.* Shakespeare is omni-present in the plays and the sonnets, and while his translators are many, it is particularly noteworthy that Pasternak should have lately undertaken the translation of many of the sonnets as well as of *Hamlet*, *Romeo and Juliet*, *Antony and Cleopatra* and *Henry IV*. Chaucer's *Canterbury Tales* and poems by Wordsworth and Keats have also been recently rendered into Russian. Many of the best translations of the ballads and other poets are by Marshak, but he is by no means the only translator in the field : *The Ancient Mariner*, for example, has been translated by Livak. But one of the most popular of British poets is Robert Burns, who is not only frequently translated but also often set to music by Soviet composers such as Shostakovich and Khrenikov. Burns's directness and simplicity are again elements which strongly attract the Soviet public. The optimism of Browning is likely to appeal but so far one has noticed only one translation by Marshak.

Among other influences we must note that of folk-songs, national epics, bardic traditions, and, of course, the rich multi-national store of the various national poetic traditions, such as the Ukrainian and Bielo-Russian, the Georgian, the Uzbek and the Kazakh. The associate Republics, as well as the autonomous Republics and Regions, and the many smaller nationalities, all provide traditions of their own, and these are a potential source of influence on Russian poetry. In this sense, there is a natural variety of forms to choose from. The whole panorama of this development, which is bound to affect the future, can only be dimly grasped as yet.

Parallel with the stimulation of the national consciousness of these peoples and of their poetic traditions, we perceive that Russian poetry, the main stream among them, has also become more consciously national. The base has been widened to allow the participation of millions of new readers; and this poetry now reflects feelings and aspirations which are more comprehensible to the new "average reader" than the more esoteric works of 1900-30. Since 1932, and even more so during the war, the emphasis has been on directness and simplicity, and the fundamental emotions of which a revived patriotism was one. Among the other emotions thus evoked, and having all the appearance of novelty after the more abstract themes of the early revolutionary poetry, are those of love, death, mother-country, hatred for the enemy, nostalgia for home and the things that have been destroyed. There is a positive assertion, too, of the national

---

*But in 1946 these implications were referred to (see leader in *Literary Gazette* of April 20th).

spirit and of Russia as an eternal cause, of faith in man and the
Socialist patrimony. There are touches of narrative humour as in
the portrait of the happy-go-lucky soldier character of Twardowsky's
Vassily Tyorkin. And underlying it all in most cases there is an aggres-
sive philosophy of optimism which takes certain premises for granted
and rejects their opposites. The war stimulated an enquiry into the
relative values of the two civilizations thus opposed. One of the
antitheses expressed in the poetry of this time is that between the
" soulless and inhuman German " and the " soulful and essentially
human Russian." This " essential humanness of the Russian nature "
is seen as a universal quality and Bielinsky is quoted for the distinction he established between Russians and foreigners : that the Russian
is at home everywhere and can assimilate the best of other civilizations
while the foreigner is by nature more narrow and restricted. This is
the " spacious Russian nature " of 19th century literature seen again
in a new light.

There is no doubt that the war gave an impetus to dormant lyricism
and made more real and concrete the national and emotional themes
that had been revived in the 1930's; and the bond between the
past and present was also reinforced. If this period shows a certain
lack of variety of theme, this is due to the all-pervading preoccupation
with the war; but while it may have been the poet's " duty " to help
in the war effort, it is also true that the circumstances of this war
were such that the poet could hardly have escaped its direct impact,
and the result is that the poetic reactions to this theme are for the most
part really *felt* although there is also a certain amount of conventional
poetizing about it among some poets. Much of the poetry of this
period will not survive except for its documentary interest, but enough
will probably last to show that this was a poetic revival when compared with the preceding decade. The post-war ambition appears to
be to create more " monumental " works and " the marble of the
Iliad " haunts the imagination of not a few poets and critics.

A feature bound to strike a Western observer is that in Soviet
poetry there is hardly a note of pessimism or doubt even when
it deals directly with the war and its horrors. The horrors and the
losses are deeply felt but the confidence in the future is such that, while
there is disillusion in the German character, there is none in human
nature itself. There is no note such as we may find in some poems of
Randall Swingler written in Salerno Bay, 1943 :*

> " O love is it worth it? And are the dead rewarded
> With a bearer bond on history's doubtful balance?
> And is the loss redeemed by a sunset glory
> A sweet transfusion of blood to a new-born world?

*Quoted from *Our Time*, February, 1946.

No it will never be worth it, not the loss redeemed.
The dead die hideously and there is no honour.
The blood that runs out in the sand can only embitter
The violence of a fate that is still unmastered."

To the Russians this might appear as an example of inadmissible pessimism, showing a poet's non-realization of his social duty in a time of national crisis. Nor would such a statement be published or, if it were, it would be heavily criticized. Therein lie both the limitation and the moral force of Soviety poetry : it is paid the compliment of being regarded as an *effective* social force. On the other hand, Soviet poetry may often appear to us over-simple and limited in its range of emotions.

It may be asked whether the Russians are more allergic to poetry? What is true is that the average Russian is not yet living in a world where man has been abstracted from a natural milieu of traditional song, as we had been in the more highly industrialized West. He has not yet lost touch with his folklore, though there was a tendency for him to do so; but everything is being done now to preserve the links. So we find that at one end Soviet poetry still flowers in the personal lyricism of Pasternak while at the other it merges with the popular song as is often the case in the poems of Issakovsky, Lebedev-Kumach and Surkov. This explains, too, the popularity of poetry readings, the frequent appearance of poets before crowded auditoriums in Moscow and elsewhere, and the constant reading that goes on of new or old works in the Writers' Clubs. We may recall that Essenin and Mayakovsky were in the habit of reciting their poems on every possible occasion, and the enormous concourse of people that followed Essenin to his grave is a testimony of the direct popular appeal that poetry can exercise.

If we have quoted Randall Swingler's poem as the type of statement that cannot be found in Soviet war poetry, another contrast is afforded by a Soviet criticism of Stephen Spender's *Ruins and Visions*.* Here the critic is appreciative enough and recalls Spender's poems of the time of the Spanish Civil War, but he is surprised to find a note of pessimism in these later poems, in which " the visions cannot be seen for the ruins," and he concludes that the poet must be in the grip of an " inner crisis." Similarly, a number of American poets, who are reviewed, are found to be " vague " and without any " purpose or direction." Here we are apparently back to that fundamental difference which seems to separate these two worlds at present. And now let us pass on to examine the actual contribution of this period.

Literary Gazette, of 14th April, 1945.

2

Children's Verse, Poster-Poems and Fables

A WORD must be said about children's verse though we cannot treat it in detail here. It is best seen in the work of Marshak, Korney Chukovsky, Mihalkov and Barto, and their literary quality is high. Marshak (b. 1887) is a master of this *genre* and combines fantasy with ingenious rhyme, simplicity and directness. As we have seen, he has translated much from the English, and among these translations we find many English nursery rhymes. He has by now many books to his credit and *The Absent-Minded Man from Basseyna Street* is a good example of his style. Korney Chukovsky is also a talented versifier, but as we have noted, his fantasy ran away with him in his *We Shall Vanquish Barmalay* and he was severely criticized for this ' aberration ' : this has not, however, affected his general reputation. But it is apparent that the children's writer, too, must steer his course between excesses of fantasy and the shallows of reality. The ideal would appear to be a mixture of fantasy and reality with the latter as a very concrete base. The moral is always present and children are encouraged to be good and patriotic. It is perhaps in Mihalkov that the note of social morality is most in evidence and that is probably the reason why his *Facts* were so favourably contrasted with Chukovsky's *Barmalay*.

Children's verse provides the background in Marshak's case at least to another popular Soviet *genre,* that of the poster-poem. This is a short and usually satirical poem of social or political portent. It proved especially effective during the war years when poems of this type were much used in the daily Press and in the *Tass Window Posters*. These pointed verses on topical themes were a useful " weapon " in satirizing the German army and the Nazis, and some of them are classics of their kind. In contrast to the British, whose natural " weapon " is their sense of humour, the Russians are more naturally inclined to satire, and they have a tradition behind them. During the war there was a conscious attempt to revive this tradition and classical models were much publicized. In the field of the poster-poem we find that Marshak was much to the fore and many of his poster-poems are pithy and telling, and among the best of their kind. Those collected in his book *The Lesson of History* are excellent examples of this genre, and Marshak was awarded a Stalin Prize in 1942 for his work in this domain. The book is illustrated by the Kukriniksi, a collective trio of artists, who rival Cruikshank, our cartoonist of the days of the Napoleonic War, for their cruel and satirical fantasy. Many of the *Tass Window Posters* were illustrated by them and their efforts certainly succeeded in making the Germans look ridiculous. Another prominent wartime poster-poet was Demyan Biedny (1883-1945), one of the original proletarian poets and ballad writers on topical themes. The change that has taken place in the atmosphere of Soviet poetry in the past decade is well illustrated by the incident of 1936, when Demyan Biedny wrote the libretto of an operetta, *Bogatyry,* in which he satirized the legendary champions of Russia only to find that the critics turned against him most violently in defence of Russian traditions.

Mihalkov, a writer of the younger generation like Simonov, was also co-author with El-Registan (d. 1945) of the new Soviet hymn. His social awareness and dexterity in children's verse served him as a spring-board for the revival in the later years of the war of another *genre*—that of the fable. Here again there was a strong though neglected Russian tradition, for in Krylov (1769-1844) the Russians had a master of the *genre* who blended the devices of the fable with the expression of what has been termed " popular wisdom." Much of Krylov has in turn become Russian proverb and there is nothing more typically Russian than this writer. The anniversary of his death was celebrated with every sign of enthusiasm in 1944.

By this date Mihalkov had also tried his hand at the fable and with him it becomes an instrument of social satire with a strong moral sting in its tail. Mihalkov does not spare his victims as can be seen from his fables, *The Vixen* and *The Piggy.* In the former, published in *Pravda* in the winter of 1945 with a telling cartoon, he satirized the have-done-wells-out-of-the-war, who are tempted by the wiles of more dashing fox-wrapped females to neglect their lawful wives and family. In the latter, he makes a slashing attack on the Russian " piggy," who is sent abroad, has matured and seen all the capitals, and, returning home " a full grown swine," keeps on insisting thereafter that everything foreign is marvellous—" so like a foreign swine himself, that even to compose this fable is disgusting."

The social implications of this use of the fable are obvious. Since the war there have also been signs that parody is being encouraged and this is some evidence of a livelier critical outlook.

3

Narrative Poetry: " Vassily Tyorkin " and " The Colours of the Brigade "

THE war on the whole favoured the revival of lyrical poetry and this was more adapted to the emotional reactions of the time. But there were also several attempts at the narrative form :

the most successful those of Alexander Twardowsky (b. 1910) and
Arcady Kuleshov (b. 1914) in their poems *Vassily Tyorkin* (1942-3
and 1945) and *The Colours of the Brigade* (1942-43). These authors
happen to be both Byelorussians but we include them in this chapter
because their works have struck a more universal note, and Vassily
Tyorkin, the hero of the poem, is an essentially Russian character.

Twardowsky is a poet who has been in print since 1924 but it was
in the 1930's that he established a more solid reputation for himself,
publishing some ten books of verse in that decade, including the
popular *The Land of Muravia* in 1937. In 1940 a volume of his
Selected Verse was published, and with the war his attention turned
to the front, and he wrote *The Word of Hate* and *Front Line Verses*
in 1941, *Verses about the War* in 1942, and *Verses about Smolensk* in
1943. His verse has a simple and direct quality, and has its roots in
folk song and folk poetry. In 1942-43 he· wrote his *Vassily Tyorkin,*
to which a further and final instalment was added in 1945.* In this
narrative poem, he has created a lively and humorous image of the
simple, cheerful and invariably successful peasant-soldier. Tyorkin is
never at a loss and carries out the most difficult missions without
winking an eye, and he has a fund of good sense and humour. " He's
a chap of simple clay—unsophisticated." After swimming an icy river,
he is rubbed down with vodka, but he says:

" On my skin the liquor's wasted :
Let it warm my cold inside. . . ."

Although absorbed in the war, he is a human character as his sense
of humour proves, and he prefers life :

" Life is sweeter than this war :
War is ruthless, like the ocean. . . ."

But in the meantime he has to carry on :

" But until my land recovers,
Till her plains are free once more,
I can't sing of peace and lovers;
While at war I sing of war. . . ."

Twardowsky's poem was immediately popular, particularly in the
army; and it is perhaps the only work of this period, except for the
short stories of V. Ilyenkov, to combine patriotism and humour.

Arcady Kuleshov's poem, *The Colours of the Brigade,* is quite a
different sort of work. It is also direct and simple, but it has an epic
touch about it. It is written in a mixture of blank verse and rhyme,
and has a slow and dignified rhythm reminiscent of the *Song of the
Raid of Prince Igor.* Its theme is the early days of the war, the days

*Published in *Znamya*, No. 8, 1945. In 1946, Twardowsky was awarded a
Stalin Prize for this poem.

of retreat and enemy pincer movements, when a brigade is cut off
and destroyed, and a soldier—the author, no doubt, since the poem is
in the first person—tries to escape through the enemy lines with the
Colours. The poem is full of observation, local colour, and echoes of
folk refrains; but in tone it is austere and sadly nostalgic :

> " All this, through a forest wending,
> Was told us by men who had seen :
> There lived in his native village
> A player of cymbals,
> Lived with his cymbals.
>
> But the enemy came bursting in.
> And again
> The dear spaces were moaning;
> The cymbals did cease their playing,
> The strings of brass,
> The strings of steel.
>
> To the war,
> Forsaking his home,
> He departed by secret paths,
> And under the paternal roof
> He hung his cymbals facing the east.
>
> And the whole of that region Byelorussian and dear,
> All that sang in it, grew and flowered,
> He took on his way—
> He found room for it all in his filial heart.
>
> He found room there for age-long forests,
> For the rivers, the hamlets, the hills and the roads,
>
> The screech of the storks
> And the silver mouth two-horned. . . ."

This quotation gives some idea of the imagery and tone of this poem,
which might easily have been written in another century, so close is
it in feeling to the folk poetry of the past.

Kuleshov is a poet who was produced by the war, and he is
one of the more promising discoveries of this period. He has written
a number of other poems, such as the *Ballad of the Four Hostages, The
Letter from Polon,* and a poem about a girl in German captivity.
But his most moving and important poem since is *House No. 24,* 1944,
in which he evokes a reoccupied town (his native Minsk) and the

ghosts that people a deserted and ruined house : " It is bitter to bring news to those no longer among the living." Kuleshov's emotional world is so authentic and rooted in primitive life that we are a thousand years away from sophistication when reading his poems.

4

The Revival of Lyricism (1). The Debate

IN the past thirty years there has been much debate among poets and critics about the functions and future of lyrical poetry. The early years of the Revolution, those of revolutionary romanticism, were lyrical enough in their manifestations : even the prose of the time was tinged with lyricism. The most advanced lyric of those days, that of the Futurists Mayakovsky, Khlebnikov and Pasternak, was based on a new syntax and the " liberation of the word "; it was, in fact, a revolt against the classical forms of lyricism. There was the feeling, too, of a new world being born, and this required a re-assessment of feelings and emotions, themes and attitudes, as well as of forms and verbs. But the disruption of older lyrical forms also encouraged the belief that the day of the lyric was over and that new poetic forms would replace it. That was Mayakovsky's expressed and Essenin's implicit belief. Essenin came to think of himself as the last songster and he dramatized himself in this attitude, and finally committed suicide in 1925. Outwardly Mayakovsky plunged with tremendous energy into the new world and the conflicts it entailed, and wrote as he thought the times dictated. But there can be no doubt that there was within him a hidden conflict and pull towards emotional and lyrical expression which he deliberately tried to suppress.

The argument against the lyric was largely based on the assumption that it reflected a subjective world for which there was no future and that the subjective world which had been expressed in the classics of that *genre* was now no longer valid. Hegel had defined the lyric as poetry that portrays " the inner world of the soul, its feelings and apprehensions, joys and sufferings "; and the need for this was considered as having passed in a more ascetic age bent on building a new world. This feeling was expressed by Mayakovsky in 1930 :

> " My verse will come, but not ornate,
>   Not like an arrow's lyrical love-flight from Eros . . .
>   . . . ponderous, rock-jagged, age-grim,
>   as when this day an aqueduct appears,
>   firm-set upon a time by the branded slaves of Rome."

140

In the first half of the 1930's the debate was still going on but in a somewhat different form. But the lyric was still regarded as a decaying poetic form. This point of view can be found in N. Stepanov, in his review of Bagritzky's book of poems, *The Conquerors* and *The Last Night,* in *Zvezda,* No. 2-3, 1933. Stepanov says: "Lyrical poetry is now in a state of breaking up. The possibility of lyricism based on the biography of the poet and verses about the 'destination of poetry' have proved too limited and emotionally subjective for the reflection of the contemporary world. It becomes progressively clear that it is essential to overcome this lyrical inertia, reiteration, and the 'literariness' of the lyric—and to speak out in a 'full voice' about our age and to make for the road leading to the epic." Stepanov thinks that this is what Bagritzky is trying to do, but he criticizes Bagritzky's romantic elements which keep him "in the circle of a subjective and romantic interpretation of reality."

But by the second half of the 1930's we find classical lyricism and the work of Pushkin held up to universal admiration; and we also find a critical defence of the lyrical form and an affirmation of its validity in the new society. We have already outlined some of the reforms that had taken place in these years and it is clear that the re-acceptance of the lyric was due to the changed atmosphere of the society that had succeeded in carrying through its industrial programme. A statement of the new attitude can be found in A. Gurstein's *The Lyric and Socialism,* where he says: "Socialist lyricism, which in the process of historical development manifested itself chiefly in the negation of the old world and in the call for struggle against it, now in the conditions of a victorious Socialism assumes a new function—that of *affirming* Socialist society and revealing the positive aspects of the new Socialist man."

In this way, the lyric is once more vindicated but it is at the same time defined. It has reality and objective significance because it will now portray an inner world which is different from the old. A new sort of man has already emerged, though he has still to develop further as a result of the social changes that are happening. There is a fundamental difference between the two worlds; the new inner world is a positive one, and will be reflected as such in the lyrics that will now be written. In fact, the main social battle had been won and it was essential now to strengthen the foundations of the new society and to build up its culture, which was also in the process of widening its basis and working out a synthesis with its past. That is the argument and process, as we see them, which determined the new attitude to the poetry of the 1940's. The inner world and the "new psychology" thus being admitted, Marx and Engels are quoted for the affirmation that the new society will be the only one where "the natural and free development of individuals is not merely a phrase." And it follows, therefore, that the "fine human words—country, happiness, love, motherhood, dream," will assume their specific significance while in "the bourgeois world they are merely a masquerade." Thus Mayakovsky's desperate cry of 1930:

> "But I mastered my impulse
> and crushed underfoot
> the throat of my songs. . . ."

proved a tragic fact, born perhaps of the necessity of his time, but no longer valid.

5

The Revival of Lyricism (2). The Poets

THE new tone of Soviet poetry in 1945 may be gauged from Antokolsky's assertion that "Poetry is one of the most potent instruments in the development of human culture. Behind it lies the same sort of antiquity as behind the sail, the axe, the brief burst of flame in the hands of primitive man. From the oldest times poetry was the symbol of overcoming, of a victory achieved, a symbol of growing creative force. The whole of folklore bears witness to this, all the legends and the epics of the peoples of the world. . . ." Let us now see what the poets did during the war and how the lyric flourished.

We shall start with Boris Pasternak (b. 1890), who is both the senior and the best known abroad. Pasternak had already made a name for himself as a fine lyricist in the 1910's and his *Sister My Life,* 1922, and *Themes and Variations,* 1923, had confirmed this impression. His lyricism is original and dynamic: it is image-creative and word-evocative. It has the spontaneity and freshness of a lyricism whose sensibility is bathed in a morning or evening twilight of youthful memories, musical chords, and an intense but impressionistic feeling for nature. There is also something in his poems of the atmosphere one finds in Rilke; and it is interesting to recall that Pasternak's father, who was a well-known painter of his day, painted Rilke when he was in Moscow. Pasternak's poems are dynamic and they build themselves up naturally on the basis of inner verbal associations although it is true that of late this verbal structure has become modified and his poems more simple in their appeal. His verbal dynamism and extraordinary range of words and associations made his poetry sometimes difficult to follow, and while he is admitted to be one of the finest of lyric writers, his poems were never widely popular and they have received perhaps less official sanction than they should. He has also never plunged directly into social activity or written topically, although in *1905* and *Captain Schmidt* he did deal with revolutionary themes in his own dynamic manner. This fact has at times seemed to isolate him and to weigh against him, but we can find no foundation for the statement made by Herbert Read in his *Poetry and Anarchism,* 1938, that Pasternak "languishes in prison." But the effect of his unpopularity has been that he has devoted more time to translation, and we have had fewer of his published works. On the other hand, he has not ceased publication as his wartime volumes testify, although they are small in bulk; and it is to be hoped that we shall hear more of him in the post-war period. The fact remains that his lyricism is more personal and less social than that of any other Soviet poet, but it is also true that in his *Spacious Earth,* 1945, many of the poems disclose a more direct approach to reality, and there are several "war poems" among them, one of which had been previously published in *Pravda.* A Soviet reaction to this last volume, in Antokolsky's review of it, is: "The new volume of Boris Pasternak is a notable event in Soviet poetry not only because he is a notable poet and that his books appear rarely, but also because having reached full maturity, Pasternak becomes more clear and simple, and his relations to life, and those around him, more human. . . ."

During the war Pasternak published two volumes of poems: *On Early Trains,* 1943, and *Spacious Earth,* 1945. The latter is really a reprint of a selection of poems from the former book with additions. *On Early Trains* contains twenty-six poems and we note that fifteen of them were written in 1941 while the remaining eleven were composed in 1936. Among these latter is a section entitled "The Artist" and there is an interesting poem which begins:

> "With artist's stubbornness inborn
> My soul's at home, when he is strong:
> Men's eyes he now avoids, word-shorn,
> Ashamed he thinks his own books wrong . . ."

In *The Thrushes,* one of his finest lyrics and one full of the country atmosphere of the Writers' Village where he lives, Pasternak affirms his artistic faith:

> "Such is the thrushes' shady bower.
> They dwell in woods spared by the rake,
> As artists should, tuned to this power.
> Theirs is the way I also take."

In the *Spacious Earth* we find the poems of 1941 with several additions of war poems. In *Spring* we have a presentiment of approaching

victory: " This spring all is very special, the sparrows chirp more
loudly. . . ." There are poems about the front, like *The Sapper's
Death* and *The Scouts*; and there is an interesting poem, *The Old
Park,* in which a wounded soldier suddenly recognizes in the hospital
the house of his childhood, and this leads to a train of historical
reflections. This poem is really symbolical and can be interpreted as
an oblique statement of the synthesis that has taken place between
the old and new :

> " The voice of this our present age,
> And visions of past time itself,
> Are healed and blended and assauged
> With patient nurse's soothing help . . ."

In another poem, *On Early Trains,* the early years of the war are
evoked and there is a sobering passage reminiscent of Blok :

> " Through the past's peripeteias,
> And years of poverty and wars,
> In silence I beheld of Russia
> Once more the inimitable traits. . . ."

Pasternak has been compared on more than one occasion to Donne
by D. S. Mirsky and others, but we can find little resemblance. In
his most dynamic and verbal moods, a more obvious comparison
suggests itself with G. M. Hopkins. But to make this comparison
effective, we must imagine a Hopkins without his religious background
and writing in such a way as to condense his verbal rhythms and
associations into a framework of classical quatrains. These quatrains
are, however, always new and surprising because of the unexpected
verbal effects and felicities.

Konstantin Simonov is a representative of the younger generation
and he was poetically formed in the middle 1930's. He makes no
bones about calling his poems " lyrics," and he has poems like *The
First Love* and a " lyrical diary of 1941-42," *With You and Without
You,* dedicated to Valentina Serova, an actress of the Komsomol
Theatre. Simonov is the pioneer of love in the new world of
affirmative Socialism. One of the highest authorities in the land is
rumoured to have remarked, on seeing one of these books of lyrics,
that only two copies should have been printed : one for him and one
for her; but that, if it is so, has not abashed this poet, who still treads
the path of love and who, having been the first " to open the secret
of his heart," is immensely popular as a result. But love has not
blinded Simonov to the realities of the day and he was also one of
the leading war poets as well as a pioneer in all the national and

patriotic themes. As may be imagined, his volume of production is much larger than Pasternak's and, as we have seen, he has written short stories, novels, diaries and plays, as well as film scenarios. He was in uniform during the war and has covered the front from the Barents Sea to the Black and from Smolensk to Stalingrad. In all these peregrinations and while writing about the stark realities of the front and poems like *Kill Him*, which enumerated all the good reasons why a German should be killed, he feels acutely all the time the absence of his beloved and evolves a dialectic of love to fill the void. Thus, a great many of his poems are about the war and about love at the same time. But there are many poems also dealing directly and exclusively with war incidents and patriotic themes. Simonov is certainly the liveliest and the most typical poet of this period and also the best guide to the general trend of feelings and emotions. Creatively he appears to be genuinely happy in this atmosphere and it will be interesting to watch his post-war development. His cycle of poems, *To A Distant Friend, Lethargy*, and *Music*, some of them written in Germany towards the end of the war and published in *Znamya*, No. 9, 1945, are remarkable for their deepened anguish, and almost metaphysical vision of love and death. The words anguish, boredom, sadness, grief, are recurrent and the contrast between " Russia " and " foreign parts " is stressed.*
The " distant friend " is the same; the " separation " is the same as throughout the war only the feeling of loneliness appears intensified :

" When by the one and only force of love,
I could have made our souls together live,
And could have told your soul : Come, live with mine,
Be bodiless, and be unseen to other eyes,
But part not from me by a single step. . . ."

And again in this poem *To A Distant Friend* we find him writing :

" To share my anguish here I do not wish,
Here rarely you will hear your spoken name,
But if I silence keep—the silence is of you,
And the air is peopled with your faces. . . ."

And in *Music* we have these lines :

" Suddenly, as in a dream, the feeling came,
That there was no one left around me,
That all were dead and everything was empty. . . ."

*Since writing this, I have come across a criticism of the poems of Simonov in the *Literary Gazette,* of April 27th, 1946. Apparently Simonov is not the only poet to have exhibited signs of " depression." Dolmatovsky and Matusovsky also show signs of it, and the critic takes them to task for seeking refuge in " love and Russia " and shutting their eyes to the critical light in which they should see the reality of foreign lands.

These later poems certainly strike a different note from the famous and optimistic poem, *Wait, I Shall Return,** which was so popular and set to music by so many composers. But it is too early to say whether this mood will continue.

Like Simonov, Alexei Surkov (b. 1899) was a soldier-poet. He is the more restricted and austere—bolshevist—vein, like Tikhonov's, of one who " In the fourth war since the age of eighteen still carries his soldier's fare." He has " experienced all, only boredom has not come our way." In *The Soldier's Heart* (poems of June, July, August, 1942), he " has gone through the hell of war, but is alive still, and ready for more." His output was large, his quality variable, and his style direct and metallic. His experience is that of a whole generation of which Saburov, the hero of Simonov's novel *Days and Nights*, is the representative and he finds his moral support in the faith he has in comrades : " How such a wicked time survive if friends prove rare and belief is lost? " And the positive faith is proclaimed in :

> " The war's news is not easy or simple;
> 'Tis bitter to trample the blood-stained dew.
> We are men of average stature,
> But we are life-makers and builders all. . . ."

Pavel Antokolsky (b. 1896) has been writing since the age of sixteen and printing since 1921. He has now over twenty volumes of verse to his credit. He is a poet of culture and has an awareness of Europe; he has written on French themes (*François Villon*, 1937) as well as translated from the French and the languages of the U.S.S.R. He is by nature a lyrical poet but with a strong leaning, as in Robert Browning, towards *dramatis personœ*—one of his books published in 1932 was called that (he was an actor once, and a producer). In it, incidentally, we find a poem entitled *The Fight for the Lyric*. Antokolsky is acutely conscious of problems of culture and history, and in his approach to Europe he tends to make the contrast between a " humanist and active " U.S.S.R., the new world, and a decaying older world threatened with destruction. In *Verses 1933-40*, we have two poems, *The Map of Europe*, 1937, and *The Latest News*, 1940, which both point this theme. In the latter the poet says :

> " Whether you return victorious,
> Or fall retreating,
> You are doomed nevertheless,
> You have but an hour to live. . . ."

---

*This has been translated by Alan Moray Williams in *The Road to the West* (Frederick Muller).

In a tone somewhat reminiscent of Blok's poem, *The Scythians*, 1918, the poet calls Europe to join the U.S.S.R., where "each wave sings of the future" before it is too late, and he ends :

> "You will not win the debate against us :
> We are humanity,
> Such as you must now become."

In the course of the war Antokolsky has published *The Half-Year* and *Iron and Fire* : the poems of these books treat of the war, the younger generation, and in all of them there is an historical perspective. All these themes were given additional point and poignancy in his long poem, *The Son*, 1943.* This is an impassioned cry of a father's grief at the loss of an only son (his own) at the front. But the poem again has an historical background. The life of the son, as seen developing from his childhood years in a positive and human direction are contrasted with the "mis-educative" influences at work in Germany preparing the way for the fatal conflict. The guilt, the blame, attaches to the German "educator," who had inculcated in the younger generation "lust and wrath" and had perverted the spiritual world. This is the murderer who must be punished. "Having died a hundred times and born anew, my son calls yours to answer." Antokolsky's poems range from more personal lyrics to those in which a social or historical consciousness predominate. His sense of drama and history may be deduced from his own statement that "The poet experiences himself in time as the son of a generation, as a participant, as a witness and as an actor. With all his emotional strength he serves the cause of history. He cannot fail to serve; if he does not wish to, he will find himself left out in the backstairs of 'minor forms.' Only such service gives art the right to a major style such as, say, that of the Renaissance or the 19th century realistic novel. . . ." As the reader will not fail to notice we are back here to that *historical* theme which is so dominant in Soviet literature and of which Antokolsky is a leading poetic example.

Margarita Aliger (b. 1915) has been writing since 1933, but she was not at all prominent until the war provided her with more emotional themes. She is a poet of impassioned mood and essentially lyrical approach—she is more naturally lyrical than any of the poets we have mentioned except Pasternak. She is ambitious of theme, too, and runs to long poems. In *Zoya*, 1942, for which she was awarded a Stalin Prize, she treats of the girl who was martyred by the Germans but she tells the story of her life and death in a series of lyrical images rather than in a strictly narrative way. Her reactions to the war and the events and the incidents of the time are to be found in many other

*Awarded a Stalin Prize in 1946.

147

of her poems, but her approach is not an objectified one and her personal life figures quite importantly in her work. In September, 1945, she published a very long poem of two thousand five hundred lines, an end of the war poem, *Your Victory*, in which she summed up her poetic experience during that period. Despite its length, the poem is again essentially lyrical in mood and feeling; and she performs a *tour de force* by evoking a whole complex of personal and national emotional experience. There is in the poem also a great wealth of detail but this does not drown the lyrical note. Like Vera Inber's *Pulkov Meridian*, *Your Victory* will prove one of the most interesting reflections and documents of this time, full of glimpses of reality, varied emotional states, sorrows and joys, and future aspirations. Unlike Simonov's later poems, it ends on an optimistic note more characteristic of Soviet poetry and her latest poems are called *Great Expectations* :

> " But the living know the word ' to live,'
> so full of sound, so full of light;
> to drink long draughts of a spring's own water,
> and breathe the honeyed summer's wind.
> ' To live ' is cherry's gummied sweetness.
> ' To live ' is made of birch-tree clumps.
> There's nothing brighter in the world,
> No, nothing simpler, more mysterious.
> The expectation of to-morrow's day,
> of morning with its azure promise,
> —all this remains, all this I have. . . ."

And the very last lines strike the historical note :

> " . . . . Only he that is greedily youthful,
> will conquer in the world after all.
> We're in the ranks and marching to attack.
> Our long vacation is not yet.
> Be ready then, my generation !
> Fare you well, my friends ! "

6

The Poets of Leningrad

THERE would be no reason to separate these poets from those we have already discussed but for the fact that they found themselves in the besieged city of Leningrad; and that their work accordingly bears the imprint of common themes and experiences differing in many ways from those of the other poets. The experience of the siege, which lasted several years, was a special one, since a large civil population found itself cut off without supplies in an atmosphere of the front line. Hunger was an additional cruel enemy and hundreds of thousands of people died of starvation. Leningrad is at the same time a town of great literary traditions and architectural beauty—until the Revolution it was the centre of Russian intellectual life; in 1930, it still represented forty per cent. of Soviet literary activity, though the tendency has been progressively to make Moscow the new centre; but even so many of the writers who now live in Moscow are of Leningrad origin. In this atmosphere, then, of classical shades and famished men and women, with the enemy literally at the gates of the city and shelling it constantly, we must imagine these poets surviving and writing, and performing various social duties. The four poets we are concerned with here are Anna Akhmatova, Nicolai Tikhonov, Olga Bergoltz and Vera Inber.

Anna Akhmatova (b. 1888) has been, ever since her début with the *Acmeist* movement in 1912, a fine writer of short dramatic or love lyrics. Her *Anno Domini 1921* was her last book for a long while, and one heard little of her in the 1920's and the 1930's; but it is clear from a book of *Selected Verse* published in 1943 that she had written a number of poems in the 1930's. It is not till 1940-43 that she seemed to re-emerge out of obscurity and figure again in print and anthologies. It is interesting to note that in 1940 she wrote a poem addressed *To Londoners* in which she expressed her horror of the bombing :

> " The twenty-fourth drama of Shakespeare
> Time now is writing with skeleton hand.
> Much rather Hamlet, Cæsar and Lear,
> We would read by the leaden river. . . ."

Anna Akhmatova did not stay in Leningrad throughout the siege, but was evacuated to Central Asia; she has, however, recorded her impressions of the early days of the siege in nostalgic lyrics written in a style that still bears the imprint of her *Acmeist* past. This is a quotation from her *The Statue of " Night " in the Summer Garden* :

> " . . . The Dionysian goblets are empty now,
> And the eyes of love are bewept.
> Those are your terrible sisters
> That are passing over our town."

We are promised in 1946 an edition of her *Collected Poetry* (1909-45), and she is also writing a long poem *Tryptych* and a series of *Leningrad Elegies.*

We should not be wrong in calling Nikholai Tikhonov (b. 1896) a soldier poet. He is by nature militant and adventurous, and easily changes the pen for the rifle or the poem for the pamphlet when necessary. He came out of the war of 1914 and the Civil War with two books of poems, *The Horde,* 1922, and *Mead,* 1923, in which he sounded an austere and virile note. He favoured the ballad form and he must have studied Kipling among other poets. He was the positive type of poet whose experience was steeped in life :

> " Life lessoned with rifle and oar;
> Strong winds blew my shoulders about,
> And lashed with ropes knotted and hard,
> To make me more skilled and reserved,
> And as plain as the iron of nails. . . ."

Later we find him going through a stage of being influenced by the Pasternakian dynamic and he was also attracted by Georgian themes. By the time of the war, however, he has returned to his more austere style. In 1935, after a visit to Paris, we find him writing some poems about Europe in which reminiscences of the last war, Verdun and the fields of Flanders, mingle with a sense of disquiet at the apparent unawareness of Europe. A militant poet by nature, Tikhonov took a very active part in the defence of Leningrad and at the end of the third month of the blockade he had written his *Kirov With Us,* 1941. In this poem Kirov is the symbol and unseen presence behind the heroic defenders of the city and the whole poem is full of the spirit of determination to withstand the onslaught and to affirm the will to victory :

> " So let our soup be water,
> And bread the weight of gold,
> We'll stand here, made of steel,
> The time for rest can wait. . . ."

This and his *Panfilov Guardsmen* are his chief poems of the period but he has written much besides*; a great deal of his effort as a Party man during these years was devoted to publicity and propaganda, and as one of the leading literary figures and the chief " bolshevik " poet, he was elected in 1944 to the Presidency of the Union of Soviet Writers, a post which involves a great deal of administrative, " critical and educative " work.

Of the two women poets who remain to be considered, Olga Bergoltz has an eye for poignant human situations : " Oh yes, we

---

*Eight poems by Tikhonov and two by Olga Bergoltz are included in *The Road to the West.*

discovered a terrible happiness when we had to share our last crumb."
(from *The Leningrad Notebook*, 1942). To the poet the beautiful
familiar city seems now like a dream : " We approached the front
by streets familiar, as in a dream remembering each. . . ." Her
Leningrad Poem is made up of various incidents observed in the life
of the city. This is a characteristic one :

> " It was December and the darkness grew.
> I was returning home with rationed bread,
> When suddenly a neighbour stopped me.
> Oh, let's exchange : this dress I'll give.
> If not. Then give it me for friendship's sake.
> Ten days have passed and still my daughter lies
> Unburied. I must find a coffin for her.
> I know where one is to be got for bread. . . ."

The moral of the poem is that the poet is prepared to give up the
bread for the living but not for the dead. It must be remembered
that at one stage of the blockade a hundred and fifty grammes of
bread a day was all that was available.

Vera Inber in the poems of *The Soul of Leningrad*, 1943, has a
tendency to introduce historical associations and to generalize, but
she is also a collector of detail. We have noted that she kept a diary
which has since been published and her aim also seemed to be to make
her poems a minute record of these tragic days. There is a wealth of
realistic record allied to a more ambitious theme in her longer poem,
The Pulkov Meridian, 1941-43. A record of her work on this poem
may be found in her diary. The poem itself is divided in four parts :
We are Humanists, Light and Heat, Fire, and *The Year.*

The poet notes the various effects of German barbarism such as the
bombing of hospitals and the destruction of art treasures, and she pro-
claims her ' humanist ' faith :

> " Yes. We are humanists. The light
> of lofty thought is dear to us.
> The glow of shining deeds is like
> a glittering goblet or a ring
> that is passed on from father to son,
> from age to age, without an end. . . ."

Her humanism stresses all the human values which are imperilled
and calls upon the " humanists " to fight this evil. This notion of
humanism as well as the idea of man as the maker of history are the
recurrent themes of wartime poetry.

7

Other Poets

OUR survey of poetry has not been nor was it intended to be
exhaustive. We have picked out the poets who have appeared
to us to be the most characteristic and interesting. But there are
many poets whom we have not so far mentioned, to say nothing
of the younger generation whose features are still not clear. The
Anthology of 1943 included the names of all the established poets who
have been active in the past decade. Among them, and leaving out
those we have mentioned, are N. Asseyev, A. Bezimensky, A. Zharov,
I. Utkin, M. Svetlov, I. Selvinsky, V. Lugovsky, V. Rozhdestvensky,
N. Ushakov, A. Prokofiev,* N. Braun, S. Kirsanov, V Lebedev-
Kumach, S. Alymov, M. Issakovsky, V. Gusev, S. Schipachev, S.
Vasiliev, E. Dolmatovsky, N. Rylenkov and A. Iashin. Many of them
have published in reviews during this period but not in book form, and
it is therefore difficult to judge their work. From what we have seen of
it, that of Selvinsky, Rozhdestvensky, Schipachev, Utkin, Asseyev and
Dolmatovsky, appears the more interesting. Schipachev in particular
has been making a name for himself as a lyrical poet in the last year
or two and the critics say that his poems reveal " the inner world of
Soviet man." His *House in Shushenko,* 1944, is a poem that combines
feeling with a sense of history and destiny : it is an evocation of
Lenin's house in Siberia and his youth in the perspective of after-
events. Another poet who has lately attracted attention and who has
a vein of fantasy, personal lyricism and romanticism in his poetry is
Leonid Martynov; and it will be interesting to watch his development.

There is the legion of younger poets but we shall not attempt to
discuss them here. Much verse was also written at the front and
the Union of Soviet Writers has been keeping in touch with these
poets and no doubt the more promising will be encouraged; and the
next few years will see a new post-war generation of poets. They are
already beginning to be printed. Among such contributions, we
came across a curiosity : a poem by a young woman soldier poet about
another woman, a Hero of the Soviet Union, who had fallen in
battle.† The author is Junia Drunina, the poem is *Zinka,* and it is
one of a cycle *About War.* " The fair-headed soldier lies dead," is
the opening and the poem ends thus :

---

*Another Leningrad poet, who was awarded a Stalin Prize in 1946 for his
wartime poem, *Russia.* On the whole, his utterance is banal and
rhetorical.

†Printed in *Znamya,* No. 8, 1945.

"... And the old mother in calico dress
Has lighted the lamp of the ikon ...
But how shall I write and tell her
Not to wait for you any more."

The Anthology of 1943, though it covers a fairly wide range of poets from Blok, Biely and Bryusov to those of the present day, was evidently compiled to emphasize the patriotic mood of the poets included. It is noticeable that two very good poets of the early 1920's, Gumilev (1886-1921) and Mandelstam (1892-1942), are excluded from the new tradition and are not published; but they are still read in second-hand editions of the early twenties.

We must also record the death in 1942 of Marina Tsvetaeva. A prominent poet at the beginning of the Revolution, she finally migrated and lived and wrote in Paris. On the outbreak of the war, she returned to the U.S.S.R., but died before gaining a footing in her re-adopted country. She must have left quite a large body of work, but she has not been quoted or referred to so far.

CHAPTER IX

THE LITERATURE OF THE NATIONALITIES

WE have referred more than once to the development that is taking place among the nationalities constituting the U.S.S.R. and the Nationalities Commission of the Union of Soviet Writers whose business it is to keep in touch with the national writers. This is an aspect of Soviet literature about which comparatively little is known but one which will become of increasing importance not only for Russian literature itself but also for the world at large. We are in the process of witnessing the formation of a variety of national literatures and traditions, especially those located in Central Asia, which had hitherto depended mainly on oral tradition but which are now entering a conscious phase of written literature with world classics to serve them as an example. The process is three-fold : it consists in establishing the national tradition itself by tracing its origin, descent and historical background; in incorporating that tradition into a contemporary Soviet nationalities outlook, and in a mutual exchange through translation of the various national classics and contemporary works with those of Russian literature; and lastly, in providing these national literatures, again through translations, with a background of world classics such as the works of Shakespeare. And this is happening in poetry, prose and the drama.

This process naturally forms part of a political development, of a growing national consciousness that is beginning to animate many of these newly-formed states. Of these, there are sixteen associate Republics : in Central Asia, we have Uzbekistan (with its capital Tashkent), Kirghizia (Frunze), Kazakhstan (Alma Ata), Turkmenistan (Ashkabad), and Tadjikistan (Stalinabad); in the Caucasus, there are Azerbaidjan (Baku), Georgia (Tbilisi), and Armenia (Erivan); in Europe we find the Ukraine (Kiev), Bielorussia (Minsk), Esthonia (Talinn), Latvia (Riga), and Lithuania (Vilna), Karelia and Moldavia. The sixteenth Republic and the largest, the R.S.F.S.R., includes in its turn many nationalities and autonomous Republics such as the Buriat-Mongol, Tartar and Ossetian, which have not yet been granted associate status.

Politically, the national development of these Republics and peoples is being fostered; but this is done on the principle of " Socialist in content and national in form "—a principle which applies to these literatures too, and by it any so-called " chauvinist " trend is discouraged. Thus, while national, historical and literary traditions may be stimulated, care is taken that they should not assume exclusive or anti-Russian forms. The Tartars may, for example, recall their warlike traditions under a Ghengis Khan or Mamai Khan or other of their past leaders, but they are expected to see these in the right contemporary perspective : the Tartars of Kazan sinned in this respect during the war and showed a tendency to " chauvinism " in some of their published works. An account of the Soviet policy towards the nationalities may be found in Stalin's book on that subject. Light is cast on it, too, in Stalin's *On Dialectical and Historical Materialism,* where it is made clear that more importance is attached to movements and trends that are beginning to manifest themselves than to those which have already reached maturity and are " about to disintegrate." In the light of this dialectical proposition, it is natural that the attention should have been concentrated on the development of nationality in Russia itself as well as among its associate peoples. By contrast with the more highly developed nations of Western Europe, Soviet Russia and its peoples have just reached a stage of national development which in countries like England and France had taken place centuries ago. This fact, together with the dialectical premise referred to, may explain the emphasis on nationalities that is an important feature of present day Soviet evolution. The fundamental notion is that the nationalities should be gradually developed to their fullest extent before they reach the next stage, which may be that of universal humanity.

The Soviet principle is therefore " Socialist in content, and national in form "; and this we see applied to the national literatures. The subject in itself is a vast one and would require special study. We can claim no specialization in this domain and can only venture on a few generalizations, which we hope will stimulate the interest of the reader and emphasize the future importance of the subject. To quote the names, too, of many writers of the fifteen non-Russian Republics would only confuse the reader, who may not be very familiar, as it is, with Russian writers. And then the fifteen Republics would by no means exhaust the whole panorama, for there are at least forty already formed national literatures and some sixty or more languages are being written in.

Leaving out the Baltic Republics, the most developed of the national literatures to date appear to be the Ukrainian, the Bielorussian, the Georgian and the Uzbek. Those of Azerbaidjan, Armenia, Kazakhstan, and Turkmenia, seem to be developing rapidly, while we have such new features as a first prose work published in the autonomous Republic of Tana-Tuva and the appearance of a Buriat-Mongol review. It may be said that the literatures of all these peoples so far are either exclusively or preponderantly poetic. Poetry and song have always been the first of literary forms in the early stages of any community, and it is not surprising, therefore, that we should find poetry as the chief medium of expression of most of these Soviet peoples who are now emerging into the light of modern history. At the same time, the foundations of prose have been already laid among some of them and are being fostered among others, as we have seen in the case of the first flowering of Tuvinian prose. Most progress in prose has been made so far in the Ukraine, Georgia and Uzbekistan.

The Ukraine occupies a place of its own. It has had very strong poetic and literary traditions for many centuries. It must be remembered that Kiev was once the capital of the most cultured and flourishing part of Russia from the 10th to the 13th centuries. It is the land of that early epic, *The Raid of Prince Igor*. But the cultured life of those centuries was put an end to for some centuries by the Mongol invasion of Khan Batu. The tradition of song and popular poetry, however, persisted, and we have a new flowering of the national genius in the 19th century with Taras Shevchenko, now regarded as the national poet, and Lessya Ukrainka. They wrote in their national language whereas Gogol, who was also an Ukranian, chose Russian as his medium. The Tsarist policy had discouraged the national languages, but now they are being stimulated. Many of the Ukrainian writers of to-day like Alexander Korneychuk, the dramatist, P. Bajan, M. Rylsky, N. Rylenkov, Pervomaysky, P. Tychina, the poets, are more than just Ukrainian writers, and figure prominently, when translated, in Russian literature. The same is true of short story writers like Dovzhenko, the film producer. Ukrainian prose and drama likewise is more developed, though in Korneychuk it has a dramatist more prominent than any prose writer we could name. But the poets are the chief pride of the Ukraine and their work has its own distinctive lyrical qualities.

Bielorussia is also mainly renowned for its poets such as Janko Kupala and Jakub Kolas, and we have already examined the work of a younger wartime poet, Arcady Kuleshov. All these Ukrainian and Bielorussian poets are very close to the soil and draw much of their inspiration from folk traditions.

Georgia is a country with a literary past and an international outlook. Many Georgian poets are alive to what has been happening in French and English poetry in the past fifty years. During the war, patriotic themes have been the most current; but we find that in a discussion of Tabidze's poems he is reproached for using " decadent " images while the patriotic poems of some of the other poets are described as being over-rhetorical. In Georgia itself there are many distinct mountain tribes or small nationalities with their own folklore and oral traditions and these are periodically written down and collected. Thus during the war an expedition set out to collect the songs of the Hevsuri and Svans—the latter are supposed to have traditions dating from the days of the crusades, and we are told that the Svan warriors still wear armour. In the domain of prose, there has been much research lately into the historical past, and while Georgian historians have been busy recalling the old Georgian frontiers, historical novelists like K. Gamsahurda have also appeared and have written about 11th century Georgia.

The writers of these nationalities produce Almanacks every now and then, and we are given proof of literary activity in Ossetia, in Daghestan, in the Bashkir Republic, in Azerbaidjan, and in Turkmenia, to name a few only. We also learn that "not all Ossetian poems during the war faced up to the realities of current life." Developments in Turkmenia have been much publicized of late and we discover the Iury Olesha, the well-known writer and author of *Envy* and *The Three Fat Men,* who has not been seen in Moscow for some years, had been living in Turkmenia and helping with the national revival going on there.

In Kazhakstan we had the old bard Djambul, who was very active and lively until his death in 1945. He was a striking example of the bardic tradition which is still alive in these Central Asiatic Republics where the bards are called *akyns.* Much of the Central Asiatic lore has been preserved by them and in their chanted poems they interweave with their lore many a contemporary topical theme such as the *kolhoz,* the deeds of the Red Army, or those of Lenin and Stalin, who assume legendary features in their verse.

Uzbekistan is particularly rich in traditions. This region had a flourishing culture in the 7th century but this was destroyed for a time by an Arab Moslem invasion in 705. This culture revived by the 12th century but then, of course, there were the invasions of Genghiz Khan. Nevertheless, flourishing poetic tradition was maintained and enriched by cultural interchange with other Asiatic peoples, Persia and the near East. This poetic tradition includes Alisher Navoy and Babar, the Great Mogul Conqueror of India. The tradition was kept up throughout the centuries so that we even find women Uzbek poets in the 19th century. The last Uzbek classic was Furkata, who died in 1909; and in the Soviet period a poet like Gafur Gulyam is one of the most representative. There appears to be much literary activity in Uzbekistan and a first attempt at the historical novel has been made by Aybek in his *Sacred Blood* and *Navoy.* A great deal of translation of the European classics is taking place. Shakespeare is now well known there*—*Othello* is one of the most popular plays among the Central Asiatic Republics. But Lope de Vega, Cervantes, Molière, Byron, and the Russian classics have also been translated; it seems that until the Revolution the only foreign classic to have been known was *Robinson Crusoe*.

In this process of inter-communication, which is going on between these nationalities, the importance of translation looms very large; and for this reason, the translator is a leading personage in Soviet literature. The translation of some of the epics of these peoples has its importance, too, for the development of Soviet literature as a whole. Among the epics to have been translated are *Manas* (Kirghizia), *Djangar* (Kalmyk), *The Man in the Tiger's Skin* by Rustaveli (Georgia), and Alisher Navoy's 15th century *Farhad and Shirin* and *Leila and Medjun* (Uzbek). The Cossack epic, *Zadonschina*, has also been recently rendered into modern Russian. All these works, with their critical commentaries, will help to enrich the national poetic traditions and that of Russian literature, which will now have a wider " international " basis upon which to work.

In the background of this very complex scene, translation becomes a problem and we find quite a lot of attention being devoted to it by the Writers' Union. There are probably fewer translators than there is work for them to do. Thus at a discussion on this theme in 1943, we are told that " Not one of the seventy books published in Georgia, not one of the twelve books published in Buriat-Mongolia, has yet appeared in Russian. . . . Before the war there had appeared eight issues of the Almanack *Friendship Between the Peoples,* but no issue has been published since the war. . . ." There is much discussion, too, of the principles of translation. The most authoritative theoretician is Korney Chukovsky, whose book *The High Art* is a classic on the subject. Chukovsky maintains that the ideal of translation should be a combination of verbal exactitude with the poetic quality of the original. But where this combination is impossible, he holds that an inspired and poetic translation is better than a scrupulously exact one. As an example of this in prose, Chukovsky cites the first Russian translator of Dickens, who was not always textually exact, but who managed to convey the spirit and humour of Dickens better than any subsequent translator. He made a similar criticism about the most recent translation of a play of Molière's. Others again criticize Chukovsky for his " too liberal interpretation of the translator's rights and duties." And so the debate continues. But it may be said that in general the quality of Russian translation is high, and there are some most excellent translators like Lozinsky, who has

*For his popularity in the Caucasian Republics, see I. Iuzovsky's book, *Shakespeare in Armenia* (1946).

recently rendered the *Divina Commedia** into Russian. The leading translators are also members of the Writers' Union and the fees they get are usually higher than our current ones.

As we have seen, the nationalities are in different stages of development and, in general, they are tending to discover prose as a new medium of expression. The process of flowering will take some time and it is impossible to say whether they will contribute anything of world significance in the future, but certainly the horizon of literature will be a more varied one in the next hundred years. In this brief survey we have only hinted at the latent possibilities in the situation.

---

*This translation was awarded a 1944 Stalin Prize in 1946.

CHAPTER X

THE NEW DEMIURGE AND THE WINDOW OF EUROPE

I

Soviet Literature and the Notion of Humanism

THE panorama of Soviet literature as it unrolls and affirms itself in the present only confirms our impression of its high integration and of a certain self-dramatization peculiar to it. Theory and practice are one, in intention and aspiration at least; and when there is a gap, as there often is, much heart-burning is experienced. This literature is ultimately in the power of a dominant theory whence it derives its impetus and limitations. The theory is at once dynamic, critical and all-embracing : it repudiates the notion of natural or vegetable growth, or of a slow and unforced flowering of literature. Here literature becomes a function or activity of society to be directed along proper channels like any other aspect of social life; and it is a mirror above all in which society is to glean and study its own progress. But the mirror is not intended for the passive contemplation of static forms : the reflected image is to point a moral, situate man in a given perspective and incite to further action. Being concerned with a goal and the future, it is dynamic in intention; and hence the perpetual tug-of-war between critic and writer—the former bent on closing the gap between artistic achievement and shifting reality and the latter bound by the laws and limitations of vision and creation.

This debate is far from resolved, as can be seen from the recurrent fear expressed that the writer may get out of touch with realitv or that he does not need " distance " between the theme selected and its final creative image. The fear of falling out of step is ever present, and the critic's function is often to point out *where* the writer should be at a given moment. Mayakovsky was the first and most naturally dynamic of Soviet writers. Since his death there has been no equally dynamic figure. Pasternak, it is true, has an inherent dynamism in his vision and the structure of his poems, but for the current taste he does not grapple immediately enough with topical problems. Prishvin,

Sholokhov and Leonov also have this quality and the two latter certainly attempt to keep up with the complex of reality, though they take their time about it, while Prishvin is preoccupied with his own special world of reality, that of nature. As for the others, the work of many of them, though topical and up-to-date, show no sign of an inherent dynamic principle. The debate between the " dynamic " critic and the " static " writer or artist explains much of the tension and drama of Soviet literature.

A further element of drama is supplied by the sense of mission or of destiny that is to be met with in the interpretation of the rôle of Russian or Soviet literature. Whereas in Mayakovsky the mission was a " revolutionary " one, in Leonov and other writers or critics of late, the question has been of " Russia and her destiny." The mission is still a " revolutionary and liberating " one, but as a result of the revival of traditions " Russia " has become a synthesis of all these aspirations. Russian literature and philosophy in the 19th century are one long book of " messianic " quotations, on the one hand, and of " realistic " definitions of the relations between Russian and Western thought, on the other.

Dostoievsky alone would supply a whole volume of such quotations. Here is one from a letter of his to A. N. Maikov, " A great renewal is about to descend on the whole world through Russian thought, and this will be achieved in less than a hundred years. But in order that this great object may be achieved, it is essential that the political right and supremacy of the great Russian race over the whole Slav world should be definitely and incontestably consummated." Or again, from *The Idiot,* this time : " Reveal to the Russian the world of Russia. . . . Show him the whole of humanity, rising again and renewed by Russian thought alone . . . and you will see into what a wise and truthful giant he will grow before the eyes of the astounded world. . . ." In *The Possessed,* we come across this : " A really great people can never accept a secondary part in the history of Humanity, not even one of the first. . . . A nation which loses this belief ceases to be a nation. *But there is only one truth,* and therefore only a single one out of the nations can have the true God, only one nation is ' god-bearing,' that's the Russian people. . . ."

The realist philosophers were not religious in tone, but they were concerned essentially with the problem of integrating the Russian people and affirming the independence of Russia. This Chernyshevsky says : " Ever since the representatives of our intellectual movement independently criticized Hegel's system, it has not submitted to any foreign authority." And the specific features of Russian classical or realistic philosophy as now defined consist in " its activity, efficiency and practical revolutionary application; its criticism of contemporary idealistic and metaphysical theories, including those of

Hegel and Feuerbach; a correct understanding of dialectics, and the application of the dialectical method in studying environment, and a sharply negative attitude towards the idealistic and abstract dialectic, which is isolated from life; *a firm conviction in the unlimited and boundless ability of man to interpret and influence the outer world both of nature and society. . . ."* In so defining the traits of the re-discovered classical philosophy, the critic of to-day integrates their premises into the *effective* heritage of contemporary Russian thought. The Dostoievsky strain, too, becomes apparent in Leonov and others; and thus these two principles, the apocalyptic and the dialectic, are subtly blended in the dialectical interpretation of our times.

"Show him the whole of humanity," this phrase of Dostoievsky's, and "this firm conviction in the unlimited and boundless ability of man" of the positive philosophers, have a common foundation in the Russian belief that man is the determining factor in shaping society and the world. In the 19th century, however, Russian thought tentatively asserted that man *could* be the maker; in the 20th century it affirms that he *is* the maker.

This has a direct bearing upon the revived notion of Humanism, the *new* Humanism, now current in Soviet literature. It was to be encountered, before Gorky died, but never has the term been so stressed as during the war and after. We may recall Vera Inber's poem, a section of which is entitled *We Are Humanists*:

"Yes. We are humanists. The light
Of lofty thought is dear to us. . . ."

We have also noted the optimism underlying Soviet thought and poetry—the optimism of Genya and his universal machine.† This optimism and the idea of Humanism derive from a faith in man and his ability to control and *transform* his environment; and also from the fact that Russia is still in many respects a virgin land full of "boundless possibilities." But it has been a virgin land for a long time without producing this optimistic belief before, and the explanation must therefore be sought elsewhere or in a whole complex of circumstances.

We must distinguish between this new humanism and the old. In his famous essay of 1919, the poet Alexander Blok was concerned with Humanism, but it was the *crisis of humanism* in the West that mainly preoccupied him just as it does Berdyaev or Maritain to-day. For Blok the world of the Renaissance-created individual and personality was coming to an end and a new world full of terrors and ecstatic music was looming on the horizon. In the West this crisis is still in

progress and is assuming ever acuter forms. But in the Soviet Union
we have this positive affirmation of a new Humanism. What are its
foundations and definition?

There have been many partial definitions. Gorky is often quoted
for his : " Man—that rings proudly." There is the belief in " the
heroic breadth of Russian man," in Russian literature as " the most
human of all," in " the love of one's country signifies the fiery desire
to see the realization in it of the ideal of mankind " (Bielinsky). But
in Alexei Tolstoy we find a more substantial definition of the new
Humanism. It reads : " Russian literature is *human* as no other
literature. But the humanism of classical literature differs in principle
from the Soviet one. In the former we see pity, suffering for man,
compassion for him. But in the latter we see a real active struggle
to build up conditions for human happiness. In the former humanity
is *psychological*. In the latter humanity is *historical*, determined by
the content itself of national ideals and strivings. In the former, man
is the object of psychological vivisection, in the latter he is *an historical
man.*"

This definition brings us back to the positive, social man, to the
maker of history, to the man who transforms social conditions and
who has the lever of history in his grasp, to the man building a new
world society. It is, in fact, the new embryo hero whom we have
discussed, the " hero of our time " for whom nothing is too difficult.
It is *the new Demiurge*, of whom Pertzov says : " In the personality
of the new Demiurge, *the conscious creator of history*, our art finds
its true pathos and deep dramatism."*

Here man is conceived of as the *subject of history;* he is integrated
in the historical process as a conscious and active element of it, shaping
its course towards a goal of which he is aware. But let us see what
Pertzov has to say further : " In its day, the young bourgeoisie raised
high the banner of the personality, breaking the feudal chains that
hampered human development. The rising bourgeoisie had need of
the idea of a free personality and equated the free individual and the
bourgeois. Its philosophers saw in the private enterprise of the
merchant or the factory owner the desired manifestations of a creative
personality. The ' natural man ' of Rousseau is free of all social ties.
. . . . Rousseau's philosophy played a revolutionary rôle and was
deeply reflected in literature. We need only recall the proud heroes
of Byron, who opposed themselves to society, or the image of René,
Chateaubriand's romantic hero, the image of a gloomy and disillusioned personality, which found its satisfaction in pitting itself
against the whole of society. Thus the idealized and poetic image of
the ' free bourgeois ' and the natural man is identical. As Taine said,

*Znamya, No. 9, 1945.

writing of Rousseau : ' Can one imagine anything more tempting than
this doctrine for the third estate? It provides it with a ready weapon
against social inequality and political arbitrariness.' . . . But for us
the natural man is not the isolated individual but the member of a
Socialist collective. The banner of the personality has now been
raised by the U.S.S.R. . . ."

The *new Demiurge,* the new creative personality, is thus seen as the
product of a new social integration, where there is no antithesis
between the individual and society and where the personality will
flourish in the closest interpenetration with society. Thus achieving
historical awareness, man would be both living in and shaping
history, since society and nationality are historic forms. In this
would seem to lie the theoretical premise of the new Soviet Humanism
as now expounded.

If we may venture a comparison between the two Humanisms,
European and Soviet, what appears to have happened is roughly this.
By the 16th century, having gradually thrown off the medieval
discipline and made many discoveries in all spheres of politics,
geography, art and science, Europe burst into a creative flowering and
at the same time affirmed the primacy of individual man. Owing to
her Byzantine isolation, Russia remained outside this process except
superficially until the 19th century, when suddenly in Dostoievsky,
though in a different social climate, we find the dialectical offshoots of
many of the Renaissance problems that had been long aired in Machia-
velli, Marlowe and Shakespeare, and many others. In the meantime,
European Humanism had become fatally and inevitably materialized,
and the Industrial Revolution was its ultimate but material expression.
Russian criticism analysed this "decay or crisis of Humanism,"
decided to avoid this seemingly inevitable process, and by contrast
emphasized the need for re-integration. Temperamentally and
historically this was a very Russian solution, since Russian society had
never evolved the complex compartmentalization and division of
labour characteristic of the West. Russian Christianity had also
taught that truth resides in the congregation of the faithful and not in
dogma or abstract authority, and there was no sharp distinction
between the theologian and the lay believer. The stress was therefore
always on unity and integration. The greatest Russian thinkers had
also decided that Western forms were unsuitable to the " god-bearing "
people, who, on the contrary, had much to teach the " disintegrating "
West. In the Revolution this principle merged with the rationalistic
dialectical one. And now we have the dual emphasis on the
integrated people as the source of truth and on the "renaissance"
man, who is both the " conqueror of nature," as Faust wished to be
(*Thinkst thou heaven is such a glorious thing? I tell thee 'tis not half
so fair as thou, or any man that breathes on earth*), and a member

of the congregation through which only can he realize himself. Thus in the Soviet Union of to-day the belated manifestations of the Renaissance and those of the Industrial Revolution have fused in a faith that is religious in intensity and whose avowed aim is the *transformation* of the world. This intensity and integration are not only kept alive but are applied to the task by the pivot of the whole system, which is the Party; and this latter has for its chief theoretical instrument the doctrine of "dialectical and historical materialism," which we see constantly applied in literature and other spheres of human activity.

2

Literature and the Dialectical Principle

WE would shirk a fundamental issue and fail to understand the character of the new Demiurge if we did not briefly examine his dialectical premises. Dialectical materialism consists of a method and a theory : the method is dialectical and the theory is materialist. The dialectical method examines nature not as an accidental collection of objects and phenomena independent of each other, but as an organically related whole. Nature therefore appears not in a state of rest or immobility, but in a state of perpetual motion and change, renewal and development, where something is always being born and developed and where something is always disintegrating and dying. Therefore the most important thing is that which is being born and developed. The development is in an ascending line and is from simpler to more complex, and from lower to higher forms. The struggle between these antitheses, between the decaying and the developing, is the inner content of the process of development.

Historical materialism is the application of the propositions of dialectical materialism to the study of social life. Hence each social movement in history must be examined not from the standpoint of "eternal justice" or other assumption but from the standpoint of those conditions which gave birth to that order. Since there are "no eternal principles," it is essential to orientate oneself on those social strata which are developing and have a future even if they are not very strong at present.

It follows that if the world and its laws can be apprehended and our knowledge of them, verified in practice, has the significance of objective truth, then there are no unknowable things in nature but only things not yet known but which will be revealed and apprehended by the forces of practice and science. If the laws of nature can be known, it follows that the history of society can also become a science. It follows that the activity of the proletariat must not be based on "good wishes," the demands of "reason" and of "universal morality," but on the laws of the development of society. The rôle of ideas and theories in history is important but a distinction has to be made between those that further development and those that retard it. And the character and development of the means of production plays a determining rôle in any society.

This very briefly is the barest outline of the principles of "Dialectical and Historical Materialism" as expounded by Stalin in 1938.* How do these principles affect Soviet literature? Our survey of the recent developments and the relations between the critics and the writers should provide the answer to this question. Soviet society is developing rapidly, its basic forms and aspirations are being constantly modified and given ever new definition; and literature is expected to interpret these changes dialectically and artistically. It is called upon to move with the times, and to foresee and give expression to any new manifestations of fact and spirit as soon as they reveal themselves. In a sense the demands made on this literature have not fundamentally changed in the past fifteen years. What has changed is the atmosphere, many of the social forms, some of the aspirations and the attitude to the national past; there has been development and the fundamental themes have acquired a new dress and accent. The horizon, too, has expanded in the post-war world and the *new Demiurge* has more space for his activities. And in the expanding world, which he sees before him, he is driven on by the motive power of his faith and dialectic. In fact, he is the Russian Faust of our time, but no complete image of him exists as yet in literature.

3

Soviet Literature Looks at the West

WE have surveyed the examples and dialectic, the themes and traditions, the criticism and the organization, which all combined form the body and spirit of Soviet literature as it enters upon a new and barely defined post-war era. At this point it may be useful to quote some views of Russian writers about the West generally.

As we have seen, the atmosphere of Soviet literature on the threshold of this new era is far from being undefined or in any sense uncertain. On the contrary, it is pervaded by a spirit of optimism and a sense of development, a feeling of national achievement and of great possibilities still unrealized. The words of Bielinsky, written in 1840, are now often quoted : "We envy our descendants who are

*This chapter (IV) forms part of *The History of the C.P.S.U.* (B.)

destined to see the Russia of 1940, standing at the head of the educated world, imposing its laws in science and art, and receiving the respectful homage of the whole of enlightened humanity. . . ." Another quotation from Bielinsky is to be encountered, that " We Russians are the inheritors of the whole world, not only of European life, and we are inheritors by right. . . ." The Soviet critics of to-day, however, sees the position in a somewhat different light. According to K. Zelinsky : " The question of the ' European heritage ' has to be put differently than it was in the times of Bielinsky and the disputes between Westerners and Slavophils. More topical is the question of the ' Soviet heritage ' for the life of Europe."* This is a common enough proposition and raises the question of the attitude of Soviet critics to Western art and literature.

A whole volume could be written about traditional Russian reactions to the West and to their projection in different terminology into Soviet criticism. Commonly, they resolve themselves into the antithesis between an integrated truth-bearing society and a disintegrated individualist mechanical world. Paradoxically, it is the Western world that appears " materialist " in the vulgar sense of the word to Russian eyes. This is a moral problem recurrent in Russian literature and this is no doubt why Berdyaev says in his *Meaning of History*: " It would appear as if to Russian thought were reserved the special mission of speculatively resolving the urgent European problems raised by the decline of the Renaissance and the crisis of Humanism."

In Chekhov we find a passage referring to Przhevalsky, the traveller and discoverer, and other men like him, where he says : " Their personality is a living document showing society that, beside men who dispute about optimism and pessimism . . . besides sceptics, mystics, psychopaths, Jesuits, philosophers, liberals and conservatives, there are also men of another order—men of action, faith and clearly conceived aim. . . ." This passage might serve as one of the broader texts for Soviet critics when dealing not with the immediate political implications but with the general trends of Western art and literature.

An antithesis which clearly emerges, and which colours the critical relation of Soviet and Western literature, is that between optimism and pessimism or scepticism. In the West the signs of pessimism have been many and various and can be traced some way back. It would be hard to find anything more revealing of this trend than an early example, Baudelaire's *Spleen* :

> " l'Espoir,
> Vaincu, pleure, et l'Angoisse atroce, despotique,
> Sur mon crâne incliné plante son drapeau noir."

Znamya, Nos. 7-8, 1944.

It was in France, perhaps, that the spiritual crisis was first manifest, and it was there that it was most logically exploited, culminating in Céline just before the war. In England, which was still drawing upon resources of Victorian optimism, the crisis did not declare itself till later, till the period of the last war and after, but even then its expression (as in James Joyce, T. S. Eliot and D. H. Lawrence) was, if not less acute, at least less general than in France.

It is not until 1946 that the awareness of this crisis becomes more common and there is a clear prose statement of it in Stephen Spender's *Notes on the Way* (*Time and Tide*, January 26th). It is worth noting and quoting from for the complete contrast it offers to the spirit and dialectic of Soviet literature. It demonstrates all those elements of the spiritual crisis of the West which serve as ammunition for the Soviet critic and which at the same time accidentally throw into relief the rôle of the new Demiurge. Thus Spender says : " The peoples of the world to-day exist in a state of anticipation of their being precipitated into a new pattern of unity or a new chaos. The whole of civilization is enclosed in one idea : the idea of the potentiality which may re-create everything or destroy everything. . . . It becomes evident that the inner life of humanity has attained the power to transform completely and totally the outer environment, so that the chaos or the order of that inner life must inevitably be reflected in man's future environment. Thus we find expressed in literature a growing insistence on *being* rather than *making*. . . . We are now entering the era when man is defenceless against himself, when nature is defenceless against man, and when the dream in the shape of an after-life suddenly becomes real in this life here and now. No wonder that to many people it seems that our civilization has entered a final phase of King Lear on the Heath. When it seems possible for man to write *Finis* on his world, it seems, from what we know of him, and from what we see taking place in the world around us, unlikely that anything will prevent his doing so. . . ."

Here we have a reaction which many in the West instinctively share and which some had already expressed in print in the 1930's or before. On the other hand, it is also evident that this reaction is a purely Western one, arising out of the problems posed by this stage of Western culture, and that it does not include the " other world," that of the Soviet Union. There, as we have seen, the optimistic notion of man as *the maker of history* and of a new Humanism is not only prevalent but is the dominating one. This contrasts vividly with the " growing insistence on *being* rather than *making*," which Spender notes and which is apparently discernible in the West. If this is so, then clearly the ultimate stage of this crisis has been reached, for the European man of the Renaissance was, until the 19th century at least, a positive character who could still believe that :

> " All things that move between the quiet poles
> Shall be at my command."

It might be argued that the discovery of atomic power is an ultimate fulfilment of this 16th century wish and that the positive man is still operative. If he is, then he would appear to be active in separate spheres of life without any unifying and compelling *credo* to guide or integrate the whole of his life; and this, indeed, is the essence of the spiritual crisis he is undergoing.

In contrast, the Russian *maker of history* is sustained by a faith and a dialectic; and he is moreover highly integrated. This integration is the result of three causes : the first is the heritage of the Russian congregational spirit; the second is that the Russian people as a *whole,* the 85% or so of the population who were peasants, have only comparatively recently emerged from the Middle Ages—they were serfs until 1861; and the third is that " integration " on the basis of the fusion of all classes with their people has become a practical policy of the Party, that guides the destinies of the U.S.S.R.; and this control eliminates the immediate possibility of any such general " spiritual crisis."

It should not, however, be overlooked that the seeds of such a crisis did exist in Russia at the turn of the century and up to the Revolution. Much of the poetry of Alexander Blok, and his essay on *The Decline of Humanism,** bear witness to this. The Revolution ultimately had the effect of eliminating this trend of thought and of imposing its own optimistic and highly integrated philosophy; and it was to encourage more positive attitudes and literary trends. Before the Revolution Russian literature was much more within the orbit of European currents of thought and it reflected the development of these in its own way. Thus we saw Parnassian, Symbolist and Futurist movements in Russia. In the 1920's there was also the " Serapion Brotherhood," who based themselves on Hoffman, and many other evidences of European modernist trends. But by the middle 1930's these had all been discouraged and the foundations of a Russian positivist and realist classical tradition had been established. This " healthy and moral " tradition reinforced the background of the positive man who had achieved the first stage of his industrial Revolution, and to whom now much of Western literature appears " abstract," " unrelated to life," or simply " decadent." And he now claims that " no other nation has a literature in which the moral code has been so strong."

In such an atmosphere, and with the critical control which we have seen exercised in the case of Zoshchenko, there can be no room for

---

*This has now been published with others of his essays in a collection entitled *The Spirit of Music* (Lindsay Drummond).

despair or the "bacteria of historical fatalism and pessimism." On the contrary there is a sense of wonder at "the grandiose perspectives" revealed from "the heights we have reached." The question arises how this positive and active principle will interact with or effect the passive state of *being* to which Spender refers in the passage we have quoted. From the Soviet point of view, according to the doctrine of dialectical and historical materialism, the positive developing principle should eventually triumph over a disintegrating one. But it must be said that most of the Soviet novels, for example, which have been translated into English, do not bring with them any great revelation of an artistic or human nature, not the kind, anyway, that *moves,* and they appear ordinary enough to the English reader or critic. It may be, as Antokolsky says in his article on *War and Culture,* that "somewhere at the front, in a dugout, the idea may have been born of an Iliad which shall enrapture us in a few decades," but there has certainly been no compelling work of that kind produced so far. But if the inter-action of two principles is to bear fruit, there should be a circulation, a current of ideas on *both* sides. It is evident that the U.S.S.R. is still on the whole hermetically sealed off from the West in everything except the classics and a few picked writers who, in its eyes, may reflect "progressive trends." It cannot be said that this critical isolation, which also involves the intercourse of writers, is good for either side; it only helps to foster misunderstanding, create tension, and provoke distorted criticism.

A recent example of the sort of impasse that can be reached in literary debate was afforded by a discussion arising out of some views expressed by John Lehmann in *New Writing* on the attitude of the writer during the war. While Lehmann showed an insufficient appreciation of the complex factors dominating the Soviet scene, A. Surkov, the poet, who replied in the Soviet Press, exhibited all the assurance and intransigeance of an "old campaigner" for whom white was white, and black was black. No doubt there was something in the argument on both sides, but the question arises how far civilized intercourse is helped by intransigeance and sometimes violence of language. But as a result of their training, assertiveness has become second nature as well as a technique in Soviet criticism when faced with controversial issues. This method, the application of the lever, has undoubtedly proved effective in the home country in every sphere of life, but when applied abroad it strikes one as a rather crude device. The question of the wartime contribution of literatures is also referred to in a Leader on *The World Significance of Russian Culture* printed in the *Literary Gazette* of the 20th of April, 1946. The relevant passage reads : " Can we say that literature abroad has passed the test? Neither the literature of England nor that of the U.S.A.— not to mention that of other countries—can boast of great achievement

in ideas or art in time of war. Not a few leading writers . . . preferred
to keep silence in expectation of better times. Richard Aldington,
Somerset Maugham, Aldous Huxley, and many many others, did not
wish to apply their energies to the liberation of the world from the
brown plague. *Nor can those books written by certain leading Western
writers with the sincere intention of helping the just cause always
satisfy the reader.* Advanced writers abroad did not feel in their work
that support of the masses and the people which is the source of Soviet
writers' strength. In wartime, each of them worked in isolation to a
certain extent. . . . Is this not why we encounter in their books now
a distinguished abstraction, now an illogicality and incompleteness of
statement, a shyness in defending anti-Fascist and democratic ideas? "
We may take it that this is a typical estimate of Western literature as
practised by the dialectically-minded and it is not without some
foundation. Since the end of the war there has been a general dusting
and brushing up going on in the dialectical armoury and especially in
those critical weapons which might be used in dealing with Western
phenomena. This is not as surprising as it may seem, and is probably
based on both defensive and offensive considerations : on the one hand,
there is undoubtedly a wish to counteract the spread of unsifted and
" undesirable " Western influences and to protect the " Socialist
patrimony "; on the other, there is the desire to consolidate wartime
achievements and to interpret them in a dialectical perspective and, of
course, to make these premises as widely accepted as possible. Thus,
in the post-war world, all the available evidence would point to a
sharpened critical attitude and a growing dialectical exclusivism as
well as to an expressed wish to assert the superiority of Russian and
Soviet culture and letters.

The rôle of Soviet literature in relation to foreign countries is now
defined as follows : " Penetrating abroad, it must counteract those
false ideas, prejudices and legends, which are instilled into the consciousness of the masses by the ideologists of capitalist reaction. It must
counterbalance the lies and slander of our enemies and give the world
a truthful and undistorted image of the Soviet Union. It must
convince the reader of the advantages of the Soviet social order."
(*Literary Gazette*, of 20th April, 1946.) It is obvious that there
is now a tendency to re-assert ideological premises and sharper
criticism. More revealing is the definition of the rôle of Soviet
writers writing about foreign countries : " Not so long ago we disc-
cussed the essential failings in the work of certain reporters who
approached the description of post-war Europe in a superficial manner.* We may also find some faults with our poets. Reading many

---

*The reference here is to a group of well-known journalists, Boris Agapov
among them, who were criticized in 1945 for their undialectical impressions of Berlin and Germany after V Day.

verses, in which are lyrically recorded the experiences of Soviet man away from his native country, we find in them now detailed observation, now a sincere expression of longing for home. But let us remember that, when Mayakovsky was abroad, he also exhibited nostalgia but he did it in another way. His verses about foreign lands were penetrated by *a sense of fundamental distance between the two worlds* and a triumphant feeling of pride of the Soviet man who, in the spacious squares of Paris or amid the skyscrapers of New York, was conscious of himself as the bearer of another and more perfect order of life, of other and loftier ideals. The Soviet artists of to-day have *even more* right to such pride!" *(Ibid)*. This passage may well make us reflect, for it preaches a new form of cultural snobism and emphasizes spiritual superiority rather than human *rapprochment*. It is, perhaps, no exaggeration to say that here is the psychological root of much that will affect us in the post-war world.

Or does the explanation of this continued exclusivism lie in these words of Iuzovsky, which we quote from an article (*Literary Gazette,* of 3rd of February, 1945) of his discussing the problems of Soviet drama : " Humanity is in the process of forming a new society. . . . Therefore there can be no peace or relaxation even after the war. . . . The duty of Soviet drama is to prepare men for the new age. . . . Soviet art alone can give an optimistic answer as distinct from that of the *escapist* literature of the West. . . . The fate of Russia is to bear the heavy Cross. . . . Let us understand this and go forward with clenched teeth. . . . Let us think of the joy of the struggle and the pride of the people selected as a weapon for liberating mankind. . . ."

This atmosphere of drama and tension, of predestination and unconscious hysteria, is often uppermost and hides from us the many human, authentic and valuable contributions of Soviet life and literature. It is the message of these latter that we should like to see emphasized more. And then perhaps Soviet literature will become more humanly positive and less assertive, more universal and less self-conscious. But the renewed insistence after the war on ideological distinction between the two worlds would seem to point the other way.

4

Literature and the New Five Year Plan

THE new Five Year Plan, the first of a new series, which was announced in March, 1946, both picks up the thread of pre-war activity and opens up new horizons not only for the Soviet citizen but also for Soviet literature. It aims not only at reconstruction, but also to increase still further the " might of the U.S.S.R." The ultimate ideological objective is still Communism, which, it is calculated, will be reached in some twenty years' time if the industrial revolution proceeds at an accelerated pace. In Russian eyes, the achievement of Communism will coincide with the attainment of an abundant and cheap supply of consumer goods and also with the raising of the political and cultural consciousness of the masses to a point where there would be a notable increase in Party membership, that is, the people and the Party will become identified, the Party is at present only about 3% of the population, but over 10% if we count the candidates and the Komsomol. The atmosphere of the first post-war Plan is again one of enthusiasm and " Socialist Competition," the idea being to fulfil and over-fulfil the Plan. Or, as the Decree states, " to reconstruct the war-damaged Regions, to restore the pre-war standard of industry and agriculture, and then to surpass that standard in a notable degree."

How does this Plan affect literature? The Decree says that it must " assure the further flowering of Soviet culture and art." From a leader of the *Literary Gazette* of the 23rd March, 1946, a further directive is apparent : " The new Five Year Plan raises a vast quantity of problems which Soviet literature cannot ignore. The Plan will inevitably call to life new forms of labour, exploits, scientific discoveries, technical inventions and improvements. To distinguish the new in life, to guess its imminence and to incarnate.that new element in artistic works was always the honourable task of Soviet literature. We must carry on the Gorky traditions of active participation in the daily creative work of the Soviet people. We must continue the labour *of creating monumental works wherein the man of our age, the man of the Stalin type, the creator of the Plans, will be revealed in his full stature;* works in which will be shown how was forged the will-power of that man, how his soul was formed and how his consciousness was strengthened, enriched and armed by the teaching of Marx, Engels, Lenin and Stalin."

Here we have, again, the bare outline of the " hero of our time," to whom we have often referred in the course of this book. The theme of the " hero " is further enlarged upon in a leader of the *Literary Gazette* of the 30th of March, 1946, wherein he is seen as " a man who has stood the test of war and has matured in its school. This hero offers the writer boundless possibilities, for his path in life was complicated. *But he will not bear magniloquent representation or rhetoric, for the deeds he has accomplished are real and tangible; nor will he suffer any diminution of his strength, or the tone of pity or compassion, for this man takes upon his shoulders big problems, always measuring them by his spiritual capacities.*" The hero thus suggested as a model for writers in 1946, in the enthusiastic atmosphere of the Plan, is not a new post-war ideal but rather the magnified and historically defined Soviet man of whom Pertzov had already sketched the outlines and had called the *New Demiurge;* and this confirms our previous analysis of the main trend of this development. In April, 1946, a " Conference of Prose Writers " met in Moscow. The writers came from all parts of the Soviet Union. We are told that "' from the very first day it was evident that they were united in a truly orthodox attitude to the immortal traditions of Russian literature, bound together in political unanimity and a profound idea and critical attitude of their high calling. *There were many disputations of a creative nature but there was not one case of a departure from the fundamental position on the question of the creative method, the leading ideas and aims of Soviet literature.* Different people, different destinies, different levels of mastery, but despite all this only one banner—that of Socialist Realism, one striving only—to create for the good of the Great Country."* This expression of loyalty and unanimity, which certainly did not exist a decade ago, tallies with M. Molotov's statement of November 6th, 1945, that the Soviet intellectual was now " fused " with the people. It is no doubt the result of the Party's success in carrying out the industrial revolution and winning the war.

While the Plan affects all Soviet citizens in various ways, and while we note the obvious directives to writers, there is so far no sign of any attempt, as there was in 1929-32, to mobilize writers to " report " on the various aspects of the Plan in progress. Writers are expected rather to be aware of its importance and significance, and to digest the experience in their own way. The centre of gravity has now swung away from interest in technical and mechanical detail or the effort the workers as a mass (Katayev's *Speed Up, Time* was a novel of this type in 1933) to that of building up a representative image of the heroic man-personality of the age. Hence the importance attached to Shakespeare as a model, the stress on biography, and the insistence that the writer should be aware of the national climate and the historical perspective in which this hero is to flourish.

In actual fact, we shall find writers engaged in working in different spheres, but their efforts will no doubt tend to have a common feature and stamp in this obsessing consciousness. Some will broach more immediate themes and will, in fact, report on the Plan, for reporting has become a habit with many. Others will still be concerned with their war experience. Others again will be delving into history or labouring to produce panoramic novels in which near-history will culminate in the Great Present. There will be many debates as to how writers should or do fit into the Plan. It is to be hoped that by comparison with earlier stages, greater respect will be paid to the rôle of the creator and the manifestations of personality; and this is

Literary Gazette of 13th April, 1946.

the only way in which the image of the hero can be animated. If he fails to come alive eventually, we shall have to conclude that the pattern is still far too rigid.

Writers are already defining their position in relation to the Plan. Maxim Rylsky, for example, argues that, while he does not approve of "anarchy or an artist's isolation," he yet understands the peculiar nature of the creative process. Mere contemplation is impossible, he says, and participation is necessary, but "*it is not visits to Kolhozes or the Donbass that can determine our part in the revival of our country* but rather our immediate participation in some creative work."* He suggests that writers would be more truly creative and constructive if they themselves helped in the reconstruction process, say, by planting an orchard or a vineyard and thus making their country more beautiful and productive. In that way their work would have deeper roots. There is certainly a more personal note about this approach to planning in 1946 than there was in the more generalized and dictated enthusiasm of 1930.

In the same way, there is a new emphasis on "æsthetic principles" and the "organic" nature of literature if we examine the following statement discussing the influence of Soviet literature abroad : "Contrary to the views of æsthetes and snobs, who attempt to represent our literature as being tendentious 'propaganda,' *it is necessary to discover the æsthetic principles* of Socialist literature, and to show how, out of the advanced political thought of Soviet writers, there organically grows up *a wealth of personal feelings and experiences,* as well as a variety of artistic devices and forms, unknown to the foreign writer. . . ." (*Literary Gazette* of 20th April, 1946). In itself this trend is a constructive one, but here again, as in so many other statements of the kind, one can detect a disconcerting insistence on affirming the superiority of Soviet literature *as a whole* rather than a reliance on a critical debate of the comparative merits of particular works or authors.

This is the stage Soviet literature has reached in 1946, on the eve of its thirtieth anniversary; and these are the main lines along which it is intended to evolve in the next four or five years—until the next Plan will assess the progress achieved and define the outlines of the next phase. The war had proved a "test of our social order, our State, our Government, our Communist Party, and our work." (*Pravda* of 11th February, 1946). Hence a new feeling of assurance and pride : "Life has shown that there are no fortresses in the world which the Soviet people cannot take under the expert and wise leadership of the Great Stalin. There were none in the past and there will be none in the future. . . ." (*Pravda* of 15th February, 1946). The talk is of "new and boundless horizons," spiritual greatness," and "the

Literary Gazette of 9th May, 1946.

moral superiority of the Soviet people." There is no suggestion any-where in print of "the realization in the heart and mind of the individual that life is too big a thing for him to deal with by human power; that the situation is beyond him. This realization is a terrible blow to pride and self-confidence. It is an admission of final weak-ness." (*The Defeat of Modern Man* in *The Listener* of 14th February, 1946). On the contrary, we behold Soviet man cresting a wave of positive and optimistic philosophy. But we also have the right to ask whether he has opened his full heart to us in literature, as many of his "classical" predecessors had done. The answer is, not yet, as Soviet critics themselves admit in their renewed search for "personal feelings." It remains to see what fruits or grapes Maxim Rylsky's orchards and vineyards will bear.

We have been concerned mainly with the background and develop-ment of Soviet literature during the war. We have attempted also to indicate some of its leading post-war trends. But there have been a number of events of more recent date in this sphere which will help us to determine more clearly the nature of this new phase in Soviet literature, for a new phase it is, corresponding to the claim that, "A new historical period has begun in the life of our country." We have already dealt with its background—the launching of the new Five Year Plan and the revived goal of Communism. Now we shall consider the directives and reforms that have since been published.

It has been clear of late that a new critical wind was blowing through the U.S.S.R. The machinery of the State and the Party was being overhauled preparatory to new tasks. The note has been criticism at home and criticism abroad; and this has coincided with a revival of Leninist-Marxist ideology and a more militant outlook. The Western Democracies have again become "imperialist" and "capitalist" ["as is known, imperialist circles in Britain and America are stretching their tentacles over oceans and seas, and trying to subordinate whole lands to their purposes" (28/6/46)]. Whatever the multiple causes of this sharp and caustic attitude, which almost suggests a return to an earlier period of militant Communism, it is no doubt also largely connected with the sorry state of international relations and the clash that has become apparent with British and particularly American interests in various parts of the world. Internally, in the Soviet Union, this situation is leading to an "ideolo-gical" mobilization of all forces to deal with "current problems," and literature and the arts have also been assigned their rôles in the new *educative* drive "to raise the communist awareness of the people and the technical standard of the masses." To this end, "all forms and means of ideological and cultural activity of the Party and State have been mobilized: the Press, propaganda and agitation, science, art, literature, the wireless, museums, cultural and educational institutions. . . ."

For some time, the leaders of the *Literary Gazette* have been more than usually critical; the writers were reproved for the way they managed their Club without due attention to ideological discussion; and it was evident that the writers were being told to bestir themselves and to face " reality." The new critical spirit, evidently of high inspiration, was soon to have its own organ in the review, *Culture and Life,* first published on the 28th June, 1946. This Central Committee publication proceeded to tell writers, artists, film directors and theatre managers what was wrong with them and what they should do : " Life requires the development of ideological and cultural work in accordance with the historic tasks confronting the Soviet State." Even the newspapers did not escape censure for lack of " bolshevik " criticism " and they were urged " to wage a pitiless campaign against .the remnants of an ancient, outworn ideology," although this seemed to contradict M. Molotov's 1945 statement that the intellectuals had now become " fused " with the people. Film directors and theatre managers were blamed for delving too much into literature and history, and for assuming that the " Soviet people after the war want only relaxation and diversions, or are satisfied with base ' amusing' little plays which portray the luxurious life of magnates. . . ." Somerset Maugham's plays were withdrawn and " servility " to Western fashions was discouraged. Part two of Eisenstein's *Ivan the Terrible* film was held back and condemned as untrue to history for portraying Ivan as " a maniacal scoundrel instead of a progressive statesman." *Novyi Mir* was reproved for " lagging behind." In fact, it would need a whole new chapter to discuss all the negative points raised by the first number of *Culture and Life.*

In its positive programme, it advocated intensive ideological training, the propagation of the Marxist-Leninist classics and the need for new books on the Social Sciences; it also announced the publication of a *ten million* edition of *The History of the C.P.S.U.* (B), the book we have discussed in our Section on *Literature and the Dialectical Principle.* Critics were told that they were " detached from life," " at the service of particular agencies and writers," they did not know how " to combine an analysis of idea content with that of artistic form," and must evolve an " authoritative literary criticism based on principle," that is, " *advanced scientific theories which make for the understanding of processes taking place in society,*" that is, " bolshevik criticism continuing the glorious traditions of Bielinsky, Chernyshevsky and Dobroliubov." The critic's duty was a " decisive campaign against hypocrisy and the stereotyped, formalism, shallowness, and servility."

The whole stress has therefore been laid on the problems of the day. Even the name of the *Historical Journal* had already been changed to that of *Problems of History*. "Current problems," "historic tasks," "awareness," "heroic efforts," "ideological content," these are now the recurrent slogans. In a sense, there is nothing new about them; but it is their renewed, intensified and planned application that makes of them at this stage a goad to further effort and psychological integration. And literature has been defined anew as "a permanent record of the great experience of building Socialism in our country and an active participant in the Soviet people's struggle to build Communism. . . ."

After *Life and Culture* had delivered its broadside, other storms broke upon the literary world. On August 14th, 1946, a *Resolution of the Central Committee* condemned the Leningrad reviews *Zvezda* and *Leningrad,* and drew attention to the unsatisfactory state of affairs in that town where Michael Zoshchenko had found asylum and was actually on the editorial board of *Zvezda.* In an earlier chapter, we had already remarked on the unpopularity in pontifical circles of both *Zvezda* and Zoshchenko. Now, in this hour of pontifical militancy, matters had come to a head. But let us pass on to Leningrad and see what happened there as a result of the Resolution.

Within a week, Zhdanov, a Secretary of the Central Committee and "boss" of Leningrad, had made a report on the Resolution to the Leningrad Party Organization which, in its turn, passed a resolution of its own. This approved the Central Committee Resolution and considered that "the City Party Committee . . . had lost sight of questions of ideological work, neglected the supervision of reviews, overlooked errors of the first magnitude committed by the editorial staff and thereby made it possible *for persons alien to Soviet literature, like Zoshchenko and Akhmatova, to occupy leading positions on the reviews."* It had also ignored "Lenin's and Stalin's directives that literature is a most important factor in the Party and State for the communist education of workers. . . ." Owing to lack of supervision, the Leningrad reviews "instead of becoming a potent channel of *education* . . . had placed their pages freely at the disposal of such bounders and dregs of literature as Zoshchenko, who preach a putrescent vacuum of ideas, cheap taste, and a non-political approach. . . ." The reviews had "popularized the works of Akhmatova, *that typical representative of an empty poetry that is alien to our people. . . ."* The reviews had also published "the works of Yakfeld, *exquisite in form but false in content;* the decadent poetry of Sadofyev, Komissarova and others. . . ." The resolution further pointed out that in the Leningrad branch of the Writers' Union a situation had arisen in which the interests of the State and the Party were being sacrificed for the benefit of personal interests and friendly relations. . . ." Further, it was considered that the Central Committee Resolution was "a document of the greatest importance for the Leningrad Party organization, demanding from it a *radical turn towards strengthening the whole of its ideological work* . . . and the necessity of abandoning their careless attitude towards literature, the theatre, the cinema, and art. . . ."

The final recommendation is at first sight surprising and shows how radical the turn had become : it asked for Tikhonov to be removed from his post as President of the Writers' Union, for having "connived at tendencies and morals alien to Soviet literature." The Central Committee was asked "to strengthen the leadership of the Union by placing at its head a more consummate leader. . . ."

By September 7th, a Resolution of the Praesidium of the Writers' Union of the U.S.S.R. had dotted the i's and crossed the t's. Zoshchenko and Akhmatova were expelled from the Union for "not participating in Socialist construction "; Tikhonov was relieved of his office; and a Plenum of Writers was summoned for October. The Resolution criticized severely certain late trends, which included "formalist conceptions," "æsthetic subjectivism," the idea of a "Socialist Symbolism " propounded by Selvinsky as an alternative to Socialist Realism, and the claim made by the Ukranian writer Petro Panch to "an author's right to ideological mistakes." The Union was also reproved for having helped to disseminate Pasternak's "a-political" poetry.

In brief, the Resolution asserted that it was "essential to bring about a radical change in the life and work of the Writers' Union." As a first step its administrative machinery was reorganized. Fadeyev was elected General Secretary, supported by four deputy secretaries, Simonov, Tikhonov, Vishnevsky, and Korneychuk, and eight members of a Secretariat.

There could be no clearer indication than these events that Soviet literature had, indeed, entered a new and more restrictive period. Contrary to the expectation of a broader and more mature postwar development, literature and the arts have again been more obviously confined to a narrower educational and interpretative rôle. No doubt the immediate objectives and more distant goal aimed at by the Party and the State are all-important in their eyes and need no special justification for this use of literature. But there can be little doubt that the political, economic and social development is taking place at far too accelerated a rate for writers to become really creatively rooted in the kaleidoscopic reality. By the time they have pondered a larger work, they may find that the whole emphasis· or trend has changed. This was a problem of which Alexei Tolstoy was very conscious. He tended constantly to re-write his works and we have come across a statement after his death, that he would probably have re-written his *Peter the Great* novels had he lived. This notion of an elastic work of art contradicts all the classical assumptions, but then it can be argued that we are living in a dynamic and not a classical age. It remains to be seen, however, whether this notion will become a universal principle or prove merely an experiment in time. In the meantime, the U.S.S.R. has gone into a monastic retreat again, for even Party members have been made to attend extra ideological courses and lectures to brush up their Marxism and critical terminology. And "hostile bourgeois ideology" will be the butt against which the new invective will be directed. This seems to suggest that we all have not been very successful so far in constructing post-war bridges.

INDEX

Index

Structure of the Writers' Union of the U.S.S.R.

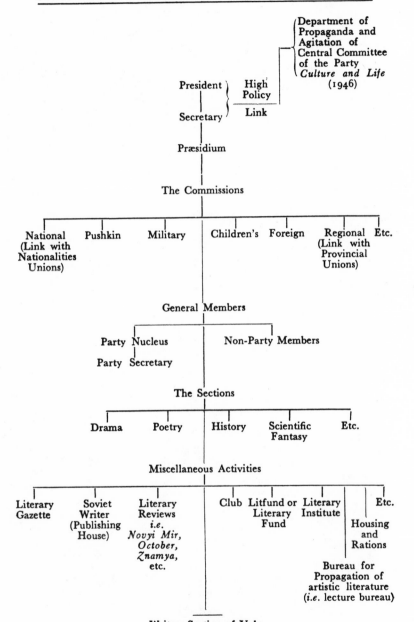

President ⎫ High
          ⎬ Policy
Secretary ⎭ Link

Department of Propaganda and Agitation of Central Committee of the Party
Culture and Life
(1946)

Præsidium

The Commissions

National (Link with Nationalities Unions) — Pushkin — Military — Children's — Foreign — Regional (Link with Provincial Unions) — Etc.

General Members

Party Nucleus — Non-Party Members

Party Secretary

The Sections

Drama — Poetry — History — Scientific Fantasy — Etc.

Miscellaneous Activities

Literary Gazette — Soviet Writer (Publishing House) — Literary Reviews *i.e. Novyi Mir, October, Znamya,* etc. — Club — Litfund or Literary Fund — Literary Institute — Etc. / Housing and Rations

Bureau for Propagation of artistic literature (*i.e.* lecture bureau)

Writers Section of Voks
(Through this channel foreign writers are received and delegations are also sent abroad)